Lockheed C-130 Hercules

Martin W. Bowman

First published in 1999 by
The Crowood Press Ltd
Ramsbury, Marlborough
Wiltshire SN8 2HR

British Library Cataloguing-in-Publication Data
A catalogue record for this book is available from
the British Library.

ISBN 1 86126 205 1

Typefaces used: Goudy (*text*),
Cheltenham (*headings*).

Typeset and designed by
D & N Publishing
Membury Business Park, Lambourn Woodlands
Hungerford, Berkshire.

Printed and bound by Redwood Books, Trowbridge.

Acknowledgements

The majority of data, individual C-130 histories and statistics etc., are taken from the *Lockheed Production List 1954–1999*, 16th edition, by Lt Col Lars Olausson, Swedish Air Force (retd), who very kindly made this definitive reference work available to me. (Copies and details of any additions, corrections etc., can be sent to Lars, at Box 142, S-530 32 Satänas, Sweden.)

I am also indebted to Francis K. Mason FRHistS AMRAeS, one of our finest aviation authors, for kindly allowing me to use his photos, and to reproduce his superb line drawings and Hercules cut-away.

I am no less grateful to all of the following people, each of whom supplied me with an embarrassment of riches, time and expertise. It is no exaggeration to say that for every photo featured in this book, there are at least five more for which, unfortunately, no room could be found: Lt Col Lennart Berns; Sgt Rick Brewell, RAF PR; Capt Mike Brignola USAF; Alan Brothers, Lockheed Martin, London; S/Sgt Colin Coupens USAF; Ray Crockett, Director of Information, Lockheed Martin, Marietta, Georgia; Don L. Dick, Media Relations, RAF Mildenhall; Gp Capt Alex Dickson OBE AE FIMgt; Graham Dinsdale; Paul Dunn; Maj Don Eaton, WOC Mombasa Public Affairs; Lt Col Walt Evans USAF; Brian Foskett, Marshall Aerospace; Ron Green; Terry Holloway, Marshall Aerospace; Mick Jennings; Gary Madgwick/The Aviation Workshop; G. McA. McBacon; Andy Sheppard, Guideline Publications; Capt Darren A. Maturi USAF; Pete Nash; Miranda Pye, Lockheed Martin, London; Mike Rondot, RAF Retd; Graham Simons; SrA Christopher C. Thomas USAF; Robert Walden; Andrew Wise, Editor, RAF News; Geoffrey Woodford.

Biographies of airmen lost in south east Asia were kindly provided by Margaret Nevin and H. W. Hoffman of 'Homecoming II' and Ted Sampley, both of whom worked tirelessly at the *US Veteran News and Report* on behalf of Vietnam War MIAs. Thanks too, go to the 2nd Air Division Memorial Library in Norwich for help with books and volumes on USAF history, people and aircraft.

Martin W. Bowman
Norwich, Jan 1999

C-130s have hauled gas, ass and trash in several wars. KC-130R BuNo 160626 of VMGR-252 is pictured at Muhharad Bahrain on 1 March 1991, just after the end of the Gulf War, where the USMC 'hauled gas for those who kicked ass.' Mike Rondot

Contents

Introduction

C-130J, the next millennium Hercules. N130JA/ZH865, the C-130J prototype, was rolled out at Marietta, Georgia, on 18 October 1995, and first flew on 5 April 1996. Lockheed Martin

Everyone knows the Hercules – even those who are unaware of its C-130 military designation know exactly what it is for and what it does, this bulky, squat, but lovable aircraft with the reassuring friendly face of a seal pup and whaled tail. In RAF circles it goes by the name of 'Fat Albert' and in Vietnam it soon earned sardonic affection as the 'trash and ass hauler' – at least, that's what the 'fast movers' called it. Its reputation was such that one US colonel proclaimed that it was the only airplane of which it could be said that if it had been grounded, then the war would have ended. Universally this 'Mr Dependable' is fondly referred to as the 'Herky Bird'.

In the twenty years since the Vietnam War this priceless aircraft has written its own chapter in aviation history as the world's most successful military airlifter. For when military cargo and heavy equipment have to be delivered into trouble zones – or soldiers and paratroops, or people, relief supplies and medical aid, or if the need to be evacuated from war and famine, then the success of the operation depends on this immensely reliable and versatile airlifter. When there are labours to be done, whether they be military support or international relief, the Hercules is usually there, swirling the dust in the middle of desert wastes, being put down on a remote jungle strip, or landing on bomb-scarred runways at war-ravaged airports, delivering cargo or airdropping supplies.

For forty years the Hercules has also come to the aid of countless thousands in every part of the world. Name a continent, and the Hercules has invariably been there, and usually more than once – seen it, done it, and if it hasn't, is doing it tomorrow. Normally it is in the background, beavering away, earning its keep, not so much an unsung hero, but more a faithful friend we have all met somewhere before and have begun to take for granted. Sometimes, though, at Khe Sanh, Entebbe and Sarajevo, to name but a few, the Hercules has taken centre stage. At Khe Sanh in 1968 some 6,000 marines were entirely dependant on air supplies, and the C-130s delivered everything, often in foul weather conditions and in the face of enemy

4

opposition, for seventy-one days almost non-stop. Pilots used what came to be known as the 'Khe Sanh' approach, a method whereby the aircraft stays high, only nose-diving towards the landing strip at the last moment so as to avoid anti-aircraft fire for as long as possible.

More than 2,100 of these much-loved aircraft have been built, and yet the design did not please everyone when it first appeared in 1954. Kelly Johnson, who generated many wonderful sleek designs – the Starfighter and the Blackbird included – at the Burbank 'Skunk Works', called the Hercules 'ugly'. Granted, the C-130 has never been sylph-like and it can be uncomfortable, especially riding back there in the hold – but ugly? Never! Its rotund appearance has tended to hide several novel features, including four turbo-prop engines capable of reverse thrust, large low-pressure tyres semi-recessed into undercarriage blisters, and a rugged, simple construction that was designed from the outset to operate from rough or semi-prepared grass- or sand-strips with the minimum of support. This 'ugly duckling' has undergone five major facelifts and countless modifications, while some show stretchmarks having been lengthened to carry civil and military cargo in the L-100 configuration. These changes have resulted in a myriad number of successful variants, including gunship, bomber, air-to-air refueller, airborne command post, AWACS, fire-fighter and even airborne hospital: but the Hercules has always managed to retain the same familiar characteristics and proven pedigree that it has enjoyed since it first took to the skies on 23 August 1954.

However, none of those variants has been more significant or as far-reaching than the latest C-130J development of the aircraft: this is truly a model for the next millennium, with databus architecture replacing conventional wiring; a revolutionary new powerplant driving six-blade, scimitar-shaped composite propellers; and a cockpit with a digital autopilot, a fully integrated global positioning system, colour weather and ground-mapping radar and a digital map display, plus an advisory caution and warning system that allows for fault detection.

Such technological advances were not even a remote possibility back in the early fifties when the United States Air Force developed requirements for a new tactical aircraft based on the lessons being learned

in the Korean War. Even so, in 1950 an idea – a pipe-dream almost – for an aircraft that could carry a 30,000lb (13,600kg) payload of freight or troops over a distance of 1,500 nautical miles and could land and take off from difficult terrain, was reportedly thrown into a brainstorming meeting at the Pentagon by an unknown USAF colonel. At this time the request was akin to trying to send a manned vehicle to the moon. Certainly, it was almost technically impossible, given the limit of engine and airframe development at this time. However, a more formal operational requirement developed from the original idea, and requests for proposals were issued to Boeing, Douglas, Fairchild and Lockheed.

mand. Ten years later, when America became involved in the Vietnam War, it was the Hercules that moved troops and equipment from the US base at Naha, Okinawa, to South Vietnam. At the peak of the war effort there were fifteen squadrons of C-130s permanently assigned for Tactical Air Command or temporary deployment duties. Although around fifty Hercules aircraft were lost in Vietnam, the C-130 had more than distinguished itself, not just in troop and cargo movements but in many other important roles, too. For instance, it was the last aircraft out of Saigon in 1975, and was jam-packed with people: there were 475 reported on board, fifty of them crammed into the flight deck!

Mass parachute jump by the RAF formation team, 'The Falcons', from C-130K XV214.
via Frank Mason

The Air Force demanded responses within two months. The Burbank advanced design department made its submission on time, and the Model L-206, as it was called, was judged the winner out of the four contenders. Lockheed had opted for an uncomplicated, workmanlike design for the airlifter, but had made what it thought was a brave decision by rejecting conventional piston engines and going for the newer and less proven technology of turboprops.

The designers proved their detractors wrong. The first Hercules entered service in 1956 with the USAF Tactical Air Com-

Since then, the Hercules has never been far from the front line. It has continued to prove to be a most flexible workhorse, while its humanitarian role may account for the great affection which the Hercules seems to inspire; it even boasts its own civilian fan club! What challenges the next millennium will pose for the aircraft, few people would dare to hazard a guess, but of one thing we can be certain, and that is that those who are fortunate to have worked with and flown on the Hercules can look back with a deep sense of pride at an airlifter that is without equal.

Plan view

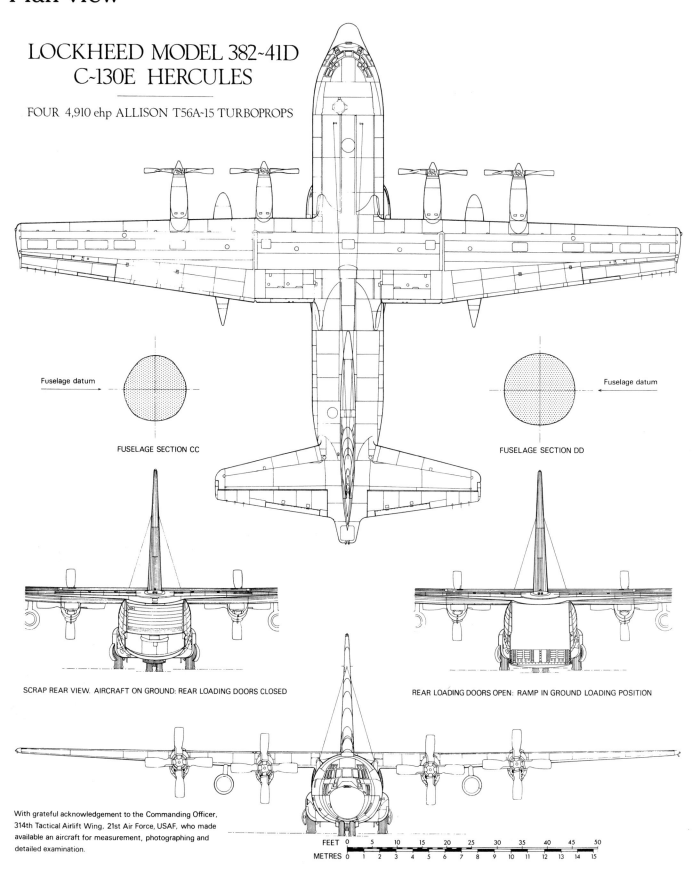

LOCKHEED MODEL 382~41D
C~130E HERCULES

FOUR 4,910 ehp ALLISON T56A-15 TURBOPROPS

Fuselage datum →

FUSELAGE SECTION CC

← Fuselage datum

FUSELAGE SECTION DD

SCRAP REAR VIEW. AIRCRAFT ON GROUND: REAR LOADING DOORS CLOSED

REAR LOADING DOORS OPEN: RAMP IN GROUND LOADING POSITION

With grateful acknowledgement to the Commanding Officer, 314th Tactical Airlift Wing, 21st Air Force, USAF, who made available an aircraft for measurement, photographing and detailed examination.

FEET 0 5 10 15 20 25 30 35 40 45 50
METRES 0 1 2 3 4 5 6 7 8 9 10 11 12 13 14 15

Plan view

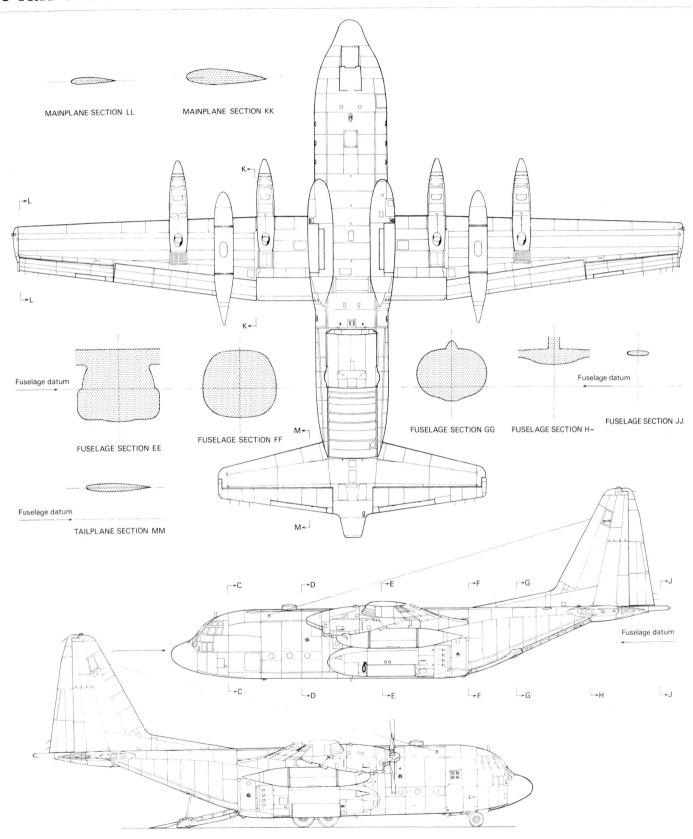

MAINPLANE SECTION LL

MAINPLANE SECTION KK

K

L

L

K

Fuselage datum

Fuselage datum

FUSELAGE SECTION EE

FUSELAGE SECTION FF

FUSELAGE SECTION GG

FUSELAGE SECTION H-

FUSELAGE SECTION JJ

M

Fuselage datum

TAILPLANE SECTION MM

M

C D E F G J

Fuselage datum

C D E F G H J

Cutaway view

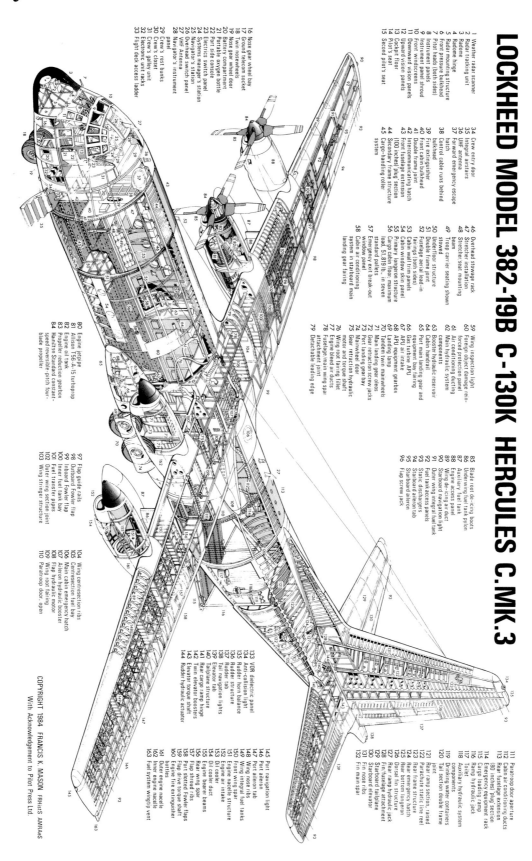

LOCKHEED MODEL 382-19B C-130K HERCULES C.MK.3

1 Weather radar scanner
2 Radar tracking unit
3 Radome hinge
4 Radome
5 Twin nosewheels
6 Forward emergency escape hatch
7 Pilot heads (both sides)
8 Instrument panel shroud
9 Front windscreens
10 Downward vision panels
11 Upward vision panels
12 Cockpit floor
13 Pilot's seat
14 Second pilot's seat
15 Flight deck access ladder

16 Nose gear wheel bay
17 Ground telecom socket
18 Nose gear wheel door
19 Nose gear wheel door
20 Battery compartment
21 Portable oxygen bottle
22 Port side console
23 Electrics switch panel
24 Systems manager's station
25 Navigator's station
26 VHF Antenna
27 Overhead switch panel
28 Navigator's instrument panel
29 Crew's rest bunks
30 Crew's closet
31 Crew's galley unit
32 Electronic unit racks
33 Radar mounting structure
34 Front pressure bulkhead

34 Crew entry door
35 Integral airstairs
36 VHF antenna
37 Forward emergency escape hatch
38 Control cable runs behind bulkhead
39 Fire extinguisher
40 Front cabin bulkhead
41 Double frame joint
42 Intercommunicating hatch
43 Front fuselage extension (100 inches) plug section
44 Secondary frame structure
45 Cargo-handling roller system

46 Overhead stowage rack
47 Stretcher installation
48 Stretcher seat mounting
49 Troop carrier seating shown stowed
50 Underfloor structure
51 Double frame joint
52 Fuselage aerial lead-in fairings (both sides)
53 Cabin wall trim panels
54 Cabin window skin panels
55 Primary longeron structure
56 Cargo cabin floor: maximum load, 51,819 lb., in seven standard pallets
57 Emergency exit break-out window panel
58 Cabin air conditioning system in starboard main landing gear fairing

59 Wing inspection light
60 Foreign object damage reinforced protection panel
61 Air conditioning ducting
62 Main hydraulic system components
63 Booster hydraulic reservoir
64 Cabin handrail
65 Port main landing gear and equipment bay fairing
66 Gas turbine APU
67 APU air intake
68 APU equipment gearbox
69 Landing ramp
70 Tandem twin mainwheels
71 Main landing gear oleos
72 Gear retraction screw jacks
73 Starboard landing gear bay
74 Mainwheel door
75 Gear retraction hydraulic motor and torque shaft
76 Port landing gear fairing fillet
77 Engine bleed air ducts
78 Fuselage main wing spar attachment joint
79 Detachable leading edge

80 Engine jetpipe
81 Allison T56-A-15 turboprop
82 Engine oil tank
83 Propeller reduction gearbox
84 Hamilton Standard constant-speed reversible-pitch four-blade propeller

85 Blade root de-icing boots
86 Underwing fuel tank pylon
87 Auxiliary fuel tank
88 Engine access panel
89 Wing de-icing air duct
90 Starboard navigation light
91 Outer wing integral fuel tank
92 Fuel tank access panels
93 Static dischargers
94 Starboard aileron tab
95 Starboard aileron
96 Flap screw jack

97 Flap guide rails
98 Outboard Fowler flap
99 Inboard Fowler flap
100 Inner fuel tank bay
101 Fuel transfer pipes
102 Wing root fairing
103 Outer wing section joint
103 Wing stringer structure

104 Wing centresection ribs
105 Centresection fuel bay
106 Main cabin emergency hatch
107 Aileron hydraulic booster
108 Flap hydraulic motor
109 Wing root fairing
110 Paratroop door, open

111 Paratroop door aperture
112 Cabin air conditioning ducts
113 Rear fuselage extension (80 inches) plug section
114 Emergency equipment rack
115 Cargo loading ramp
116 Ramp hydraulic jack
117 Toilet
118 Auxiliary hydraulic system
119 Drinking water containers
120 Tail section double frame joint
121 Rear ramp section, raised
122 Parachute static line reel
123 Rear ramp structure
124 Rear emergency hatch
125 Rear bottom longeron
126 Dorsal fin structure
127 Rear ramp hydraulic jack
128 Fin/fuselage attachment
129 Starboard tailplane
130 Starboard elevator
131 Fin nose ribs
132 Fin main spar

133 VOR dielectric panel
134 Anti-collision light
135 Rudder horn balance
136 Rudder structure
137 Rudder tab
138 Tail navigation lights
139 Elevator tab
140 Tailplane structure
141 Rear cargo ramp hinge
142 Twin elevator boosters
143 Elevator torque shaft
144 Rudder hydraulic actuator

145 Port navigation light
146 Port aileron tab
147 Port aileron
148 Wing nose ribs
149 Port integral fuel tanks
150 Front wing spar
151 Engine nacelle structure
152 Engine air intake
153 Oil cooler
154 Oil cooler duct
155 Rear wing spar
156 Engine bearer beams
157 Rear slotted Fowler flaps
158 Port drive torque shaft
159 Flap shroud ribs
160 Engine fire extinguisher bottles
161 Engine nacelle
162 Inner engine nacelle
163 Fuel system wingtip vent

COPYRIGHT 1984 FRANCIS K. MASON FRHistS AMRAeS With Acknowledgement to Pilot Press Ltd.

CHAPTER ONE

A Feat of Strength and Endurance

On 21 June 1932 at a bankruptcy court a group of investors led by Robert E. Gross, a San Francisco investment broker, bid $40,000 for the assets of the defunct Lockheed Aircraft Company. As there were no other bids, Judge Harry Holzer accepted their offer, adding 'I sure hope you fellows know what you're doing!'. Gross became chairman and treasurer of the new Lockheed Aircraft Corporation, while Lloyd C. Stearman was elected president and general manager. Under the new regime Lockheed moved away from their famous Orion and Vega single-engined designs, to twin-engined planes, the first of which was the successful Model 10 Electra transport, and later, the Model 12 Electra Junior fast executive transport. In 1936 Lockheed delivered its first military aircraft to the US Navy, Coast Guard and AAC, and plant facilities were increased to build the Model 14 Super Electra, which would fly on 24 July 1937.

Lockheed tried hard to carve a niche in the highly competitive transport market

First flight by the second YC-130 prototype (1002, 53-3397), on 23 August 1954 from the Lockheed Air Terminal, Burbank, California, pictured crossing the Sierra Nevada mountain range during the 61-minute flight to Edwards Air Force base in the Mojave desert, with Stanley Betz and Roy Wimmer at the controls.
Lockheed

with the Models 10, 12 and 14, and later Model 18, and eventually had a breakthrough on 23 June 1938, when Britain placed an order for 200–250 Hudson aircraft. World War II saw the Lockheed Aircraft Corporation grow enormously. On 31 March 1940 the workforce stood at 7,000 employees; in 1941 it had risen to 16,898 personnel. Between 1 July 1940 and 31 August 1945 Lockheed turned out 19,077 aircraft, including P-38 Lightnings, Hudsons and Lodestars, and 2,750 B-17 Flying Fortresses, to become the fifth-largest US aircraft producer.

Post-war, Lockheed sought other markets, notably in the field of civil and military propeller-turbine and jet transports. In 1955 the Model 188 Electra turbine-

Marietta, 15 miles (24km) from Atlanta, Georgia, and the complex was used to revamp B-29s and then build 394 Boeing B-47E Stratojets. The vast 76-acre (31ha) site was now destined to build another aircraft in far greater numbers, because on 2 February 1951, the USAF issued a request for proposals (RFP) to Boeing, Douglas, Fairchild and Lockheed for a medium transport complying with a specially prepared general operational requirement (GOR). Experience had revealed serious operational limitations in the Fairchild C-119 tactical troop and cargo transport, which was underpowered and offered little improvement over the earlier C-46 and C-47 transports. A replacement for the 'Flying Boxcar' therefore became of paramount

the time. Such was the urgency that the four manufacturers were expected to submit their final proposals within two months. Some sources predicted that the winner of the GOR could ultimately expect to build as many as 2,000 aircraft.

The new medium-size transport had to fulfil three main criteria. First, it had to be able to carry ninety-two infantrymen or sixty-four paratroopers over 2,000 miles (3,220km) for tactical missions, or for logistic missions, a 30,000lb (13,608kg) load (including bulldozers, trucks, road-graders and howitzers) over 950 nautical miles (all without refuelling); second, it had to operate if required from short and unprepared airstrips; and it had to be capable of slowing down to 125kt (232kmph)

Line-up of very early production C-130As at Marietta. The first seven C-130As were ordered by the Air Force on 10 February 1953, and in April 1954 the Pentagon ordered a further twenty C-130As. All of these aircraft were delivered without nose radome, but were later modified to carry AN/APS-42 or AN/APN-59 search radar. Lockheed

powered airliner entered the design stage. American Airlines and Eastern Airlines between them ordered seventy-five Electras, and by the end of 1955 Lockheed had received orders for another sixty-one. A military development, the P3 (P3V) Orion long-range patrol aircraft, went on to achieve great success, as did the Constellation family of piston-engined transports, 856 of which were built, and a further 1,051 P2V Neptunes.

In January 1951 Lockheed reopened Plant 6, a government-built factory at

importance, especially with the escalation of, and American involvement in, the Korean War, which had broken out in June 1950. As already mentioned in the introduction, at a brainstorming meeting at the Pentagon that same year an unknown USAF colonel is reported to have said that what the Air Force really needed was an aircraft that could carry a 30,000lb (13,608kg) payload of freight or troops over a distance of 1,500 nautical miles, and could land and take off from difficult terrain – a feat almost impossible to achieve at

for paradrops (made through two side doors) and even more slowly for steep 'assault' landings. A critical requirement was that it had to perform with one engine out over the drop zone, and this had to be taken into consideration. At Lockheed-Burbank, Art Flock and his design team under the supervision of Willis Hawkins, head of the advanced design department, went to work on temporary design designation L-206. Hawkins opined that it would have to be an amalgam of jeep, truck and aircraft, and Flock and his team

53-3129, the first production C-130A-LM which was rolled out at Marietta on 10 March 1955, took off for the first flight at Marietta, Georgia, on 7 April 1955 with chief pilot Bud Martin at the controls. Lockheed

53-3129, pictured passing Stone Mountain, near Atlanta, Georgia, was nearly lost on 14 April 1955 when an inflight fire broke out in the no. 2 engine during a landing at Dobbins Air Force Base. The fire took hold and broke off the left wing before fire crews extinguished the blaze. A new wing was fitted, and 53-3129 went on to complete a memorable career as The First Lady, seeing service as a JC-130A space vehicle tracker at the Atlantic missile range then as a transport, and later as an AC-130A gunship in south-east Asia. Lockheed

(Right) C-130A-LM 55-0023 (3050) City of Ardmore, the fiftieth Hercules built, was the first of three in the first delivery to a Tactical Airlift Command operational squadron (772nd Troop Carrier Squadron, 463rd Troop Carrier Wing), at Ardmore AFB, Oklahoma, on 9 December 1956. Crew L–R: Joe Garrett and Capts Gene Chaney, Richard Coleman and T/Sgt Al Marchman, flight engineer. City of Ardmore was damaged by ground fire in Vietnam in March 1968, was repaired, and served the Air Force until the late eighties before being acquired by the Texas Museum of Military History (now the Linear Air Park, at Dyess AFB) in 1989. Lockheed

C-130A 55-0004 which joined the 314th TCW, Tactical Air Command in October 1957. This aircraft was finally retired at the end of the 1980s. Lockheed

explored all possibilities before reaching the final design. Al Lechner busied himself with the general configuration, including the wing and fuselage, while Jack Lebold dealt with the undercarriage, and Willard Tjossen and Merrill Kelly concerned

themselves with the preliminary design of the engines.

Although it was intended as a medium-sized tactical transport, Flock opted for four engines instead of two, even though this decision took much soul-searching, as

it would make the L-206 more expensive than its competitors. In a surprise move, the slimline 3,750eshp Allison T56-A-1A turbine driving three-bladed, variable-pitch, constant-speed propellers was chosen. No turbine-powered transports had

Some thirty-five C-130As were converted to other variants, including twelve (57-0484/495) which were modified to C-130D, a ski-equipped version conceived in the late 1950s for service with the 61st TCS in Alaska and Greenland in support of the Distant Early Warning (DEW) line radar stations. Six C-130Ds (57-0484/0489 – 57-0485 Snowshoe, pictured) were converted to C-130D-6 standard during 1962–63 by removal of their skis. Lockheed

ever been produced in the USA before, but these would give the L-206 a top speed of 360mph (580kmph), faster than any other tactical transport, and pitch could be reversed to enable crews to stop quickly and back up the aircraft on a short field.

Equally as ingenious was the name bestowed on the new aircraft: for a company which historically has always named its aircraft after constellations in the heavens, 'Hercules' was the only possible selection. In

only 3.4ft (1.04m) off the ground, or at truckbed height. Standard tie-down rings were fitted in the floor and on the walls of the cargo compartment to secure pallets, containers and vehicles. The inward-opening top half of the cargo door allowed the Hercules to airdrop equipment and cargo the width of the cargo compartment. The entire plane was pressurized, despite difficulties caused by so many openings (in addition to the rear ramp, a 6.7ft (2.04m)

and a systems manager (a loadmaster made up the fifth member of the crew) in a 'greenhouse' with twenty-three windows designed to give 20 degrees of down all-round visibility, especially during landings at rudimentary airstrips. A strong undercarriage had tandem main landing-gear wheels which retracted into fairings on the sides of the fuselage. A 132ft (40m) span, high aspect-ratio, angular wing was laid across a flat fuselage and provided excellent

C-130A-LM 54-1625 was delivered to the 314th TCW in August 1957; it was modified to JC-130A, and then in 1967 to AC-130A configuration in the 16th SOS, when it was named War Lord. The gunship was shot down over the Ho Chi Minh Trail on 21 April 1970. Lockheed

classical myth Hercules was a hero noted for his great strength and courage, and for the performance of twelve immense labours.

Other important Hercules' features included a 41ft 5in (12m 62cm) long cargo compartment of nearly square cross-section (10.3ft/3.14m wide and 9ft/2.74m high) for a total volume of 4,500cu ft (127.4cu m), with a hydraulically operated, two-segment, rear loading ramp, with the forward section hinged downwards to a maximum of 13 degrees to act as a ramp, and the aft segment hinged upwards. To achieve ease of loading and unloading, the cargo floor was

wide and 6ft (1.83m) high, upward-hinged door was situated on the port side of the fuselage just aft of the crew entrance door, and there were also paratroop doors on both sides of the rear fuselage just forward of the ramp. It had to be pressurized because one of the prerequisites to military service was that, having delivered troops and cargo, the new transport had to be able to accommodate seventy-four litter patients and two medical attendants, and evacuate them from that battle area.

Above the blunt nose, a spacious flight deck accommodated two pilots, a navigator

ground clearance. The 38ft (11.6m) high vertical stabilizer was designed to offer easy access to the aft fuselage, and would also permit pilots good control response on low-speed approaches. Inside the fuselage, folding canvas seats were provided for seventy-eight ground troops (with a maximum of ninety-two infantrymen being accommodated in a high-density configuration), or sixty-four paratroops. Alternatively, fifty-five seats facing aft could be installed when operating in the personnel transport role, or seventy-four litters and two attendants (or seventy

C-130A-LM 54-1639 (3026) is lifted over the production line at Marietta; in the background are Boeing B-47 Stratojet bombers. 54-1639 was delivered to the 314th TCW in August 1958, and was subsequently modified to JC-130A configuration. She finished her military career with the ANG, in 1989, and was the used for parts by TBM Inc. The aircraft is currently being restored as a tanker. Lockheed

(Below) Australia was the first overseas customer for the Hercules, ordering twelve C-130As, including A97-207 (57-0500/3207) which served No. 36 Squadron, RAAF, for twenty years, December 1958–78, this aircraft was subsequently loaned to rock star Bob Geldof for relief operations in Ethiopia where it was operated by International Air Aid. After a long career as N22FV, EL-AJM The Wizard of Oz, and other registrations with various operators, the aircraft is currently used by NASA at Dryden. MAP

(Bottom) C-130A A97-208 (57-0501/3208) was delivered to No. 36 Squadron, RAAF, in December 1958 also. It was taken into store at Laverton in 1978 and was later sold, in 1983, to the French government (Sécurité Civile) for Chad (TT-PAA). Gary Madgwick/The Aviation Workshop

litters and six attendants) could be fitted for casevac duties.

Most Lockheed people were greatly impressed with the final design, although notably 'Kelly' Johnson did not favour the 'bulky' shape. The L-206 certainly did not emerge a pretty aircraft, but the dependable, sturdy new transport was not designed to break the sound barrier. It was not designed to break anything: from the outset it was a thoroughbred, but a workhorse and not a steed, conceived only to toil and sweat down in the dust, ice lakes and jungle clearings, places where grace and beauty have no place – designed to get the job done, and get out again, preferably all in one piece. However, provision *was* made for a few social graces: the entire fuselage was air-conditioned and heated, and as has already been mentioned, pressurized. The Hercules was one of the first aircraft to use air bled from the engines to supply the air-conditioning and pressurization systems.

The Lockheed proposal was submitted in April 1951 along with the three other manufacturers. The Lockheed design team need not have worried about losing out to twin-engined designs on price: despite its size, and other factors, the new plane's overall performance and its superb handling ability outweighed any fiscal disadvantages, and on 2 July Lockheed was declared the winner. One of the plane's

The C-130B first flew on 20 November 1958, and in December a contract was issued for 123 C-130B models for Tactical Air Command. 58-0719 (3514) (pictured) was delivered to the 463rd TCW in July 1959; it was written off on 11 November 1965 after being spun by an engine groundtest at Forbes Field, Kansas, when it hit C-130B 58-0730, setting both aircraft on fire. Lockheed

Overseas customers for the C-130B were Canada (four), Indonesia (nine) and South Africa (seven), while Pakistan and Iran each received four aircraft from the US under the Military Assistance Program. Pictured is the third C-130B (62-3490/3700) for the Imperial Iranian Air Force, which as 5-103 served No. 5 Air Transport Squadron before being sold to Pakistan (AS-HFQ); it was written off on 8 July 1969 when it burned during refuelling at Islamabad. via Frank Mason

many advantages over its rivals was the fact that it weighed much less – 10,000lb (4,550kg) or more – than its competitors, its basic mission weight being only 108,000lb (9,000kg). This was due to the widespread use of machined skins with integral stiffening – one section for the upper and lower wing surfaces was 48ft (15m) long – which largely eliminated riveting, and in the process, produced a much stronger and more robust surface structure. More weight was saved by using 300lb (136kg) of titanium on engine

the USAF that the production models (Model 182) be built in Marietta. This proposal was accepted, and by the time the first seven C-130As were ordered, on 10 February 1953, most of the design team had moved to Georgia. Al Brown was chosen as C-130 project engineer.

The first C-130 prototype (1001/53-3396), which was to become famous as the Hercules, was initially used for static tests. The second YC-130 prototype (1002/53-3397) first flew at the Lockheed air terminal on 23 August 1954 with Stanley Betz

trial programme was carried out at the Air Force flight test centre at Edwards. Soon the Hercules was exceeding the original performance specifications, turning in cruising speeds of up to 20 per cent faster, an initial rate of climb and service ceiling some 35 per cent better, a landing distance down by 40 per cent, and one-engine-out climb rate up by a very impressive 55 per cent.

In April 1954 the Pentagon ordered a further twenty C-130As, and in September another order was issued for forty-eight more. The C-130A differed from the YC-

The C-130E first flew on 15 August 1961, and deliveries of the first of 377 C-130Es for the USAF began in April 1962. C-130E 69-6581 (4357) was delivered to the 61st TAS in 1969. Operating with the 37th TAS, this aircraft crashed on take-off from Ramstein AB, West Germany, on 14 November 1981 following a fin-stall caused by a missing washer on the rudder booster. *Lockheed*

nacelles and wing flaps, while another new development in the form of high-strength aluminium alloys, was used throughout the aircraft's overall structure. In an age when complexity in aircraft design seemed to be the byword, the simple Hercules design consisted of only about 75,000 parts.

Lockheed were awarded a contract for two YC-130 (Model 82) prototype/service-test aircraft, which would be built at Burbank, and on 19 September 1952, the Pentagon issued a letter contract for seven production aircraft. Lockheed proposed to

and Roy Wimmer at the controls, and Jack Real and Dick Stanton, flight engineers, on board. To keep expenditure down and to create space for flight-testing equipment, both prototypes were finished without the navigator's station, and were not fitted with radar, nor with the majority of the furnishing, while only minimum radio was installed. 53-3397 was airborne in 800ft (250m) from the beginning of its take-off roll, and made a 61min flight to Edwards AFB in the Mojave desert in California without a hitch. Most of the subsequent

130s principally in having provision for two 450 US gallon (1,703 litre) external fuel tanks outboard of the outer engines, and in being powered by more powerful T56 engines. The first twenty-seven aircraft were delivered without nose radome, but were later modified to carry AN/APS-42 or AN/APN-59 search radar. The first production C-130A-LM (53-3129) was rolled out at Marietta on 10 March 1955. Chief pilot Bud Martin and co-pilot Leo Sullivan flew it on 7 April 1955, and flight engineers Jack Gilley, Chuck Littlejohn

(Left) **The** Svenska Flygvapnet **(Swedish Air Force)** became the first European air force to operate the Hercules, leasing C-130E 64-0546/4039 from Lockheed in February 1965 after the aircraft had been sold back before delivery to the USAF. In 1982, 4039 (designated Tp 84 '84001' in Swedish service) was modified to C-130H configuration. Six additional C-130H models had by then entered service. 84001 is a regular attraction at European air shows and is pictured here at Air Fete 1997. Author

In all, nine overseas customers – Argentina, Australia, Brazil, Canada, Iran, Saudi Arabia, Sweden and Turkey – acquired 109 C-130Es. Some twenty-four Es were bought for Nos 435 and 436 Squadrons, Royal Canadian Air Force (130315/4070, pictured, joined No. 436 Squadron in April 1966). Author's Collection

and Bob Brennan checked out the systems. 53-3129 flew perfectly, but it was nearly lost a week later, on 14 April, at the end of a test flight in which each engine was feathered and air-started. All went well, but an inflight fire broke out in the no.2 engine during a landing at Dobbins Air Force base. The pilot Leo Sullivan and co-pilot Art Hansen got the C-130 down safely at Dobbins, but here the fire took hold and broke off the left wing before fire crews extinguished the blaze; fortunately no-one was injured. The cause of the fire was later traced to a quick-disconnect fuel hose behind the engine firewall which had worked loose (the coupling was fitted to each engine to permit the USAF to change power plants quickly). The problem was soon rectified and a new wing was fitted, and 53-3129 was flying again within a few months. This particular C-130 was dubbed *The First Lady* and went on to complete a memorable career, seeing service as a JC-130A space-vehicle tracker at the Atlantic missile range, then as a transport, and later as an AC-130A gunship in south-east Asia. 53-3130 took over as the new structural test aircraft, using much of the heavy instrumentation from 53-3129.

Now occurred a greater problem so acute that it threatened the whole Hercules programme: the reduction-gear system in the Curtiss-Wright variable-pitch three-bladed propeller units were electrically-driven, and an electrical malfunction began causing a series of uncontrollable pitch changes and also severe propeller vibration. By the time the tenth C-130A was rolled out, both Lockheed and the USAF were of the opinion that the problem with the propellers was not going to go away, and from 26 November 1955 a switch was made to an Aeroproducts' hydraulically operated design, first tested on the sixth C-130A. This partially cured the problem, but another change was made, in which the 15ft (4.57m) prop units were completely replaced with four-bladed 13.5ft (4.11m) Hamilton Standard hydraulic propellers. This ultimately proved the best solution, and the Hamilton-Standards were eventually retrofitted to most C-130As.

The Hercules was now in the ascendancy, in more ways than one. The prototype was turning in a very impressive climb-out performance in distances as short as 600ft (180m), and landing and coming to a stop well within 1,000ft (300m). The order book was increased in August 1955 when

A picture that says it all! C-130E 64-0542 (4032) **Haul On Call** was delivered to the 314th TCW in February 1965, and served eight other units before being assigned to the 317th TAW at Pope AFB in 1978. At the time of writing this aircraft is still going strong, serving in the 53rd AS, 314th AW, at Little Rock AFB, Arkansas. Andy Sheppard

a fourth contract was issued for eighty-four Hercules. Total Hercules orders now stood at 159, discounting the two prototypes.

In June 1956 two C-130As were delivered to the USAF Air Proving Ground Command at Eglin AFB for Category II and operational suitability tests, which they passed with flying colours. The C-130s also came through gruelling tests in cold climates and a programme of heavy lift cargoes and air drops. Finally, on 9 December 1956, the first operational C-130s for the USAF were delivered, when five were flown from Marietta to the Tactical Air Command's 463rd Troop Carrier Wing, at Ardmore AFB, Oklahoma. First to arrive was 55-0023 *City of Ardmore,* the fiftieth Hercules built. During the acceptance ceremony, Robert E. Gross, the chairman of Lockheed, formally handed over the Hercules to Gen Otto P. Weygand, chief of TAC. Addressing the 5,000 people present, Weygand told them that 'the C-130 will play a most important role in our composite air strike force, for it will increase our capability to airlift engines, weapons and other critical supply requirements'.

Altogether, the 772nd, 773rd and 774th Troop Carrier Squadrons (TCS) in the 463rd TCW (which lost one squadron when re-equipping, as did follow-on units) received about thirty-eight Hercules. By the end of the year, the 314th TCW at Sewart AFB, Tennessee, also took delivery of its first C-130A, and by the following summer, the 50th, 61st and 62nd Squadrons had been allocated forty-eight C-130As. By the end of 1958, C-130As equipped six TAC squadrons in the US, three PACAF squadrons (the 21st, 815th and 817th in the 483rd TCW at Ashiya AB) in Japan, and three USAFE squadrons (the 39th, 40th and 41st in the 317th Wing at Evreux) in France. During 1958 the pioneer Hercules squadrons of the 463rd Wing at Ardmore moved to Sewart AFB, and this base became the hub of C-130 operations for the next three years. Altogether, 192 C-130As (and twelve ski-equipped C-130Ds) were delivered to TAC, while fifteen C-130As were delivered to the Air Photographic and Charting Service, Military Air Transport Service (MATS). Among the many modifications and sub-modifications, seventeen C-130As (and one JC-130A) became AC-130A gunships, sixteen were modified to JC-130A missile trackers for the USAF Space Systems Division, and eight became DC-130A drone launchers, while three became WC-130A weather

reconnaissance aircraft. In September 1958 an order for twelve C-130As (with T56-A-11 engines) was received for the Royal Australian Air Force (RAAF). It brought final C-130A production to 233 (including the two prototypes).

C-130 Main Models

In December 1958 a contract was issued for 127 C-130Bs (Model 282) for Tactical Air Command (C-130B 57-0525 first flew on 20 November 1958). The C-130B differed

In March 1960 the first forty-six GV-1 tanker versions (re-designated KC-130F in 1972) for the USMC were delivered. Pictured are BuNos 150688, 150687, 150686, 149816 and 149814 of VMGR-352 (which began receiving GV-1s late in 1962) heading out over the Pacific on 22 October 1963 from MCAS El Toro, California, to rendezvous with the F-4B Phantoms of VMFA-314 en route to their Far East destination. Refuelling the fighters 750 miles out to sea, the tankers had taken off two hours before the F-4Bs. Operating in VMGR-152, 149814 collided head-on with F-4B 151456 when refuelling other F-4Bs over South Vietnam on 18 May 1969. A. Scruggs, USMC via Francis K. Mason

The C-130H-LM (Model 382C) was the fourth main variant of the Hercules, and the first three production H models (NZ7001/3) were delivered in April 1965 to the RNZAF for issuing to No. 40 Squadron. NZ7004 and -05 followed in January 1969. (Pictured is NZ7002.) All five are still in operation with the RNZAF in late 1998. Gary Madgwick/The Aviation Workshop

The C-130K/Hercules C.Mk.1. (Model 382-19B) version for the RAF, which first flew on 19 October 1966, was similar in most respects to the C-130H. Some sixty-six C-130K models were built by Lockheed, with some components by Scottish Aviation; they were fitted by Marshall of Cambridge (Engineering) Ltd, with British electronics, instrumentation and other equipment before delivery to RAF Air Support Command. XV191 was delivered to No. 36 Squadron in August 1967 and is one of twenty-five aircraft which were modified to C.Mk.1P configuration with inflight-refuelling probes. C.Mk.1Ps and C.Mk.3Ps (twenty-five of which are to be replaced by C-130Js/ -30s) remain in service with the RAF, the largest Hercules operator after the USAF. MoD

from the C-130A in that its internal fuel capacity was increased by 1,820 US gallons (6,889 litres), it had heavier operating weights, and it was powered by 4,050eshp T56-A-7 engines. Ultimately some 230 C-130Bs were built. The US Navy (USN) received seven C-130F transports, the US Coast Guard (USCG) twelve HC-130B rescue aircraft, the US Marine Corps (USMC)

version were replaced by 1,360-gallon (5,148-litre) versions, with the larger external tanks being resited between the engine nacelles. Beginning with the ninth C-130E, the forward cargo-loading door (6.7ft by 6ft/2.04m by1.83m) on the port side was dispensed with. Deliveries of the first of 389 C-130Es for Military Airlift Command (MAC) began in April 1962. The USCG

are fitted with an improved braking system and redesigned centre-wing box assembly to extend the service life of the airframe. Sixty-six C-130K-LM (Model 382-19B) Hercules were built by Lockheed, with some components by Scottish Aviation, with British electronics, instrumentation and other equipment installed by Marshall Engineering, Cambridge, before delivery to RAF Air

C-130s mothballed at the MASDC (Military Storage and Disposition Center) in the early 1970s. The nearest aircraft, minus its engines and landing gear, is C-130A 53-3133 (3005), the seventh Hercules ordered for TAC and delivered to the 3206th TW at Eglin AFB in January 1956. Mick Jennings

forty-six KC-130F tankers, and MATS had five WC-130B weather reconnaissance aircraft. A further twenty-nine examples were ordered for the air forces of Canada, Indonesia, Iran, Pakistan and South Africa.

The C-130E (Model 382-4B), which first flew on 15 August 1961, was the third major Hercules production aircraft and was designed for longer-ranged logistic missions. Internal fuel capacity was increased from 5,050 US gallons (19,116 litres) for the C-130As, to 6,960 gallons (26,347 litres) for the C-130Es, while the two 450-gallon (1,703-litre) underwing tanks of the earlier

received one EC-130E electronics platform, and the USN had four C-130G TACAMO communications platforms from the production lines. Eight foreign countries (Argentina, Australia, Brazil, Canada, Iran, Saudi Arabia, Sweden and Turkey) ordered another ninety-seven production Es, to bring total C-130E production to 491.

The next major variant was the C-130H-LM (Model 382C), which was first delivered to the RNZAF in March 1965. C-130Hs are basically similar to the C-130E, but are powered by T56-A-15 engines, usually derated from 4,910 to 4,508eshp. They

Support Command. The C-130K first flew on 19 October 1966, and as the Hercules C.Mk.1, entered service with No. 2 OCU at Thorney Island in April 1967. Thirty C-130Ks were brought up to a standard approaching that of the L-100-30, with the fuselage stretched by 15ft (4.57m). Some 1,092 C-130H/K models were built. This includes 333 variants for the US armed forces (including the ANG, AFRes and USCG), and 693 C-130Hs for the US armed forces and forty-six countries excluding the UK. USAF versions of the C-130H include fire-suppression foam in the fuel

(Left) C-130H production line at Marietta in 1974. The nearest aircraft is 4556, destined for the Venezuelan Air Force (FAV) in February 1975 as 4224; it is followed by C/No. 4557, destined for delivery to the USAF in October 1974 – coded 73-1592, it has a Boron-epoxy composite reinforced centre wing. The latter aircraft entered service with the 314th TAW in January 1976; it lost its No. 3 propeller in flight in March 1992, was repaired, and is still in service with the 41st ECS, 355th Wing in Air Combat Command at Davis-Monthan AFB, Arizona. Lockheed

The nose and the rear fuselage of C-130H 4928 is mated with the centre section, largely built in Scotland by Scottish Aviation, on the Marietta production line. 4928 was delivered to the Algerian Air Force in July 1982 and coded 7T-WHJ. Lockheed

(Below) When this photograph was taken in 1975, C-130H (4584) was scheduled to become 1212 for Abu Dhabi. However, it was sold back to Lockheed in exchange for 4985. 4584 was sold to the Canadian Armed Forces (130337) in August 1986, and entered service in May 1987 with No. 436 Squadron. It transferred to No. 435 Squadron in 1989, and continues to operate with this unit at Trenton. Lockheed

tanks for improved survivability; however, international C-130H versions do not include fire-suppression foam.

Designations C-130L and C-130M were not used. C-130J/-30 (Models 382U/V) are being built to replace C-130s in service with the RAF, the launch customer, and in the US, those with MAC, AFRes and ANG. N130JA, the C-130J (RAF Hercules C.4/ZH865) prototype, was rolled out at Lockheed-Marietta on 18 October 1995, and flew for the first time on 5 April 1996.

By the mid-1990s there were still in active service over sixty C-130As out of the 231 C-130As built, approximately 130 C-130Bs out of 230 delivered, and of the 491 C-130Es built, more than 310 were in worldwide service with the US armed forces, and about ninety others in operational use with armed forces of various countries. Of the 1,092 C-130H models built, US government agencies were operating more than 300 C-130H models in a variety of special versions,

and about 350 standard C-130H models were in operation with the armed services of more than forty-six overseas countries. In addition, about eighty of the 116 L-100, -20 and -30 aircraft built were also in service with military and non-military operators.

When the millennium arrives the Hercules will have been in continuous production for over forty-five years, through at least *eighty-five* original and modified versions. Now that's versatility for you!

Reflected glory. C-130H (4785) A97-005 of No. 36 Squadron, RAAF, one of twelve H models for Australia, was delivered in August 1978.
Lockheed

Despite this newspaper advertisement, in Europe the much championed FLA concept, which has been on the drawing board since 1982, is an unknown quantity and the airlift market seems to have been left wide open for Lockheed.

(Above) **C-130H 82-0052/35-1072 (4980), the 1,700th C-130 built (and the second of fifteen C-130Hs for Japan) was handed over by USAF Col Ronald D. Patchett, who in turn officially presented the aircraft to Maj Masamichi Shishido of the Japan Self-Defence Force, Air Transport Wing, on 12 December 1983. Japan thus became the fifty-fifth nation to operate the Hercules, which, by the time this photo was taken, had been produced in more than forty versions and derivations.** Lockheed

C-130H 91-1231 (5278) of the 165th TAS, ANG, the 2,000th Hercules built, pictured at Split, Croatia, on 23 March 1994, during Operation Provide Promise. **This aircraft – which has since acquired the name** Man O'War – **was the first with SATIN (missile warner; chaff and flare dispenser), and was officially delivered to the 165th TAS, ANG, on 14 May 1992.** Author

CHAPTER TWO

Models and Variants

YC-130-LO (Model 082-44-01)

The two prototypes/service test aircraft (C/N 1001/1002, 53-3396/53-3397) were the only two Hercules built at Burbank; they were powered by four 3,250eshp Allison YT56-A-1A axial-flow propeller turbines driving three-blade Curtiss turbopropellers. The first aircraft was used initially for static tests and the first flight was made by 53-3397 at the Lockheed Air Terminal on 23 August 1954. The YC-130s were later operated by Allison for engine tests, and were re-designated NC-130s in 1959. 53-3396 was disassembled in October 1960, and 53-3397 in 1962.

C-130A-LM (Model 182-44-03)

This was the first production version, of which 204 were built at Marietta in Georgia. These differed from YC-130s in that they had provision for two 450-US gallon (1,703-litre) external fuel tanks outboard of the outer engines, and were powered by 3,750eshp Allison T56-A-1A

or T56-A-9 engines. The original Curtiss three-blade propellers were fitted to the first fifty or so C-130As, but during the course of production these were replaced, first by Aeroproducts propellers, and finally, in 1978, by Hamilton-Standard four-blade units. All C-130As had provision for four 1,000lb (454kg) thrust Aerojet 15KS-

1000 JATO (jet-assisted take-off) bottles on each side of the rear fuselage to improve short-field performance, thus reducing take-off ground run at the design mission weight of 108,000lb (48,988kg) from 1,000 to 790ft (305 to 240m).

Rough-field tests proved that the side-hinged nose-gear doors were easily dam-

Specification – Lockheed C-130A Hercules	
Powerplant:	Four Allison T56-A-9 turboprops, each rated at 3,750eshp
Weights:	Operating 61,842lb (28,051kg); max. take-off 124,200lb (56,340kg); max. payload 36,600lb (16,600kg)
Dimensions:	Span 132ft 7in (40.41m); length 97ft 9in (29.79m); height 38ft 3in (11.66m); wing area 1,745sq ft (162.12sq m)
Performance:	Max. speed 383mph (616km/h); cruising speed 356mph (573km/h); rate of climb 1,700ft/min (518m/min); ceiling at 100,000lb 34,000ft (10,360m); take-off to 50ft 3,720ft (1,135m); landing at 100,000lb from 50ft 2,600ft (792m); range with max. payload 1,830 miles (2,945km); range with max. fuel 3,350 miles (5,390km)

C-130A 55-0005 (3032), delivered to 314th TCW, TAC, in September 1957. It transferred to the South Vietnamese Air Force in November 1972. MAP

aged, and starting with the fifteenth production aircraft, these were replaced with units sliding fore and aft of the wheel well. The first twenty-seven C-130As were delivered with a 'Roman nose', but beginning with the twenty-eighth production aircraft, the now familiar 'Pinocchio nose' radome was added to house AN/APN-59 search radar in place of the earlier AN/APS-42. (The last ten of the first twenty-seven were retrofitted with the new radome also.) Other production changes included the installation of a crash position indicator in an extended tail-cone; wing centre-section modifications to extend the life of the airframe; the installation of the Tactical Precision Approach System; and the deletion of the upward-hinged, forward cargo door. Provision was made later for some C-130As to carry two 500-US gallon (1,893-litre) auxiliary fuel tanks in the fuselage, while others were equipped to carry a 450-gallon (1,703-litre) non-jettisonable pylon tank beneath each wing outboard of the engines.

The C-130A was first flown at Marietta on 7 April 1955. Starting in October 1956, 192 C-130As were delivered to the USAF, and fourteen modified RC-130As were acquired. Beginning in December 1958, twelve C-130As powered by T56-A-11s were delivered to the RAAF, who operated the type for twenty years. Thirty-five C-130As were modified to AC-130A, C-130A-H, DC-130A, GC-130A, JC-130A, NC-130A, RC-130A, TC-130A, C-130D, C-130D-6 and RC-130S configurations. Two C-130As (55-046 and 55-048) were temporarily fitted with underwing refuelling pods for evaluation by the USMC.

In 1986, an NC-130A (55-022) belonging to the 4950th Test Wing, Aeronautical Systems Division (ASD) was modified as a sensor and seeker testbed for terminally-guided air-to-ground missiles. For that purpose, the aircraft was fitted with a retractable, gimballed ventral turret for the airborne seeker evaluation test system (ASETS). During the same year, two C-130As were specially configured for aerial spray operations to replace the unit's Fairchild UC-123Ks. The last C-130As in military service equipped the 155th TAS, Tennessee ANG; they were replaced by C-141Bs in 1991. Outside the military, many have been converted for civil use and as forestry tankers.

AC-130A-LM

54-1626, an early production JC-130A, was first evaluated as a 'gunship' under Project *Gunboat*, beginning on 6 June 1967. The AC-130A, sometimes referred to as *Plain Jane*, was modified by the Aeronautical Systems Division, Air Force Systems Command, at Wright-Patterson AFB, Ohio, to carry four General Electric 20mm M-61 cannon mounted on the port side of the fuselage, to fire obliquely downward. The following were also installed: Starlight Scope (a night observation device), side-looking radar, a computerized fire-control system, a beacon tracker, DF homing instrumentation, FM radio transceiver and an inert tank system; in addition, a semi-automatic flare dispenser and a steerable 1.5 million candlepower AN/AVQ-8 searchlight containing two Xenon arc lights (infra-red and ultra-violet) were mounted on the aft ramp.

Plain Jane was battle-tested in south-east Asia during October–December 1967 and from February–November 1968. It proved so successful that the Pentagon awarded a contract to LTV Electrosystems of Greenville, Texas, for the modification of seven more JC-130As to AC-130A configuration. Delivered between August and December 1968, they differed from the prototype in being fitted with improved systems, including the AN/AAD-4 SLIR (side-looking infra-red) and AN/APQ-136 moving target indicator (MTI) sensors , and an AN/AWG-13 analogue computer. Used in the fighting in south-east Asia, the AC-130As proved very effective, especially against vehicles along the Ho Chi Minh trail at night.

C-130A (55-0011) was modified under the 'Super Chicken' or 'Surprise Package' programme to meet a requirement for improved all-weather capability and with larger guns. The 'Surprise Package'/'Cornet Surprise'/'Super Chicken' AC-130As carried two 7.62mm guns, two 20mm cannon forward and two 40mm Bofors clip-fed cannon aft of the wheel fairing. An AN/ASD-5 'Black Crow' truck ignition sensor was installed in the prototype, but was not originally included in the subsequent aircraft. Also fitted were Motorola AN/APQ-133 beacon tracking radar, and an AN/ASQ-24A stabilized tracking set containing ASQ-145 LLLTV (low light-level television).

Nine further C-130As were modified to the AC-130A 'Pave Pronto' configuration with AN/ASD-5 'Black Crow' truck ignition sensor reinstated, also the AN/ASQ-24A stabilized tracking set with AN/AVQ-18 laser designator and bomb damage assessment camera, SUU-42 flare ejection pods, dual AN/ALQ-87 ECM pods under the wings, and some other improvements. The earlier AC-130As were retrospectively brought up to 'Pave Pronto' and 'Pave Pronto Plus' standard. In south-east Asia the AC-130As used their laser designation/rangefinder equipment to mark targets for F-4 Phantoms carrying laser-guided bombs (LGBs). Five were destroyed in combat between 1969 and 1972.

The eighteen C-130A/JC-130As modified as gunships were 53-3129, 54-1623,

C-130A-II 56-0525 (3133), one of twelve SigInt aircraft, of the 7406th Combat Support Squadron, 7407th Combat Support Wing, pictured in August 1966 at Rhein-Main AB, West Germany. It served this unit until 1969 when it passed to Air America, an airline with CIA links; it was returned to C-130A configuration in 1973, finally seeing out its career in 1986 with the 356th TAS. Even then, the aircraft was in demand, being used at Rome Laboratory, Rome, New York, for electro-magnetic pulse and ECM testing.
MAP

DC-130A BuNo. 158228 (3048) of Fleet Composite Squadron -3 (VC-3), armed with three BQM-34 Firebee target drones, pictured in August 1975. This aircraft was retired in 1979. Avtel Services Inc., of Mojave, California, continues to operate DC-130As on Teledyne Ryan and Northrop drone operations for the USN. USN

54-1625/1630, 55-011, 55-014, 55-029, 55-040, 55-043/044, 55-046, 56-469, 56-490 and 56-509.

C-130A-II-LM

Beginning in late 1957, twelve C-130A-II COMINT/SIGINT (communications intelligence/signals intelligence gathering) versions were obtained by modifying C-130As (54-1637, 56-0484, 56-0524/0525, 56-0528, 56-0530, 56-0534/0535, 56-0537/0538 and 56-0540/0541). Each was fitted with direction finders, pulse and signal analysers, receivers and recorders, and was capable of accommodating twelve to fifteen ECM operators. Up until about 1971 the C-130A-IIs were operated by the 7406th Operations Squadron, 7407th Combat Support Wing, at Rhein-Main AB in West Germany, and from Athens, Greece, on Operation *Creek Misty* and other eavesdropping missions along the Iron Curtain and in the Middle East. 56-0528 was shot

down by Soviet fighters over Armenia during an eavesdropping sortie on 2 September 1958. All remaining C-130A-IIs were replaced by C-130B-IIs in 1971.

DC-130A-LM

In 1957 two C-130As (57-496 and 57-497) were modified as drone directors to carry, launch and direct remotely piloted vehicles (RPVs) such as the Ryan Firebee drone. These were followed in the 1960s by 56-491, 56-514, 56-527, 56-461, and 57-523 (an ex-RL-130A), and a C-130D (55-021). Originally these were designated GC-130A but from 1962 all were known as DC-130A. The DC-130A carries four drones beneath the wings, with specialized guidance equipment operators in the fuselage. The first two DC-130As were transferred to the USN as BuNos 158228/158229. Many had their original 'Pinocchio nose' replaced with an extended (thimble) nose radome housing the AN/APN-45, and some had an

added microwave guidance system in an undernose (chin) radome. Beginning in 1969, five DC-130As were transferred to the USN and to VC-3 (Composite Squadron Three), where they were given BuNos 158228, 158229, 560514, 570496, and 570497. Following Navy service, the last three were operated under contract, first by Lockheed Aircraft Service, and then by Flight Systems Inc. from Mojave Airport, California.

GC-130A-LM

This was the initial designation given to the DC-130As, later applied to permanently grounded Hercules that are, or have been, used as instructional airframes.

JC-130A-LM

Sixteen C-130As (53-3129/53-3135, 54-1624, 54-1627/54-1630, 54-1639, 56-490, 56-493, and 56-497) were modified in the late 1950s and early 1960s to track missiles

One of sixteen RC-130As which served with MATS' 1375th Mapping and Charting Squadron, 1370th Photomapping Group, Air Photographic and Charting Service. (Note the large camera hatches and the dielectric panels in the under-fuselage). This unit, re-designated 1,370th Photomapping Wing in 1960, was inactivated in June 1972, and fifteen of the RC-130As were returned to C-130A standard. Lockheed

RC-130A inboard profile.

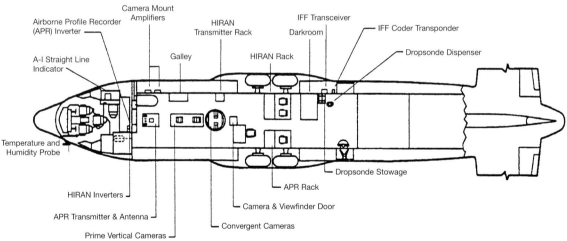

Camera Mount Amplifiers
Airborne Profile Recorder (APR) Inverter
HIRAN Transmitter Rack
IFF Transceiver
Darkroom
IFF Coder Transponder
A-I Straight Line Indicator
Galley
HIRAN Rack
Dropsonde Dispenser
Temperature and Humidity Probe
HIRAN Inverters
APR Transmitter & Antenna
Prime Vertical Cameras
Convergent Cameras
Camera & Viewfinder Door
APR Rack
Dropsonde Stowage

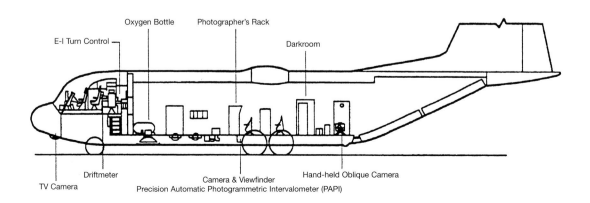

E-I Turn Control
Oxygen Bottle
Photographer's Rack
Darkroom
TV Camera
Driftmeter
Camera & Viewfinder
Precision Automatic Photogrammetric Intervalometer (PAPI)
Hand-held Oblique Camera

during tests over the Atlantic range. Based at Patrick AFB, Florida, at least eleven were used in conjunction with submarine-launched Polaris ballistic missiles. Six (54-3129, also 54-1627 to 54-1630, and 56-490) were later modified to become AC-130A gunships, while the remainder were converted to NC-130A and RC-130S configuration.

NC-130A-LM

Five C-130As (54-1622, 54-1635, 55-022/023, and 56-491) were temporarily used for special tests by the Air Force Special Weapons Center at Kirtland AFB, New Mexico. Three subsequently reverted to C-130A standard. The NC-130A designation was then used in 1968 to identify Airborne Seeker Evaluation Test System (ASETS) Aircraft.

TC-130A-LM

The nineteenth C-130A was modified to serve as the prototype for the proposed crew trainer version. The USAF had no requirement for a dedicated Hercules training aircraft and so it was modified again, to become the prototype for the RC-130A (see next entry).

RC-130A-LM

During the mid-1950s, TC-130A 54-1632 was modified as a prototype photographic-mapping aircraft. Equipment fitted included electronic geodetic survey apparatus, cameras, and a darkroom for in-flight photo processing. Its success in this role led to the last fifteen C-130As (57-0510/0524) being delivered in March 1959 to RC-130A standard, to the 1375th Mapping and Charting Squadron, 1370th Photomapping Group at Turner AFB, Georgia. This unit, redesignated 1370th Photomapping Wing in 1960, later moved to Forbes AFB, Kansas; it was inactivated here in June 1972. All except 57-0523 (which became a DC-130A) were remodified to C-130A configuration, stripped of their survey equipment, and served as transports with AFres and ANG units.

C-130B-LM (Model 282)

This was the second production series of the Hercules, and it was a more powerful version than its predecessors, due largely to the implementation of 4,050eshp T56-A-7 engines which drove four-bladed Hamilton Standard propellers. Other major improvements included a stronger landing gear, and additional tanks in the

wing centre section, inboard of the engines; these tanks increased the internal fuel capacity from 5,250 to 6,960 US gallons (19,873 to 26,346 litres), and meant that the pylon tanks could be deleted. The forward cargo door was permanently sealed, and a deeper cockpit with bunks for a relief crew was fitted. These improvements, plus in some aircraft the strengthening of the wing centre section to improve fatigue life, increased the gross weight from 124,200 to 135,000lb (56,336 to 61,235kg). Those aircraft fitted with an AN/URT-26 crash position indicator had the same extended tail-cone as similarly modified C-130As. A Tactical Precision Approach System was also installed.

The first aircraft (57-525) was flown at Marietta on 20 November 1958, and the C-130B first entered service with the 463rd TCW at Sewart AFB, Tennessee, in June 1959. A total of 231 C-130B versions were built, beginning in December 1958, comprising as follows: 118 C-130Bs for Tactical Air Command; forty-three C-130Bs for overseas customers (Canada, Indonesia, Iran, Jordan, Pakistan and South Africa); and seventy basically similar aircraft which were built as HC-130Bs for the US Coast Guard, WC-130Bs for the USAF, and as GV-1s (KC-130Fs), GV-1Us (C-130Fs), and UV-1Ls (LC-130Fs) for the US Navy and US Marine Corps. Thirty-seven USAF aircraft were modified as C-130B-Hs (RC-130Bs) JC-130Bs, NC-130Bs, VC-130B, and WC-130Bs, while two Indonesian aircraft (T-1309/T-1310) were modified as tankers with underwing refuelling pods, and became KC-130Bs. From 1988 Singapore also operated three KC-130Bs (720, 724 and 725). (The five new-build WC-130Bs (62-3492/3496) were remodified to C-130B configuration.) Aircraft basically similar to the C-130Bs were built as C-130BLs (LC-130Fs), WC-130Bs, GV-1s (KC-130Fs), GV-1Us (C-130Fs) and R8V-1Fs (SC-130B/HC-130Bs).

C-130B-II

Thirteen 'Sun Valley II' C-130Bs (58-711, 58-723, 59-1524/1528, 59-1530/1533, 59-1535 and 59-1537) were modified as electronic reconnaissance aircraft. They carried long-focal-length oblique cameras and reconnaissance systems and entered service in May 1961 with the 6,091st Reconnaissance Squadron at Yokota AB, Japan (556th RS from 1 July 1968). They replaced the unit's 'Sun Valley' and 'Smog

Count' Boeing RB-50Es used on Photo surveillance duty along the Korean DMZ (demilitarized zone). All thirteen C-130B-IIs were subsequently remodified as C-130Bs by removal of all reconnaissance equipment.

C-130BL-LM

This designation was assigned by the USAF to the first four 'ski birds' acquired for, and on behalf of, the US Navy to assist in Antarctic exploration as part of Operation Deep Freeze. In USN service the aircraft were originally designated UV-1L, but they were subsequently redesignated LC-130Fs in September 1962.

HC-130B-LM

Originally designated R8V-1Gs (USN) and SC-130Bs (USAF) prior to 1962, these twelve search and rescue aircraft were redesignated HC-130B in September 1962. All twelve were delivered to the US Coast Guard (USCG serials 1339/1342 and 1344/1351). They differed from C-130Bs in having the crew rest-bunks replaced by a radio-operator station and on-scene commander station, clear-vision panels fitting over the parachute doors after the cabin was depressurized, and provision for carrying life rafts and rescue kits. By using just two engines once the search area was reached, HC-130Bs could remain on station for up to seven hours. The HC-130Bs remained in service for almost twenty years before they were put into store at MASDC in the early 1980s.

JC-130B-LM

Fourteen C-130Bs (57-525/529, 58-713/717, 58-750, 58-756 and 61-962/963) were modified for aerial recovery of satellite capsules. Six were operated by the 6593rd Test Squadron, Air Force Systems Command, at Hickam AFB, Hawaii for aerial recovery of capsules ejected by Discovery military satellites. (Tracking equipment was carried in a radome atop the JC-130B fuselage, and a retrieval system was trailed from the rear cargo ramp to snatch the capsule parachute while in flight.) At least one JC-130B was used to evaluate the Fulton STAR (surface-to-air recovery) personnel retrieval system which was later fitted to the HC-130H and MC-130E. One JC-130B was modified as a VC-130B VIP transport before this aircraft, and most of the other JC-130Bs were converted back to C-130B configuration.

C-130B 57-0528, delivered to TAC in March 1959, was modified to JC-130B with a large radome atop the forward fuselage and wing-tip-mounted pods. MAP

Fourteen C-130Bs were converted to JC-130Bs for aerial recovery of satellite capsules with tracking equipment carried in a radome atop the fuselage, and a retrieval system trailed from the rear cargo ramp to snatch the capsule parachute while in flight. Most JC-130Bs were converted back to C-130B configuration.
Lockheed

KC-130B-LM

Two Indonesian Aircraft (T-1309/T-1310) and three Singapore aircraft (720, 724 and 725) were modified as tankers with refuelling pods containing hose-and-drogue assemblies in place of underwing tanks.

NC-130B-LM

This was the Lockheed-developed STOL version of the Hercules, initiated after the US Army expressed an interest in a short-take-off-and-landing aircraft. C-130B 58-712 was converted as a STOL prototype to test a boundary layer control system, having a rudder of increase chord and single-hinged flaps in place of Fowler flaps. Air bleeds, from two Allison YT56-A-6s operating as gas generators located under the outer wing panels in place of the external tanks, were blown over the flaps and rudder to enhance lift and controllability. All was in vain, however, as the US Army cancelled its requirement for the proposed C-130C production before 58-712 flew on 8 February 1960 in STOL configuration. In all, the NC-130B logged twenty-three hours of flight before being placed in temporary storage. The STOL system was later removed, and the aircraft fitted with standard wings and rudder from a damaged Hercules for delivery to NASA as N929NA (later N707NA), to take part in the *Earth*

C-130B 58-0712 (3507) before delivery was modified to BLC (Boundary Layer Control) test aircraft intended for the proposed C-130C STOL US Army version *(left)*. Fitted with blown flaps and control surfaces and compressors on the outer wings, it flew for the first time on 8 February 1960. 58-0712 was modified to NC-130B using the wing from a crashed L-100 (4109) and delivered to NASA, Johnson Space Center, Texas, in July 1968. It was sold to NASA, registered N707NA, in September 1969, and re-registered N929NA in October 1973 for earth survey work. In 1979, as part of the Airborne Instrumentation Research Program (AIRP), N929NA traversed over 25,000 miles (40,225km) of the Arctic, bringing back data to help pave the way for future offshore oil exploration in America's Arctic regions. It is pictured *(below)* in Norway's Spitzbergen islands – note the huge round nose, from a retired NASA P-3 Orion, containing a C-band microwave antenna, a four-channel radiometer (a key remote-sensing instrument) and the standard C-130 radar navigation antenna. The belly of the aircraft contains a camera bay, and a special thermometer with an eleven-channel scanner along with an eight-channel scanner and an 'active' microwave antenna. On the upper side of the rear ramp are located three additional microwave antennas, and still another on the 'platypus' extension behind the tail, while on the lower ramp two antennas could be extended out from the open ramp door, enabling clear ground view without aircraft interference. Re-registered N707NA in February 1982, it is still flying today, with NASA Dryden, at Edwards AFB, California. Lockheed

Survey Programme. One JC-130B (58-717) assigned to the 6,593rd Test Squadron, was also designated NC-130B for use on special tests.

RC-130B-LM *See* C-130B-II entry.

SC-130B-LM

This was the re-designation of the R8V-1Gs; later they became HC-130Gs, and finally HC-130Bs.

VC-130B-LM

One JC-130B (58-714) was temporarily modified as a staff transport before being remodified to the C-130B configuration.

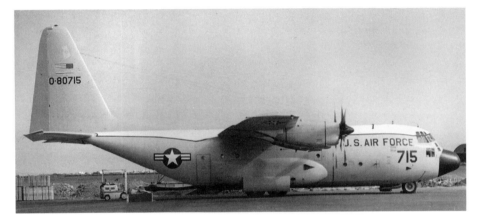

The single VC-130B VIP transport, 58-0715 (3510) converted from a JC-130B and serving with the 1174th Support Squadron at Norton AFB in December 1969. The aircraft was converted to C-130B standard in 1976, and it entered storage at AMARC in 1993. MAP

WC-130B-LM

Five weather-reconnaissance aircraft (62-3492/3496) were produced in 1962 for the Air Weather Service by Lockheed. That same year, they entered service with the 55th Weather Reconnaissance Squadron at Ramey AFB, Puerto Rico, where the WC-130Bs replaced Boeing WB-50Ds on hurricane- and typhoon-hunting missions in the region. In the 1970s, eleven C-130Bs (58-726/727, 58-729, 58-731, 58-733/734, 58-740/741, 58-747, 58-752 and 58-758) were modified to WC-130B standard. When suitably modified WC-130E/H aircraft were obtained in the mid-1970s, most WC-130Bs were returned to C-130B configuration for service in AFRes and ANG units. 58-731, a Kaman AWRS (Airborne Weather Reconnaissance System)-equipped aircraft, was the exception, being transferred in 1975 to the National Oceanic and

Atmospheric Administration (NOAA), US Department of Commerce, at Miami, Florida first as N8037 and then as N6541C.

C-130C-LM

This was the proposed STOL US Army version for which the NC-130B-LM (58-712) had served as a prototype. It was not built.

C-130D-LM

A ski-equipped version was originally conceived in the late 1950s for service in Alaska and Greenland with Alaskan Air Command in support of the Distant Early Warning (DEW) Line radar stations. The forty-eighth C-130A (55-021) was modified to become the ski-equipped prototype, which, while retaining its wheeled undercarriage, was fitted with 5.5ft (1.68m) wide, Teflon-coated aluminium skis: the nose-unit skis were 10.3ft (3.14m) long, and the main skis 20.5ft (6.25m) long. The ski-equipped prototype first flew on 29 January 1957, and underwent testing in Minnesota and Greenland – only to be returned to C-130A configuration immediately afterwards. This aircraft later became a DC-130A drone director and was issued to the US Navy as BuNo. 158228.

In the meantime, twelve production ski-equipped C-130Ds (57-484/495) for TAC were built with late production C-130A airframes and powerplants. These were delivered to the TCS on 29 January 1959. Furthermore, two C-130As (57-473 and 57-474) were modified as C-130Ds but later were returned to their original

configuration, while six C-130Ds (57-484/489) were converted to C-130D-6 standard during 1962–63 by removal of their skis. C-130D-6 (3203) *The Harker* (formerly *Frozen Assets*) stalled while overshooting at Dye III 320km east of Söndreström on 5 June 1972 and was written off. Beginning in the summer of 1975, the rest were assigned to the 139th TAS, New York ANG, which operated the five 'ski-birds' until their replacement by LC-130Hs in November 1984–April 1985.

GC-130D/GC-130D-6

This was the designation given to at least three permanently grounded GC-130Ds used as instructional airframes.

C-130E-LM (Model 382)

Tactical Airlift Command's C-130A and C-130B had proved exceptional tactical transports. By 1964 the TAC needed additional C-130 models, and this requirement coincided with that of Military Air Transport Service (MATS), in June, for turbine-powered aircraft to replace part of its burgeoning fleet of obsolescent piston-engined transports. The third major production version of the Hercules was therefore designed with longer-ranged logistic missions in mind.

To meet the MATS payload-range performance requirement, maximum take-off weight on the first 323 C-130Es for the USAF, and the first thirty-five export models, was increased from 124,200lb (56,336kg) for the C-130A to 155,000lb /70,307kg (or to 175,000lb (79,379kg), by limiting manoeuvres to reduce load factors from 2.5 to 2.25), and by increasing the fuel capacity to 9,226 US gallons (34,923 litres). The latter increase was achieved by replacing the two 450-gallon (1,703-litre) underwing tanks of the C-130B by 1,360 US gallon (5,148 litre) underwing units, with the larger external tanks being moved to a position between the engine nacelles. Starting with the 359th C-130E (68-10934), the fuel capacity was increased to 9,680 US gallons (36,642 litres). The 4,050hp T56-A-7 engines used on the C-130B were retained, the increase in the C-130E's operating weight resulting in stronger wing spars and thicker skin panels, as well as strengthened landing gear. The first flight of a C-130E (61-3258, C/N 382-3609) was made at Marietta on 15 August 1961, with deliveries to the 4442nd Combat Crew Training Group, TAC, at Sewart AFB, commencing in April 1962.

(Above) WC-130B 62-3496 (3722), the last of five weather-reconnaissance aircraft which entered service with the 55th Weather Reconnaissance Squadron at Ramey AFB, Puerto Rico, in November 1962, on hurricane- and typhoon-hunting missions in the region. In the 1970s, eleven C-130Bs were modified to WC-130B standard, and when suitably modified WC-130E/H aircraft were obtained in the mid-1970s, most of the WC-130Bs were returned to C-130B standard for service in AFRes and ANG units. Lockheed

(Below) C-130D 57-0493 (3200) of the 139th TAS, New York ANG, taxiing near an Early Warning Radar outpost of the Dye Line in Greenland in the la te 1970s. This aircraft is now under restoration at the Pima County Air Museum at Tucson, Arizona. Lockheed

C-130E 63-9815 (3976) was delivered to MAC in August 1964 and was issued to the 1611th ATW in February 1966. It is pictured here serving with the 1,115th MAS at Duke Field with white top and grey bottom, in 1969. In 1972–73 the aircraft operated with the Military Assistance Advisory Group in Abu Dhabi before joining their 316th TAW. It currently serves in the 171st AS, 127 Wing, ANG, at Selfridge ANGB, Mt Clemens, Missouri, assigned to Air Combat Command. MAP

(Right) C-130E A97-180 (65-12904/4180) of No. 37 Squadron, RAAF, pictured at Sydney, Australia on 19 October 1988. Eight years earlier this aircraft (and A97-178) operated Red Cross relief flights to Kampuchea. The aircraft was one of twelve C-130Es delivered to the RAAF in 1966–67. Author

Specification – Lockheed C-130E Hercules	
Powerplant:	Four Allison T56-A-7 turboprops, each rated at 4,050eshp
Weights:	Operating 73,563lb (33,368kg); max. take-off 155,000lb (70,308kg); max. payload 45,579lb (20,674kg)
Dimensions:	Span 132ft 7in (40.41m); length 97ft 9in (29.79m); height 38ft 3in (11.66m); wing area 1,745sq ft (162.12sq m)
Performance:	Max. speed 384mph (618km/h); cruising speed 368mph (592km/h); rate of climb 1,830ft/min (558m/min); ceiling 23,000ft (7,010m); take-off to 50ft 5,580ft (1,700m); landing at 130,000lb from 50ft 3,750ft (1,143m); range with max. payload and reserves 2,420 miles (3,895km); range with max. fuel 4,700 miles (7,560km)

During production, the first sixteen C-130Es had the forward cargo-loading door on the port side sealed; from the seventeenth aircraft onwards it was removed entirely, to be replaced by new outer skin panels. Other ongoing improvements included the fitting of the AN/URT-26 crash position indicator in an extended tail-cone, the provision of both AN/APN-169A station-keeping equipment (SKE), and the Tactical Precision Approach System, as well as wing centre-section modifications to improve fatigue life. In 1970–71 the Adverse Weather Aerial Delivery System (AWADS) was installed aboard many tactical C-130Es. In later years, USAF, AFRes and ANG C-130ES have been upgraded by the installation of a self-contained navigation system (SCNS), enhanced SKE, and updated AWADS.

In total, Lockheed built 491 C-130Es, including one generally similar EC-130E and four C-130Gs for the US Coast Guard and the US Navy respectively; the USAF received 377 aircraft, including 255 for TAC and 122 for MATS, whose successor, Military Airlift Command (MAC), assumed complete control of airlift operations in the mid-1970s. (Now, Air Combat Command uses almost all USAF C-130Es for its operations.) Some 109 additional Es were exported to nine overseas countries, the Canadian RCAF being the first to receive them, in December 1964. Argentina, Australia, Brazil, Iran, Saudi Arabia, Sweden and Turkey, are the other C-130E customers, while Israel received ex-USAF C-130Es. Sixty USAF C-130Es were modified to fulfil seven different roles, detailed as follows:

C-130E-I

On 12 August 1958, during joint service tests, Marine S/Sgt Levi W. Woods was successfully plucked from the ground by a specially modified PB-1 using the Fulton STAR (surface-to-air recovery) personnel airborne recovery system. This provided for a line to be attached to the person to be rescued, held aloft by a helium balloon to be snatched by folding, pincer-like tines on the nose of the rescue aircraft. While the USN continued with their own Project 'Skyhook', USAF interest in the STAR system waned – until, that is, a pressing need to recover downed airmen and other service personnel deep in enemy territory arose in south-east Asia during the Vietnam War.

At Pope AFB, North Carolina, in 1965, trials involving a C-130E fitted with a fixed ring device on the nose proved successful. Seventeen further C-130Es (62-1843, 63-7785, 64-0508, 64-0523, 64-0547, 64-0551, 64-0555, 64-0558/0559, and 64-0561/0568) and one NC-130E (64-0572) were subsequently modified with the STAR system for special operation behind enemy lines, fitted with upgraded avionics for adverse weather operations. In 1967 they entered service with the 'Combat Spear' detachment of the 314th Troop Carrier/Tactical Airlift Wing, and then with the 15th Air Commando Squadron, 14th ACW. Although the STAR system was actively operated, there is no evidence that any recoveries actually took place. Instead, the C-130-Is (now known as 'Combat Talons') were used on more conventional, but equally risky, sorties in Vietnam, flying day and night airlift and adverse

weather resupply missions for special forces operating behind enemy lines. 64-0563 was destroyed during a mortar attack at Nha Trang on 25 November 1967, 64-0547 was shot down by a SAM in North Vietnam on 9 December, 64-0508 was shot down by ground fire during a night SAR mission near An Loc, South Vietnam on 28 December and crashed in Laos, and 64-0558 was lost in a mid-air collision with an F-102A near Myrtle Beach, South Carolina, in 1972. The remaining C-130E-Is became C-130H(CT)s, and two were modified as MC-130-Ys, and one as an MC-130E-C.

C-130E-II (ABCCC)

The war in south-east Asia revealed the need for ABCCC (Airborne Battlefield Command and Control Centre) aircraft,

(Above) C-130E 64-0558 (4059) was delivered to TAC in July 1965, and later modified to C-130E-I configuration with Fulton recovery gear and JATO bottles for service with Detachment 2, 1st SOS, and later, the 318th SOS. This aircraft was destroyed in a collision with a Convair F-102A near Myrtle Beach, South Carolina, on 5 December 1972. Lockheed

(Below) EC-130E 62-1818 (3780) Bad Boy, pictured at Keesler AFB, Biloxi, Missouri, on 13 October 1993. Built as a C-130E, the aircraft was modified to C-130E-II (ABCCC) in 1972 for service with the 7th ACCS, and modified again in 1977 for in-flight refuelling. In April 1980 it was one of the aircraft that took part in the abortive operation to Tabas, Iran. It currently serves the 42nd ACCS, 355th Wing, at Davis-Monthan AFB, Arizona. Author

whereby a commander could directly influence and co-ordinate operations involving ground personnel and the air components, and direct them in a unified manner against the enemy. This requirement led, in the early 1960s, to the C-130-II designation being applied to ten C-130Es (62-1791, 62-1809, 62-1815, 62-1818, 62-1820, 62-1825, 62-1832, 62-1836, 62-1857 and 62-1863). Each carried an AN/ASC-15 command battle staff module housing LTV communications and control systems, and accommodation for up to sixteen operators. Combat deployment with the 314th TCW, operating from Da Nang AB, South Vietnam, began in September 1965. The C-130E-IIs were re-designated EC-130Es (see **EC-130E/ABCCC** entry) in April 1967.

AC-130E-LM 'PAVE SPECTRE' I

In April 1970 a decision was made to convert, at Warner-Robins Air Material Area (WRAMA), two C-130Es to prototype AC-130E gunship versions. The C-130E's higher gross weight, stronger airframe and increased power offered greater payload and longer loiter time than the original AC-130A gunships. Originally the AC-130Es were armed with two 40mm Bofors cannon, two M-61 20mm cannon, and two MXU-470 7.62mm miniguns; eventually a 'Pave Aegis' array was carried, consisting of two miniguns (often deleted), two M-61 cannon, and a 105mm howitzer in place of one of the 40mm guns.

In February 1971, nine additional C-130E conversions were ordered. These were not dissimilar to 'Pave Pronto' AC-130As; however, by the time that the first AC-130Es were completed in July 1971, they represented such a quantum leap in avionics over the earlier 'Pave Pronto' gunships that they became known as 'Pave Spectre I's. AN/APN-59B navigation radar and a moving target indicator were carried in a nose radome, and a head-up display (HUD) was located in the cockpit. Also fitted were the following: AN/ASQ-5 'Black Crow' truck ignition detector sensor; AN/ASQ-145(V) LLLTV; AN/ASQ-24A stabilized tracking set with a laser illuminator and rangefinder; AN/AAD-7 FLIR; AN/APQ-150 beacon tracking set; and a 2kw AN-AVQ-17 searchlight. SUU-42A/A chaff and flare dispensers were located between the engine nacelles, and AN/ALQ-87 ECM pods were fitted on the outer wing pylons.

The 'Pave Spectre Is' (69-6567/6577) entered service in south-east Asia in the spring of 1972 and were used to great effect against NVA tanks and vehicles using the Ho Chi Minh trail at night. All but 69-6571, which was shot down near An Loc, South Vietnam, in March 1972, were upgraded in 1973 to AC-130H standard.

DC-130E-LM

Seven early-production C-130E airframes (61-2361/2364, 61-2368/2369 and 61-2371) were modified as launch-and-guidance aircraft for drones or RPVs (remotely piloted vehicles). Underwing pylons permitted four drones, or two drones and two external fuel tanks (on the inboard pylons) to be carried. Internally, provision was made for consoles and work stations for two launch control officers and two airborne remote-control officers. The DC-130Es differed from the DC-130As in having a chin radome containing a microwave guidance system in addition to the thimble radome which housed tracking radar. They entered service with the 408th/100th Strategic Reconnaissance Wing, and were used extensively in south-east Asia before being returned to C-130E configuration, and reassigned to the 314th TAW.

EC-130E

This designation has been used to identify six distinct Hercules variants, although the only one built to the actual EC-130E designation was a C-130E delivered to the US Coast Guard (USCG 1,414) in August 1966 for use a Loran (**LO**ng **RA**nge **N**avigation) A & C calibration aircraft. (During development it was designated S(for 'search') C-130E, but because the 'search' prefix was considered inappropriate for an electronic calibration aircraft, this was changed to EC-130E before delivery to the USCG. Later, this aircraft was re-designated HC-130E.)

EC-130E (ABCCC)

The EC-130E designation was next used in April 1967 to identify ten ABCCC (Airborne Battlefield Command and Control Centre) aircraft previously designated C-130E-IIs (62-1791, 62-1809, 62-1815 – destroyed by a rocket on the ground at Da Nang on 15 July 1967 – 62-1818, 62-1820, 62-1825, 62-1832, 62-1836, 62-1857 and 62-1863). These aircraft were operated in south-east Asia by the 7th Airborne Command and Control Squadron (ACCS). (62-1809 was destroyed in a collision with RH53D at Posht-i-Badam, Iran, during the attempt to rescue US hostages, on 24 April 1980.) At least four remaining EC-130Es were retrofitted with 4,058eshp (de-rated from 4,910eshp) T56-A-15 engines and fitted with an in-flight refuelling receptacle atop the forward fuselage. (Despite the changes these aircraft retained their EC-130E designation, and were not re-designated 'EC-130H' as is sometimes reported.) Since 1990, at least two EC-130Es received new Unisys ABCCC III capsules to replace the Vietnam era ABCCC II capsules. These have much new equipment, including upgraded satellite communications equipment, JTIDS data link, and secure communications facilities. The two ABCCC III EC-130Es became operational only twelve days before Operation 'Desert Storm', during which they controlled almost half of all attack missions flown during the war. Also, they were used to co-ordinate SAR missions, flying a total of 400 hours during more than forty sorties.

EC-130E(CL), EC-130E(RR) 'RIVET RIDER', 'CORONET SOLO'

Other aircraft designated EC-130Es at one time or another are five 'Comfy Levy'/'Senior Hunter' (63-7783, 63-7815, 63-7816, 63-7828 and 63-9816) and three 'Rivet Rider'/'Volant Scout' electronic surveillance aircraft (63-7773, 63-7869 and 63-9817). The first five aircraft were modified in 1979 to EC-130H(CL) configuration for the jamming and acquisition of electronic intelligence, by Lockheed Aircraft Service, for the Pennsylvania ANG's 193rd TEWS (in turn, re-designated 193rd ECS and 193rd SOG) at Harrisburg. ANG personnel fly these aircraft, but it is believed that mission specialists are provided by the National Security Agency, and that tasks are performed under the direction of USAF Electronic Security Command. Beginning in June 1987, all EC-130CL/RRs were retrofitted with T56-A-15 engines as well as in-flight refuelling receptacles and IRCM jamming equipment.

In June 1992, the three remaining EC-130E(CL) aircraft (63-7773, 63-7869 and 63-9817), plus 63-7783 (which was modified to EC-130E(RR) in April 1980), were brought up to 'Volant Solo' standard for 'PSYOP' missions. These were characterized by the addition of large blade aerials ahead of the fin and beneath the wing outboard of the engines; they became 'Coronet Solo' when the Pennsylvania ANG changed from TAC status to MAC control in March 1983.

Experience that was gained in the Gulf War revealed the need to install a new TV broadcast system suitable for operation

(Above) **EC-130E 63-9817 (3978), one of four 'Rivet Rider' aircraft of the 193rd TEWS, 193rd TEWG/193rd SOS, 193rd ECG, ANG, at Harrisburg IAP, Pennsylvania. Used initially as 'Coronet Solo' aircraft for 'PSYOP' missions, they were characterized by large blade aerials ahead of the fin and beneath the wing outboard of the engines. They became 'Volant Solo' in March 1983 when the Pennsylvania ANG changed from TAC status to MAC control, and thenceforth have been used as airborne radio/television relay and transmission stations to provide emergency broadcasts in the event of a national disaster or an emergency during special operations.** Lockheed

(Below) **Experience gained in the Gulf War, 1991, revealed the need to install a new TV broadcast system suitable for operation anywhere in the world. The four EC-130E (RR) aircraft in the 193rd ECG, ANG were therefore modified to 'Commando Solo' configuration between 1992 and 1993, their fin leading-edge blade aerials replaced by four fin-mounted TV antenna pods, and UHF/VHF antennas associated with TV broadcast signals located under the outer wing panels.** Gary Madgwick/The Aviation Workshop

anywhere in the world; in 1992–93 63-7773, 63-7869, 63-9817 and 63-7783 were hence modified to 'Commando Solo' configuration. The dorsal fin leading-edge blade aerial was deleted, and replaced by four fin-mounted, protruding antenna pods dedicated to low-frequency TV broadcasting, and a UHF/VHF antenna associated with TV broadcast signals, in two 23ft × 6ft (7m × 1.8m) pods, one mounted under each wing near the blade antennas. Other modifications include the addition of trailing wire antennas, one released from the 'beavertail' and used for high-frequency broadcasts, and a second, which is lowered from beneath the EC-

HC-130E-LM *see* EC-130E *entry.*

JC-130E-LM
This designation was applied to the first C-130E (61-2358) which in March 1964 was modified for unspecified trials at the Air Force Flight Test Center at Edwards AFB and El Centro. The aircraft was subsequently returned to C-130E standard in 1972.

MC-130E-C 'RIVET CLAMP'
MC-130E-Y 'RIVET YANK'
MC-130E-S 'RIVET SWAP'
These designations applied to fifteen special operations support (SOS) C-130E-1

retrofits include inertial navigation system (INS), IRCM pods, chaff and flare dispensers, radar warning receiver, and a system permitting precision air drops of special forces teams. Their serial numbers are as follows:

MC-130E-C Rivet Clamp:
64-523, 64-551, 64-555, 64-559, 64-561, 64-562, 64-566, 64-567, 64-568, 64-572.

MC-130E-S Rivet Swap:
64-571

MC-130E-Y Rivet Yank:
62-1843, 63-7785, 64-564, 64-565.

MC-130E-C RIVET CLAMP 64-0555 (4056) Triple Nickel Ethel **(formerly C-130E/C-130H(CT)), in the 8th SOS, pictured at RAF Fairford,** Author

130E and held vertically by a 500lb weight, and used for AM broadcasts.

During Operation *'Uphold Democracy'*, 'Commando Solo' broadcasts played a vital role in avoiding the necessity for an invasion of Haiti. The 'Commando Solo' configuration is also applicable in emergency in peacetime: thus EC-130Es can be used as airborne radio/television relay and transmission stations to broadcast public information and evacuation instructions in response to natural disasters such as hurricanes or earthquakes.

'Combat Talon Is', and they were obtained by upgrading and modifying eleven C-130H(CT)s, three C-130E-Is and one NC-130E (64-571 *Night Prowler*, reportedly used for ELINT). These improvements included a change to T56-A-15 engines, also the installation of an in-flight refuelling receptacle on top of the forward fuselage, and AN/APQ-122(V)8 dual-frequency I/K band radar with terrain following. MC-130E-C 'Clamp' aircraft were fitted with the Fulton STAR recovery system (the 'Yank' and 'Swap' are not). Other

Operating with the 1st SOS, 64-564 was lost in a crash on 26 February 1981 near Tabones Island, Philippines, during a low-level turn. In 1992, 63-7783 was modified to 'Commando Solo' configuration. In July 1994 MC-130E-C 64-567 in the 8th SOS flew ex-President Manuel Noriega from Panama to Miami.

NC-130E-LM
This was the designation given to two C-130Es (64-571 and 64-572) used for trials associated with the C-130E-1/MC-130E

project at Edwards AFB, California, and Wright-Patterson AFB, Ohio. 64-571 became an MC-130E-S, while 64-572 was remodified in 1977 as a C-130E-I, and in turn, as a MC-130E-C in 1979.

WC-130E-LM

The weather reconnaissance/hurricane- and typhoon-hunting version obtained by modifying six C-130Es (61-2360, 61-2365/2366 and 64-552/554) during the 1960s. All passed to the 815th TAS in 1989–91 for use in the transport mission role, while retaining their WC-130E config-uration. They were subsequently passed to the Aerospace Maintenance and Regenera-tion Center (AMARC).

C-130F-LM

The US Navy utility transport model cor-responding to the C-130B of the USAF. Seven were delivered as GV-1Us (BuNos 149787, 149790, 149793/149794, 149797, 149801 and 149805). They were re-desig-nated C-130Fs in September 1962.

KC-130F-LM (GV-1)

Marine Corps interest in a Hercules tanker version led to two USAF-loaned C-130As (55-0046 and 55-0048) being fitted with hose/drogue refuelling pods; they were then evaluated by the Naval Air Test Center (NATC) at Patuxent River, Mary-land, in 1957. The evaluation proved suc-cessful, and deliveries to the USMC began in 1960. Initially the GV-1s and GV-1Us (as they were known prior to September 1962) were powered by 4,050eshp T56-A-7 engines, but later they were modified to use the T56-A-16 version. Eventually, forty-six dual-role transport/tankers were ordered, to be achieved by the conversion of C-130B airframes. As tankers they car-ried one 1,800 US gallon (6,814 litre) tank (or two of these in overload condition) inside their fuselage, and 934lb (424kg) refuelling pods beneath their outboard wing panels, so that they could refuel

Aircraft basically similar to the C-130Bs were built as LC-130Fs, GV-1s (KC-130Fs), GV-1Us (C-130Fs) and R8V-1Fs for the US Navy and UBMC. Pictured is GV-1U (C-130F) BuNo149794 (3661) Sky Pig, of VR-22, USN; it was damaged by typhoon 'Omar' on Guam on 27 August 1992, and was broken up by an explosive ordnance disposal team. MAP

KC-130F BuNo. 148891 (3605), of VMGR-352 delivered to the USMC in April 1961, refuelling two F-8 Crusaders of VMF-451. The internal arrangement of the tanker includes accommodations for five crew on the flight deck, two observers at the aft doors (note the large observer window, added to both aft personnel doors), and either one 3,600 gallon (16,367 litres) or two 1,800 gallon (8,184 litres) cradle-mounted fuel tanks in the cargo compartment. Lockheed

simultaneously two fighters or attack aircraft. Each pod contained a hose and drogue unit with a 91ft (27.74m) hose – normally this extended to 56–76ft (17.07–23.16m) – and a refuelling basket, but it did not contain fuel. These HRU pods were fitted with three coloured lights: red indicating that pressure was off; yellow that the aircraft was ready to transfer fuel; and green that fuel was flowing. In USMC service the aircraft were given the following identification: BuNos 147572/573, 148246/249, 148890/899, 149788/789, 149791/792, 149795/796, 149798/800, 149802/804, 149806/816 and 150684/690.

KC-130F BuNo. 149798, the twenty-third KC-130F completed, had its in-flight refuelling pods removed, and was then fitted with Hytrol anti-skid brakes and modified nose-gear doors for delivery to the Naval Air Test Center, Patuxent River, on 8 October 1963: here it began trials to test the feasibility of operating the Hercules as a COD (carrier onboard delivery) aircraft. The KC-130F carried out ninety-five take-offs and 141 landings using a simulated *Forrestal*-class carrier, laid out at Patuxent River; it was then used in carquals on board USS *Forrestal* (CVA-59) itself during operations off the coast of Massachusetts on 30 October. In the first phase Lt (later Rear Admiral) James H. Flatley, USN, carried out fifty-four approaches, of which sixteen resulted in 'bolters' (touch-and-go landings). He later made more landings, stopping in a range of between 270 to 495ft (82

KC-130F BuNo. 150690 (3742) (pictured in March 1975) was delivered to the USMC in November 1962, and was used as the 'Blue Angel's' support aircraft from 1973 until 1983. USN

KC-130F BuNo. 149798 Look Ma, No Hook lifting off from the forward deck of the USS Forrestal (CVA-59) during carrier trials in October 1963. Lockheed

to 151m) without using an arrestor hook, and take-offs in the range of 745ft (227m) or less, without using the carrier's catapults. The landing weight was progressively increased from 85,000lb (38,555kg) to a record of 121,000lb (54,885kg), and Flatley demonstrated that the KC-130F could have delivered 25,000lb (11,340kg) loads to a carrier operating 2,500 nautical miles (4,630km) from the nearest land base. However, the idea was considered impractical as it required the flight-deck to be cleared of almost every other aircraft.

LC-130F-LM

There were four of these ski-equipped aircraft (BuNos 148318/ 321), based on the C-130B variant, with 4,050eshp T56-A-7 engines. They were acquired by the USAF as C-130BLs on behalf of the US Navy, which re-designated them as UV-1Ls (after September 1962 the UV-1L designation was superseded by the LC-130F designation). All were fitted with Navy communications equipment and skis similar to those of Air Force C-130Ds, for use by VX-6 (later VXE-6) in Operation *Deep Freeze* in Antarctica, where they replaced Douglas R4Ds.

JATO-assisted take-offs were frequently employed, but three serious accidents occurred when the bottles separated and damaged the aircraft surfaces. The worst of these happened on 1 December 1971 when BuNo. 148321 *The Crown* had to abort take-off from Carrefour 'D-59', 746 miles (1,200km) from McMurdo: it sank in the ice and was abandoned. It was finally dug out in December 1986, and after temporary repairs, was flown out in January 1988 to Christchurch, New Zealand, for permanent repair; it was returned to VX-6 at NAS Point Magu, California, in September 1989. BuNo. 148318 *City of Christchurch* hit a snow-wall taking off from McMurdo on 15 February 1971 and burned. BuNo. 148319 *Penguin Express* was damaged when a JATO bottle broke loose during take-off from Dome Charlie on 15 January 1975; it was repaired with a new wing and flown out of Antarctica in December 1976. BuNo. 148320 *The Emperor* was also damaged when a JATO bottle broke loose during take-off from Dome Charlie on 4 November 1975.

VXE-6 was disestablished in 1998/99, and the LC-130Fs were withdrawn from use in the Antarctic.

CG-130G-LM

This designation described four US Navy transport aircraft (BuNos 151888/891), corresponding to the C-130Es but fitted with Navy radio equipment and powered by 4,910eshp T56-A-16 engines. These aircraft served briefly in the transport role with VR-1 at Norfolk, Virginia, and with VR-21 at Barber's Point, Hawaii, before being modified for strategic communications as EC-130G TACAMO aircraft (*see* next entry).

EC-130G(TACAMO)

The designation given to the four C-130Gs (BuNos 151888/891) after they had been

BuNo. 148321 (3567) The Crown, a ski- and JATO-equipped LC-130F of VX-6, blasts off a snowfield in Antarctica. This aircraft was delivered to the USN in August 1960 and it made its first flight into the Antarctic in the winter season of 1962. It crashed during take-off from Carrefour 'D59', 746 miles (1,200km) from McMurdo on 15 January 1975 when a JATO bottle broke loose, and it sank into the ice. The aircraft was freed from the ice in December 1986, temporarily repaired, and flown out in January 1988 to Christchurch, New Zealand, for permanent repair. After ten more years' service with VX-6/VXE-6, The Crown was withdrawn from use in 1999. Lockheed

modified during the period 1966–1970 to TACAMO (TAke Charge And Move Out) configuration, and fitted with 5,000ft (1,524m) long, trailing antennas extending from the ventral loading ramp just below the rear fin. In this role the aircraft acted as relay stations, receiving VLF (very low frequency) and UHF communications from the National Command Authority (NCA) airborne national command posts (ABNCPs) via satellites and other emergency radio links, and then retransmitting the instructions in VLF to ballistic missile submarines at sea. All four EC-130Gs were operated by Fleet Command and Control Communication Squadrons Three and Four (VQ-3 and VQ-4). BuNo. 151890 was written off at Patuxent River after being damaged by an inflight fire in the no. 1 fuel tank in January 1972. In May 1990, BuNo. 151891 was modified to TC-130G as a testbed for equipment being developed for the EC-130Q, including wing-tip electronic pods; from October 1991 it was used as the 'Blue Angels' support aircraft. The original TACAMO aircraft were joined by a number of EC-130Qs, though eventually both the EC-130Gs and -130Qs were replaced by Boeing E-6A Mercury aircraft.

HC-130G

This designation was used briefly only to refer to the twelve aircraft delivered to the US Coast Guard (USCG serials 1339/1342 and 1344/1351) in the early 1960s. The aircraft involved were soon re-designated however (see **HC-130B** entry).

TC-130G

After retirement from the TACAMO mission, it was intended that the three EC-130Gs would be brought up to TC-130G standard for the trainer/utility transport role. However, none of the aircraft had retained their rear cargo ramp, and so 151891 was fitted out as the 'Blue Angels' support aircraft. 151888 and 151889 *were* re-designated TC-130G, but the former was sent to AMARC in 1990, and the latter was broken up in March 1994, having been used for spares while in storage at NAD Cherry Point, North Carolina, from 1992–93.

C-130H-LM

The first C-130H (4052/NZ7001) flew on 19 November 1964. Initially this most numerous version of the Hercules was built with the overseas market in mind, the first three models being delivered to

the RNZAF in March 1965. However, sales only really took off when the Air Force showed interest in the early 1970s, the first models being delivered to the USAF in 1974. Some fifty air forces have bought the C-130H, making it the most widely used model of the Hercules: in total, 1,092 C-130Hs have been built.

Outwardly C-130Hs were basically similar to the C-130E, but were powered by T56-A-15 engines normally derated from 4,910 to 4,508eshp. Other improvements included a redesigned outer wing and stronger centre-wing box assembly to improve the service life of the airframe, a more efficient braking system, and updated avionics. At first, provision for JATO was made, but this facility was abandoned in 1975. From 1993 the Night Vision Instrumentation System was introduced,

and TCAS II was included in new aircraft from 1994.

Beginning in 1979, C-130Hs were delivered to the AFRes and the ANG, the first time that these reserve forces had received new-build Hercules. Some of these aircraft have been, and indeed are still being used in fire-fighting missions. Specially modified aircraft are operated by the 757th AS, AFRes, based at Youngstown-Warren Regional Airport, ARS, Ohio, for aerial spraying, typically to suppress mosquito-spread epidemics.

Variants obtained by modifying existing C-130H airframes include the DC-130H, NC-130H, VC-130H and WC-130H. Related models are the HC-130H, KC-130H, C-130K, HC-130N, HC-130P, EC-130Q, KC-130R and LC-130R. A Swedish C-130E (Flygvapnet serial 84002) was

Sales of the C-130H only really took off when the Air Force showed interest in the early 1970s, the first of eighty-four being delivered to Military Airlift Command in 1974. C-130H 74-2061 (4644) in the 772nd ALS, pictured at Rhein-Main AFB, West Germany, was delivered to the 463rd TAW in October 1977, and is still in service with the 39th AS, 317th AG, 15th Air Force, Air Mobility Command, at Dyess AFB, Texas. By 1996 the USAF, ANG and AFRes had between them received 222 C-130Hs. USAF photo by George Wegemann

Specification – Lockheed C-130H Hercules	
Powerplant:	Four Allison T56-A-15 turboprops, each rated at 4,508eshp
Weights:	Operating 76,505lb (34,702kg); max. take-off 155,000lb (70,308kg); max. payload 42,637lb (19,340kg)
Dimensions:	Span 132ft 7in (40.41m); length 97ft 9in (29.79m); height 38ft 3in (11.66m); wing area 1,745sq ft (162.12sq m).
Performance:	Max. speed 385mph (620km/h); long range cruising speed 332mph (535km/h); rate of climb 1,900ft/min (579m/min); ceiling at 130,000lb 33,000ft (10,060m); take-off to 50ft 5,160ft (1,573m); landing at 100,000lb from 50ft 2,400ft (731m); range with max. payload and reserves 2,356 miles (3,791km); range with max. fuel 4,894 miles (7,876km)

brought up to C-130H standard in 1982. Two Royal Morocaine (Royal Maroc Air Force) C-130Hs (4888 N4162M/CNA-OP and 4892/CNA-OQ) were delivered in August 1981, with SLAR (sideways-looking airborne radar) on the left main undercarriage fairing for use in detecting Polisario infiltrations in the western Sahara.

C-130H-(CT)

This designation was given to C-130E-Is fitted with T56-A-15 engines and improved electronic equipment as part of the C-130E-I *Combat Talon* special operations programme. Nine later became MC-130Es and -Cs, and two became MC-130E-Ys.

C-130H-30 (previously C-130H(S))

This version combined the features of the C-130H with the longer fuselage (15ft/4.6m) of the L-100-30. The first two C-130H-30s (4864 and 4865, TNI-AU A-1317 and A-1318 respectively) were delivered to 32 Squadron in the Indonesian Air Force in September 1980. At the time of writing, a total of fifty-six new build, and two modified from C-130H configuration, have been built for thirteen air forces.

C-130H(AEH)

This aircraft was designed to provide medical care at remote disaster areas: Lockheed Aircraft Service, Ontario, California, first modified a C-130H ordered by the Kingdom of Saudi Arabia (c/n 4837/N4098M)

Two C-130Hs were modified as VC-130H VIP transports for the Royal Saudi Arabian Air Force, and two more (N4101M/4845) and N4099M/4843, behind) for the Royal Flight operated by Saudia. Lockheed

In June 1986, C-130H 85-1362 (5072) Spirit of Texas – seen here passing Dallas-Fort Worth – became the first H model received by the 181st TAS, 136th Tactical Airlift Wing, ANG, at JRB Fort Worth, Texas, which began replacing its ageing C-130Bs. ANG

as an airborne emergency hospital (AEH), complete with operating room, intensive care unit, and all necessary equipment and supplies. Electrical power for the medical equipment and air conditioning on the ground was provided by auxiliary power units house in non-standard underwing tanks, and could be operated continuously for up to seventy-two hours. Since delivering this first AEH in January 1980, LAS has modified and delivered to the Royal Saudi Air Force eight other C-130AEHs of various configurations (two modified C-130Hs, and six modified L-100-30s: 4954/HZ-117, 4950/HZ-MS05, 4952/HZ-MS06, 4956/HZ-MS09, 4957/HZ-MS10 and 4960/HZ-MS14), each having surgical capability. One version carries its own ambulance to transport triage teams to the scene of a disaster if it is away from where the aircraft is able to land; another can be quickly converted into a medical evacuation vehicle with the capacity to airlift fifty-two litter patients in a single flight.

C-130H-MP (PC-130H)
A multi-role maritime patrol and search-and-rescue version of the C-130H: the first three were initially produced for Malaysia in 1980 (4847, 4849 and 4866). A fourth

(4898/TNI-AU AI-1322) was delivered to Indonesia in November 1981, but was lost when it crashed into Sibyak volcano. These aircraft, powered by T56-A-15 engines, were fitted with seats and a rest area for a relief crew, also searchlights on the wing leading edge, observation windows on each side of the forward fuselage, an observer station in the port paratroop door, and a pallet-mounted flare launcher and rescue kit. A Hasselblad camera operating in tandem with the aircraft's navigation system and onboard computer could produce a matrix showing the time and position of any object photographed. Optional equipment included sea search radar, LLLTV, an IR scanner and passive microwave imager.

C-130H(S)
Subsequently re-designated **C-130H-30**.

AC-130H-LM
In June 1973 the ten surviving AC-130Es (69-6571 was shot down over South Vietnam in March 1972) were provided with 4,508eshp T56-A-15 engines, thereby upgrading them to AC-130H standard. In 1978 provision was made for in-flight refuelling with a boom receptacle atop the fuselage, aft of the flight deck. Retrofits

include a digital fire control computer, electro-optical (EO) sensors and target acquisition systems, including forward-looking infra-red (FLIR) and LLLTV. Fire-control computers, navigation, communications, ECM, and sensor suites have all been upgraded. AC-130Hs were deployed to the Middle East for the Operation *Desert Storm* mission in the Gulf War, 1991. 69-6567 in the 16th SOS was shot down on 31 January 1991, 110km south-south-east of Kuwait City. They have also taken part in operations in Bosnia, Liberia and Somalia; during the latter, on 14 March 1994, 69-6576, in 16th SOS, crashed in the sea 7km south of Malindi, Kenya, after take-off from Mombasa when a howitzer round exploded in the gun tube and caused a fire in the left-hand engines. In January 1998, 69-6568 was delivered as the (MC-130P) prototype for the 'Special Operations Force Improvement' (SOFI) update programme. At the time of writing, eight AC-130Hs serve with the 16th SOS; however, these will be progressively replaced by new-build AC-130U gunships.

DC-130H-LM
It was intended that two HC-130Hs (C/Nos. 4116 and 4131/65-971 and 65-979)

C-130H 64-14852 (4036) was the first H model and was delivered to AFSC at Edwards AFB in December 1965. It was modified to JHC-130H and then HC-130H, and was issued to the 57th ARRS in September 1971. After serving this unit, and then the 305th and 301st ARRS, it was issued to the 71st ARS in March 1992; it was painted grey in March 1994, being modified to HC-130P in December that year. Ron Green

C-130H 73-1594 was delivered to the 314th TAW in December 1974 and was assigned to the 41st ECS in March 1982; it was modified to EC-130H in May 1983 and given a lizard scheme. It was then assigned to the 43rd ECS (SB) (pictured) in July 1987; it joined its current unit, the 41st ECS, (DM) in March 1992.
Mick Jennings

be modified late in 1975 as drone directors, but the ending of America's involvement in the Vietnam war obviated the need for this, and in the final outcome, only 65-979 was converted to DC-130H standard, though both aircraft were transferred to the 6514th Test Squadron. In 1998, 65-971 was still flying as an MC-130P with the 5th SOS, while at the time of writing, 65-979 was still operating as an NC-130H.

EC-130H 'COMPASS CALL'/CCCCM

In the early 1980s this designation was used to identify four EC-130Hs (64-14859, 64-14862, 65-962 and 65-989) as well as twelve C-130Hs (73-1580/1581, 73-1583/1588, 73-1590, 73-1592, 73-1594 and 73-1595), modified for use as 'Command, Control and Communications Countermeasures' (CCCCM) jamming platforms. The last twelve aircraft were easily identifiable by a blister fairing on both sides of the rear fuselage, and undertail 'trestle-like' antenna array. Additional ram air inlets in the undercarriage bays provided cooling air for the onboard electronic equipment. The EC-130Hs played a vital role in disrupting Iraqi military communications at strategic and tactical levels in the Gulf War. At the time of writing, three of the original HC-130Hs modified to EC-130H (64-14862, 65-0962 and 65-0989) (64-14859 was

remodified to C-130H standard in 1996) are among the EC-130Hs operated by the 41st, 42nd and 43rd ECSs, 355th Wing, 12th Air Force, at Davis-Monthan AFB, Arizona. As new-build C-130J aircraft are procured, priority for replacement will be given to special mission aircraft.

EC-130H(CL) 'SENIOR SCOUT'

Two C-130Hs (4735/74-2134 and 5194/89-1185) were modified in March 1994 and January 1993 respectively: they were used for the jamming and acquisition of electronic intelligence.

HC-130H/HC-130H-7

Originally the HC-130H (crown bird) designation was for forty-five USAF rescue and recovery aircraft, built to replace the Douglas HC-54s used by the Air Rescue Service in the airborne rescue mission control function. A radio operator station was installed in place of crew bunks against the aft cockpit bulkhead, the bunks being relocated to within the main cargo compartment. An observation window with swivelling seat was sited on each side of the forward fuselage. Provision was made in the fuselage for a 1,800 US gallon (6,814 litre) auxiliary fuel tank, and for rescue equipment. The latter comprised three MA-1/2 kits (each kit consisting of

five cylindrical bundles linked by four buoyant 210ft/64m polyethylene ropes; bundles one and five contained life rafts, and bundles two, three, and four, waterproof supply containers). Ten launch tubes were installed in the rear ramp for parachute flares, smoke and illumination signals, or marine location markers.

The first HC-130H was delivered on 26 July 1965, and all were equipped with the nose-mounted Fulton STAR (surface-to-air recovery) personnel recovery yoke (although this was often removed in service). The first Fulton STAR live pick-up and dual pick-up took place on 3 May 1966 at Edwards AFB, California. Two days later, three men were plucked up from the Pacific Ocean surface, this particular exercise demonstrating the HC-130H's ability to recover the crew of Apollo spacecraft. Four aircraft (64-14858, 64-14854, 64-14857 and 65-979) were modified for in-flight recovery of space capsules after re-entry, before being assigned to the 6593rd Test Squadron at Hickam AFB, Hawaii. Subsequently they were re-designated JC-130H (64-14858), JHC-130H (64-14854 and 64-14857) and NC-130H (64-14854, 64-14857 and 65-979). At the request of NASA, all USAF HC-130Hs were fitted with a Cook aerial tracker (AN/ARD-17) in a fairing above the forward fuselage, to locate space capsules during re-entry. In fact, no spacecraft recovery missions involving HC-130Hs ever took place and no astronauts were ever recovered; but beginning in December 1965, HC-130Hs saw widespread use in south-east Asia as airborne co-ordination aircraft during combat rescue missions. Using its locator beacons, the Cook aerial tracker now proved valuable in locating downed personnel.

Two HC-130Hs became DC-130H drone control aircraft, one was temporarily designated JC-130H, four became EC-130Hs, and fifteen were modified as WC-130Hs.

The HC-130H designation was also applied to twenty-four basically similar aircraft built for the US Coast Guard (USCG 1452/1454, 1500/1504, 1600/1603 and 1710/1715) These, however, were not fitted with the ARD-17 Cook aerial tracker, nor the Fulton STAR recovery yoke, and they did not carry HRU pods.

The HC-130H-7 designation was used to identify eleven US Coast Guard aircraft (USCG 1700/1709 and 1790) powered by 4,050eshp T56-A-7B engines in place of T56-A-15s. Coast Guard versions have been fitted with side-looking airborne radar (SLAR) and forward-looking infra-red (FLIR) pods for drug surveillance operations. Experiments have been conducted using the Lockheed SAMSON ('Special Avionics Mission Strap On Now) system, which comprises a pod-mounted FLIR, an optical data link, and a control console with display and recorder.

Retrofits have included updated navigation equipment, and cockpit lighting has been modified to permit operations with night vision goggles (NVGs), while most of the surviving examples were brought up to HC-130P standard with wing-mounted HRU pods containing hose-and-drogue equipment for the in-flight refuelling of helicopters. At the time of writing, HC-130Hs are serving at six Coast Guard Air Stations in the USA, and at Argentia, Newfoundland, Canada.

(Above) **HC-130H Hercules 65-0964 (4104) and 65-0970 (4112) of the 67th ARRS. 65-0964 was modified to WC-130H in 1975, and is still flying today with 39th RQS, 939th RQW AFRes at Patrick AFB, Florida; 65-0970 is flown by the 303rd RQS, 939th RQW, AFRes at Portland IAP, Oregon.** USAF

Originally built as an HC-130H, 65-0979 (4131) was delivered to the 36th ARRS in March 1966, then later modified as one of two DC-130Hs in 1977. It carried a record external load of 40,000lb (18,144kg) as part of trials with 5-ton RPVs with the 22nd Tactical Drone Squadron. In September 1977 the aircraft was modified again, to NC-130H, and subsequently served in the 514th TS, before being assigned in 1995 to its current unit, the 418th FLTS, 412th TW, AFMC, at Edwards AFB, California. Lockheed

JC-130H-LM

The designation given to HC-130H 64-14858 while it was assigned to the 6593rd Test Squadron at Hickam AFB, Hawaii. This aircraft was returned to HC-130H configuration and subsequently modified to HC-130P standard, and finally to MC-130P, in February 1996.

JHC-130H-LM

The designation given to seven HC-130H aircraft so modified during 1965–66 (64-14852/14858): all were returned to HC-130H standard in 1986–87, then some to HC-130P configuration in 1989. (64-14854 and 64-14858 also operated later as MC-130Ps, while HC-130H 64-14857 went to AMRC in 1995 and is reported to have been acquired by the Royal Jordanian Air Force in 1997. HC-130P 64-14856 crashed into the sea 70 miles (113km) west of Eureka, CA, on 22 November 1996 after all its engines stopped because of fuel starvation.

HC-130(N)

This designation applied to six C-130H airframes, namely 88-2101 *City of Anchorage*; 88-2102, delivered in October 1990; 90-2103, delivered in November 1992, and 93-2104/2106, delivered in October 1995: they went to the Alaska ANG for the dual helicopter in-flight refuelling and rescue and recovery missions. Basically similar to the HC-130P, they have updated avionics, HRU pods beneath the wings, and auxiliary fuel tanks in the fuselage.

WC-130H 65-0966 (4107) of the 403rd Air Wing, AFRes, pictured at Keesler AFB, Biloxi, Missouri, on 13 October 1993. This aircraft was originally delivered to the 54th ARRS in November 1965 as an HC-130H. One of only a few WC-130Hs remaining in the Air Force inventory, this aircraft continues to serve in the 53rd WRS, 403rd Wing. Author

HC-130N 69-05827 (4376) in the 67th ARRS, pictured during a stopover in Iceland. This aircraft received the lizard camouflage scheme in 1986 and acquired the name The King; then in 1995 it entered service with the 5th SOS and was called The Cyclone Death Duck. The aircraft was re-designated MC-130P in February 1996. USN photograph by Phan Kirk M Fasking

KC-130H-LM

Twenty-two air tankers built new and six C-130Hs modified to KC-130H standard, have been produced for eight overseas air forces: Argentina, Brazil, Canada, Israel, Morocco, Saudi Arabia, Spain and Singapore. They were fitted with wing-mounted HRU refuelling pods, and one or two 1,800 US gallon fuel tanks in the fuselage hold.

LC-130H

The designation for seven ski-equipped C-130Hs: four aircraft (83-490/493) were first delivered to the New York ANG in 1985 to replace the C-130Ds equipping the 139th TAS. Three more (92-1094 *Pride of Grenville*, 92-1095, and 92-1096 *City of Christchurch NZ* were delivered to the 139th TAS during October–December 1995.

MC-130H-LM COMBAT TALON II

Designed to supplement and eventually replace the MC-130Es used by the 1st Special Operations Wing for *Combat Talon* clandestine and special operations. In 1984 the USAF ordered the first of twenty-four C-130Hs (83-1212) for modification to MC-130H Combat Talon II standard, with IBM Federal Systems Division handling systems integration, and E-Systems installing the specialized avionics. Electronic and equipment fit included AN/APQ-170 multi-role radar (ground-mapping, navigation, terrain following, and terrain avoidance), INS, high-speed low-level aerial delivery and container release system, and automatic computed air-release point, as well as AN/AAQ-15 IR detection system, AN/AAR-44 launch warning receiver, AN/ALQ-8 ECM pods, AN/ALQ-172 detector/jammer, AN/ALR-69 radar warning receiver, IR jammer, and chaff/flare dispensers.

The first MC-130H was delivered to the 8th SOS at Hurlburt Field, Florida, in June 1990. All twenty-four MC-130Hs (83-1212, 84-475/476, 85-011/012, 86-1699, 87-023/024, 87-125/127, 88-191/195, 88-264, 88-1803, 89-280/283, 90-161/162) were delivered to the USAF by November 1991.

NC-130H-LM

Re-designated **JHC-130H**s.

VC-130H-LM

Six C-130Hs modified as VIP transports for the Egyptian Air Force (4803 and 4811, in 1984 and 1979 respectively), and four for Saudi Arabia (4605, 4737 for the RSAF, and N4101M/4845 and N4099M/ 4843 for the Saudi Royal Flight, operated by Saudia). All are distinguishable by having enlarged, relocated square fuselage windows, airline seating, galley and toilet, and extra sound-proofing.

WC-130H-LM

The designation given to fifteen HC-130H/C-130Hs (64-14861, 64-14866, 65-963/965, 65-966/969, 65-972, 65-976/977, 65-980, and 65-984/985) modified as weather-reconnaissance aircraft with Fulton STAR recovery system removed (but retaining radome) and special equipment fitted. 65-965 was lost in the Taiwan Strait on 13 October 1974 during penetration of typhoon 'Bees'. The fourteen remaining aircraft were transferred to the AFRes, 65-972 being transferred to AMARC in December 1997, leaving thirteen in AFRes service at the time of writing. Ten of these (64-14861, 64-14866, 65-963, 65-966/968, 65-977, 65-980, 65-984 and 65-985) currently equip the 53rd WRS, 403rd AW, at Keesler AFB, Biloxi, MS, pending replacement by the WC-130J.

YMC-130H-LM

Three USAF C-130Hs (74-1683, 74-1686 and 74-2065) received 'Credible Sport' modifications in 1980 to YMC-130H configuration, for possible use in the abortive Operation *Eagle Claw*, the attempted rescue of hostages in Iran. For this purpose they were fitted with an in-flight refuelling receptacle, DC-130 type radome, and downward-pointing braking retrorockets to reduce landing run. 74-1683 crashed at a demonstration at Duke Field on 29 October 1980 when the retrorockets fired too early. The two other YMC-130Hs were returned to C-130H standard in November 1984. 74-2065 is, at the time of writing, still in service with the 40th Airlift Squadron, while 74-1686 was put on display at Warner-Robins AFB Museum in March 1988.

C-130J-LM *See* Chapter 9.

C-130K-LM (C.Mk.1/C.Mk.1P/ C(K) Mk.1/W.Mk.2./C.Mk.3)

The sixty-six C-130Ks (XV176/223 and XV290/307) built by Lockheed, with some components made by Scottish Aviation; they were fitted by Marshall of Cambridge (Engineering) Ltd with British electronics, instrumentation and other equipment. Upon completion they were delivered to RAF Support Command. At first it was considered having these aircraft powered by Rolls-Royce Tynes, but in the end all were fitted with Allison T56-A-15s; they were similar in most respects to the C-130Hs. The C-130K first flew on 19 October 1966, and as the Hercules C.Mk.1, the type entered service with No. 242 OCU at Thorney Island in April 1967. One aircraft (XV208) was modified by Marshall for service with the RAF's Meteorological Research Flight at RAE Farnborough. Designated Hercules W.Mk.2, this aircraft first flew on 31 March 1973; it is characterized by a long instrumentation boom on the nose, and this has meant relocating the radar scanner onto a pod above the flight deck, scientific instruments into the fuselage and instrumentation pods beneath the wing.

During the period 1979–85, thirty C.Mk.1s were brought up to a standard approaching that of the L-100-30, with the fuselage stretched by 15ft (4.57m). The first Hercules brought to C.Mk.3 standard by Lockheed (XV223) was flown at Marietta on 3 December 1979; the remaining twenty-nine Hercules C.Mk.3s came from Marshall. The modification programme was completed in November 1985. Operation *Corporate*, the British operation to retake the Falklands in 1982, meant that the Hercules range had to be extended to enable them to support the Task Force from Ascension Island. Beginning in April 1982, Marshall's urgently installed 15ft in-flight refuelling probes to twenty-five C.Mk.1s, which were re-designated C.Mk.1P. They also began modification of six C.Mk.1s to serve as C(K).Mk.1 tankers, fitting them with a refuelling probe and a hose-drum unit; and beginning in 1986, in-flight refuelling probes were fitted to the thirty C.Mk.3s to convert them to C.Mk.3P configuration.

C-130L-LM and C-130M-LM

These designations were not used.

HC-130N-LM

Fifteen search-and-rescue aircraft (69-5819/5833), originally for the recovery of aircrew and the retrieval of space capsules: eleven were re-designated MC-130Ps in 1996; nine of these operate in the special operations squadrons, and two in the 67th ARRS. Four (69-5824, 69-5829, 69-5830 and 69-5833) remain as HC-130Ns, operating in the SAR role with the 39th RQS, 939th RQW (USAFRes), at Patrick AFB, Florida.

HC-130P-LM

Twenty combat aircrew recovery aircraft (65-988, 65-991/994 and 66-211/225),

(Above) The C-130K/Hercules C.Mk.1. for the RAF was similar in most respects to the C-130H, and the first of sixty-six models flew on 19 October 1966. The type entered service with No. 242 OCU at Thorney Island in April 1967. XV179 (pictured) was delivered to the OCU in May 1967 in the characteristic sand/brown camouflage scheme of the period. In May 1982 it was modified for the Falklands War by Marshall Engineering to C.Mk.1P configuration, with the addition of a 15ft (4.6m) refuelling probe; on 18 June 1982 it set an endurance record of 28hrs 4mins aloft. Marshall Aerospace

(Below) XV208 was delivered to No. 48 Squadron RAF in November 1967, and in 1972–73 was modified by Marshall Engineering for service with RAF's Meteorological Research Flight at RAE Farnborough. Designated Hercules W.Mk.2, this aircraft first flew on 31 March 1973; it has a long instrumentation boom on the nose, scientific instruments in the fuselage, and instrumentation pods beneath the wing. MoD

C-130K XV1900 was delivered to No. 36 Squadron in August 1967; it was subsequently 'stretched' by Marshall Engineering to C.3 standard, and finally to C.3P configuration with the addition of an in-flight refuelling probe. Betty Boop, as this aircraft was now named, received its overall grey scheme in July 1994. Sgt Rick Brewell RAF

(Right) HC-130P 66-0217 (4173), delivered to the 3rd ARRS in October 1966, was re-designated MC-130P in February 1996 and repainted grey. MAP

designated in 1966: they are similar to HC-130H (retaining that type's AN/ARD-17 Cook aerial tracker antenna and the Fulton STAR recovery system) but fitted with underwing drogue pods and associated plumbing for in-flight refuelling of rescue helicopters. The HC-130Ps entered service late in 1966, and were immediate- ly deployed to south-east Asia. 66-214 and 66-218 in the 39th ARRS were destroyed by satchel charges at Tuy Hoa, South Viet- nam, on 29 July 1968. 66-211 was lost when its right wing snapped in severe tur- bulence at low level 15.5 miles (25km) north of Magdalena, New Mexico, on 2 April 1986. In 1996 thirteen aircraft (65- 991/994, 66-212/213, 66-215/217, 66- 219/220, 66-223 and 66-225) were re- designated MC-130P. These currently operate in special operation squadrons. 65-988 currently operates in the 71st RQS, and three (66-221/222 and 66-224) operate in ARRS squadrons at the time of writing.

MC-130P-LM COMBAT SHADOW

Re-designation in 1996 for twenty-eight active-duty aircraft, formerly HC-130N/P: nine are assigned to the 9th SOS at Eglin AFB, Florida, and five each are assigned to the 17th SOS, Kadena AB, Japan, and to the 67th SOS, RAF Mildenhall, Suffolk, UK. The 5th SOS, AFRes, at Duke Field, Florida, has five aircraft, and the 58th SOW at Kirkland AFB, New Mexico, has four, the latter all for training. The MC-130P's primary role is to conduct single-ship or formation in-flight refuelling of special operations forces' helicopters in a low-threat to selected medium-threat environment. All MC-130Ps have been modified with new secure communications, night vision goggle (NVG)-compatible lighting, and advanced dual navigation stations with digital scan radar, self-contained ring-laser gyro INS (integrated navigation system), FLIR and GPS. They have also received upgraded missile warning systems, and countermeasures for refuelling missions in hostile environments. Fifteen have been fitted with an in-flight refuelling receptacle.

EC-130Q BuNo. 159469 (4595) was delivered to VQ-4, based at Patuxent River, in July 1975, for airborne communication with USN nuclear submarines. Just visible are the additional wire aerials extending to the fin and tailplane, as well as an aerial trailing from the ramp guide. This aircraft was re-designated TC-130Q before being released to AMARC in September 1991. Registered N54595, it was acquired by Airplane Sales International in June 1996. Lockheed

EC-130Q-LM

This is the US Navy designation given to eighteen improved TACAMO airborne communications relay aircraft (BuNos 156170/156177, 159348, 159469, 160608, 161223, 161494/161496, 161312/161313 and 161531) built with C-130H airframes, but with 4,910eshp T56-A-16 engines. Delivered between 1968 and 1984, they were used to supplement, and then replace, all EC-130Gs in service with VQ-3 at NAS Agana, Guam, and VQ-4 at NAS Patuxent River. (BuNo. 156176 crashed into the sea after a night take-off from Wake Island on 21 June 1977.) The new models were characterized externally by wing-tip ESM pods housing electronic and communications equipment, and with dual trailing antennas. Extended from the tail-cone and through the rear ramp, the antennas were fitted with stabilizing cones and were respectively 26,000ft (7.9km) long and 5,000ft (1.5km) long. Usually, the long antenna was streamed 16,000–20,000ft (4.9 to 6.1km), with the EC-130Q flying in tight orbits to keep both antennas almost vertical.

The TACAMO equipment was successively improved for more effective EMP (electro-magnetic pulse) 'hardening' (protection against EMP effects such as occur in the wake of a nuclear explosion). In the late 1980s this equipment was removed

from the EC-130Qs and installed in the Boeing E-6As which supplanted them, starting with VQ-3 at NAS Barber's Point, Hawaii, between 1989 and 1990, then with VQ-4 at NAS Patuxent River, Maryland, 1991–92. Following the removal of the TACAMO equipment, the seventeen EC-130Qs were either sold off, cannibalized or scrapped, although three (156170, 159348 and 159469) were re-designated TC-130Q in 1990 and used as trainers and utility transports. 156170 and 159469 were later transferred to AMARC, and subsequently registered to Airplane Sales International. 159348 is now on static display at Tinker AFB.

TC-130Q

Three EC-130Qs were re-designated as TC-130Qs in 1990 (156170, 159348 and 159469), and then used as trainers and utility transports. (See **EC-130Q** entry.)

KC-130R-LM

Fourteen tanker/transport aircraft (BuNos 160013/160021, 160240 and 160625/160628) with pod-mounted hose-and-drogue systems, for the USMC. All the aircraft were delivered between September 1975 and the middle of 1978. Based on the C-130H airframe and powered by

4,910eshp T56-A-16 engines, they were fundamentally similar to the KC-130H for export customers. The KC-130R could, however, carry 13,320 US gallons (50,420 litres) of fuel, compared to the earlier KC-130F which could carry 10,600 US gallons (40,125 litres).

LC-130R-LM

Six ski-equipped versions (BuNos 155917, 159129/159131 and 160740/160741), based on the C-130H airframe but with 4,910eshp T56-A-16 engines. All were obtained with National Science Foundation funds to supplement LC-130Fs in the Antarctic, but were operated on the NSF's behalf by the US Navy's VX-6 (later VXE-6). 155917 crashed when landing at Amundsen-Scott South Pole Station on 28 January 1973. 159129 was damaged when the nose ski broke off on take-off from Dome Charlie, Antarctica, on 15 January 1975. The aircraft was repaired on site in January 1976 and returned to service, but was later involved in a collision with a fork-lift at NAD Cherry Point, in November 1997; it was then transferred to AMARC. 1591131 crashed at site D59, Antarctica, when it was landing with spares for LC-130F 148321 on 9 December 1987, and was written off. 160740 was

(Above) USMC F-4J Phantoms of VFMA-212 are refuelled by KC-130R Bu No. 160020 of VMGR-352 near Hawaii on 2 October 1979. This aircraft was delivered to VFMA-212 in October 1976. The USMC and all but two of the international KC-130 operators utilize the same integrated fuel system that supports both fixed-wing and helicopter aerial refuelling. The system provides 300gpm flow rate simultaneously from both pods. M.E. Cotton USN

(Below) LC-130R BuNo. 159130 (4516) was delivered to VXE-6 in December 1973 (pictured at RAF Lyneham in the 1970s), and was still in service in February 1998. Mick Jennings

damaged at Starshot Glacier, Antarctica, in December 1984 and was repaired *in situ*; in 1998 it was transferred to the 139th AS, 109th AW, ANG, at Schenectady County Airport, New York. 160741 was also transferred to this unit in 1998/1999.

RC-130S BIAS HUNTER

Two JC-130As modified by E-Systems with BIAS (Battlefield Illumination Airborne System) as a result of a recommendation made in March 1966 as part of Operation *Shed Light*, a high-priority research and development programme initiated by the Air Force to attain a night-strike capability along the Ho Chi Minh Trail. As a result, in 1967 two (originally four) JC-130As (56-493 and 56-497) were modified as hunter-illuminators for strike aircraft flying close air-support sorties in south-east Asia at night. A large fairing housing fifty-six searchlights with a combined illumination of 6.14 million candle-power was mounted on each side of the forward fuselage, and various sensors, including infra-red devices, were fitted for location of the enemy. The project was stillborn, however. In a hostile environment such as south-east Asia where the 'Bias Hunters' were expected to maintain tight orbits at low altitude to illuminate their targets, the RC-130S aircraft would have soon fallen victim to enemy return

fire, so the BIAS programme was swiftly terminated. In 1969–70 the searchlights and other equipment were removed, and 56-493 and 56-497 reverted to C-130A configuration. Both were operated by AFRes and ANG units until 1988, when 56-497 was placed in storage at AMARC. 56-493 ended its career as a logistic support aircraft with the 152nd TFTS, 162nd TFG, Arizona ANG, at the Tucson IAP.

C-130T

This designation applied to twenty examples (BuNos 164762/763, 164993/998, 165158/161, 165313/314, 165348/351, 165378/379) ordered for service with US Navy Reserve logistics support squadrons. They were basically similar to the C-130H, but with 4,910eshp T56-A-423 engines and updated avionics. The first example was handed over to VR-54 at New Orleans, Louisiana, in August 1991. The twenty aircraft are currently operated by four USN Reserve units: VR-53 at NAS Washington, DC; VR-54 at NAS New Orleans, LA; VR-55 at NAF Moffett, CA; and VR-62 at NAS Brunswick, ME.

KC-130T

The tanker version for the USMC. It was based on the C-130H airframe and similar to the KC-130R, but was also fitted with an updated avionics suite to incorporate a new

VMGR-234 crew examine the port in-flight refuelling drogue of KC-130T BuNo. 162308 (4972) which was delivered to the USMC in October 1983. There are two types of drogue: high speed for fixed wing, and low speed for helicopter refuelling that is normally accomplished at 105–120 kts IAS. The low-speed drogues have been tested up to 10,000ft (3,000m). Lockheed

KC-130T BuNo. 160022 (5040) of VMGR-234, which received this aircraft in August 1985. Author's collection

autopilot, AN/APS-133 search radar, and an inertial navigation system plus Omega and TACAN; it was powered by T56-A-423 engines rated at 4,910eshp. A total of twenty-six KC-130Ts (162308/311, 162785/86, 163022/23, 163310/11, 163591/92, 164105/06, 164180/81, 164441/42, 164999/5000, 165162/63, 165315/16, 165352/53) have been acquired. KC-130Ts are in service with VMGR-234 at JRB Fort Worth, Texas, and with VMGR-452 at Stewart IAP, New York.

KC-130T-30

Two examples (BuNos 164597 and 164598) of this derivative were assigned to VMGR-452, a US Marine Corps Reserve tanker/transport unit, at Glenview, Illinois, in October–November 1991. They differ from previous models in that they have stretched fuselages, being some 15ft (4.6m) longer than the standard tanker. This in turn increases fuel capacity and raises the amount that may be passed to receiver aircraft via the wing-mounted refuelling pods.

AC-130U SPECTRE

This designation describes thirteen gunships (87-0128, 89-0509/14, 90-0163/67, and 92-0253) based on the C-130H airframe, with integrated avionics by the North American Aircraft Operations Division of Rockwell International Corporation. Production began with the airframe 87-0128, which was flown from Marietta to Palmdale in July 1988, for fitting out. It eventually emerged as an AC-130U in December 1990, and was then assigned to the 6510th Test Wing at the Air Force Flight Test Center, Edwards AFB. Beginning in 1990, twelve more AC-130Us nave been delivered, and all are operated by the 4th SOS, 16th SOW, at Hurlburt Field, Florida.

The AC-130U has greater altitude capability, and combines impressive firepower, reliability and superior accuracy with the latest methods of target location. This has involved updating the sensor suite, inputs from which are processed by IBM IP-102 computers at the 'battle management center' in the rear fuselage. The 'Black Crow' truck ignition sensor and radome, and the separate beacon tracking radar used on earlier gunships, have both been omitted. Observer stations are included on the rear ramp and starboard forward fuselage side. Spectra ceramic armour, three underfuselage chaff and flare dispenser (capable of dispensing 300 chaff bundles and either ninety MJU7 or 180 M206 IR decoy flares), Texas Instruments AN/AAQ-117 FLIR countermeasures, and ITT Avionics AN/ALQ-172 jammer, are all fitted to increase the aircraft's chance of survival in a low-to-medium-threat environment. Standard armament consists of a trainable GAU-12/U 25mm Gatling gun in place of the AC-130H's two 20mm cannon, one 40mm Bofors gun, and a 105mm howitzer. All weapons can be slaved to the digital Hughes AN/APQ-180 fire-control radar, AN/AAQ-117 FLIR (mounted under the port side of the nose), or to the Bell Aerospace all-light-level TV (ALLTV) (turret-mounted in the port main undercarriage sponson) for truly adverse weather ground-attack operations. Other equipment includes a HUD, combined INS, and Navstar Global Positioning System (GPS).

EC-130V

The designation for the single US Coast Guard airborne-early-warning example (CG1721), modified from HC-130H configuration. Having operated several USN Grumman E-2C Hawkeye early-warning

aircraft on surveillance operations intended to cut the flow of drugs into the southern USA, the US Coast Guard soon reached the conclusion that it required a platform with similar detection capabilities but possessing greater endurance. This aircraft was first delivered to Clearwater CG station, Florida, in HC-130H configuration in October 1988. General Dynamics carried out the conversion to EC-130V standard at Fort Worth, Texas, installing an AN/APS-125 radar dish – almost identical to the array fitted to the E-2C – above the aft fuselage section; other modifications included additional intakes for the cooling of onboard electronic equipment, as well as unidentified antenna fairings on both sides of the forward fuselage and above the nose radome ahead of the cockpit. Pallet-mounted displays and consoles sited in the hold area allow the EC-130V to carry up to three system operators.

The aircraft flew for the first time in this configuration on 31 July 1991, and the USCG operated it from Clearwater until April 1992. That summer the white and red livery was overpainted with camouflage and the aircraft was then delivered to the 514th Test Squadron, USAF, as 87-0157. In October 1993, 87-0157 was re-designated NC-130H and later flown by the 418th TS until January 1998. It went to the Naval Air Test Center at Patuxent River for service assessment the same year.

Projected military developments of the Hercules have been numerous, such as the HOW (Hercules-on-Water flying-boat with hydro-ski) and the C-130SS (Stretch/STOL) with stretched fuselage, enlarged tail surfaces, double-slotted flaps, roll-control spoilers and aerial refuelling receptacle, which Lockheed proposed as an alternative to the Boeing YC-14 and McDonnell Douglas YC-15. Lockheed

CHAPTER THREE

Air War, Vietnam

Vietnam was formerly part of French Indo-China, together with Laos and Cambodia which lie along its western border, and is bounded in the North by China. After the defeat of the French forces in July 1954 it was split into two countries, the Republic of South Vietnam and the Communist North, using the 17th Parallel as the dividing line. The victors were the Communist Viet Minh forces led by Gen Giap, and they planned to take control of the South using a new Communist guerrilla force called the Viet Cong (VC) or the National Liberation Front (NLF). The VC campaign increased in intensity in 1957 until finally, in 1960, Premier Diem appealed to the United States for help. Special 'advisers' were sent in, and in 1961 President Lyndon B. Johnson began the negotiations which led to total American involvement.

In February 1965 the Viet Cong stepped up its guerrilla war, and the first American casualties in Vietnam occurred when the VC attacked US installations in the South. The US retaliated with strikes by US naval aircraft from carriers in the Gulf of Tonkin against VC installations at Dong Hoi and Vit Thu Lu. The guerrilla war escalated until in 1965, the South Vietnamese administration was on the point of collapse. The US responded with a continued build-up of military might, beginning with Operation *Rolling Thunder*, as the air offensive against North Vietnam was called.

'Trash and Ass Haulers'

It soon became obvious that transports and their crews would be needed in large numbers to support US intervention in southeast Asia, not only to carry out airlift operations, but to perform many other rôles besides. In south-east Asia the Hercules was to see widespread service, not only with the USAF, but with the US Navy, the USMC (as the KC-130F), the Coast Guard, and the VNAF (Vietnamese Air Force), in what was to become a long and bloody conflict against a very determined

and implacable enemy. Beginning in 1972, Project *Enhance Plus* gave the VNAF over 900 badly needed helicopters, fighters, gunships and transports, including thirty-two hastily withdrawn C-130As from ANG units in the US. In addition, the RAAF operated C-130Es on airlift duties between Australia and South Vietnam. These were from No. 36 Squadron, and from 1966, No. 37 Squadron. No. 40 Squadron, RNZAF, operated five C-130Hs on logistic flights between New Zealand and Saigon and Vung Tau, South Vietnam from 1965 to 1975.

The primary function of the Hercules was aerial transportation, but they would also be used for infra-theatre aeromedical evacuation, as 'airborne battlefield command and control centres' (ABCCCs), AC-130 gunships (these and other special operations' Hercules are covered elsewhere), rescue aircraft, flare-dropping aircraft, and even 'bombers'. There was a price to be paid, and it would be high.

In the period from February 1958 until 1965, about a dozen C-130s had been lost worldwide. Then from 1965 to 1972, fifty-five Hercules (including gunships) were lost in south-east Asia alone, and more than half of these in the single year 1967–68. Moreover the airlift crewmen killed or MIA numbered 269. One of the first Communist successes against US airfields was at the major port and jet-capable airfield at Da Nang in Quang Nam Province on 1 July 1965 when the Viet Cong (VC), equipped with mortars and light artillery, landed by sea and proceeded to destroy eight aircraft. Among the losses were two C-130As, namely 55-0039 and 55-0042 in the 817th TCS, 315th Air Division. Three more C-130As were lost before the end of the year, including one which struck the water before landing at Qui Nhon, a port in Binh Dinh Province, South Vietnam. In 1966 eight Hercules were lost; in 1967, fourteen; and in 1968 operations intensified and the heaviest losses among Hercules in Vietnam were recorded, with a total of sixteen C-130s being lost.

C-130, The Workhorse of the War

More than any other aircraft, the Hercules was destined to become *the* workhorse of the Vietnam War, just as the Dakota had proved itself to be in World War II. Beginning in the spring of 1965, Fairchild C-123 Providers and de Havilland Canada C-7 Caribous were stationed permanently in-country, but the transport-dedicated versions of the Hercules were rotated in and out of strips nearest the combat zones in South Vietnam from bases in the Pacific Air Forces (PACAF) region.

As at the outbreak of the Korean War fourteen years earlier, America was largely ill-prepared for 'conventional' warfare on the Asian mainland. PACAF was a nuclear-deterrent force, like the majority of US commands at this time, a third of its 600 aircraft being made up of F100D/F tactical fighters. Only fifty-three C-54 and C-130A aircraft comprised its transport fleet, the majority of units being stationed in Japan, the Philippines and Taiwan. In Japan, C-130As of the 815th TCS, 315th Air Division, were based at Tachikawa AB, and those of the 35th and 817th TCS, 384th TCW, at Naha AB, Okinawa; a few aircraft of the 315th Air Division were also detached at Naha. In the Philippines, three squadrons operated in the 463rd TCW at Clark AB, and two others operated from Mactan AB. In Formosa (Taiwan) three C-130 squadrons in the 374th TCW operated from Ching Chaun Kang AB.

Before total US intervention in Vietnam, the PACAF Hercules had been used mainly for logistic support between the home bases and bases in Thailand and South Vietnam. After the spring of 1965, however, the Hercules became the prime transport aircraft in the Pacific theatre. Its first task was to airlift troops and equipment to South Vietnam from Okinawa: thus from 8–12 March 1965, C-130s deployed a Marine battalion landing team to Da Nang; and on 4–7 May, they carried the Army's 173rd Airborne Brigade to South Vietnam in 140 lifts.

Paratroopers in the 101st 'Screaming Eagles' Airborne Division wait prior to being airlifted into action in Vietnam aboard C-130As of the 314th Tactical Combat Wing. The aircraft, from left to right, are: 56-0491 (3099); 56-0487 (3095); 56-0492 (3100), which suffered a no. 1 engine failure during take-off on 2 May 1964 and veered off the runway; 54-1640 (3027); and 56-0486 (3094). USAF

PACAF was not designed for counter-insurgency (COIN) operations, and so at the outset, the first aircraft to deploy to Vietnam were mostly provided by Tactical Air Command on a rotational basis. After April 1965, four Tactical Air Command squadrons, deployed from the US on ninety-day tours of temporary duty (TDY), backed up PACAF's own four C-130 squadrons; by the end of 1965 there were thirty-two Hercules operating in-country, positioned at four bases. All came under the unified control of the Common Service Airlift System (CSAS) and its Airlift Control Center (ALCC) which were subordinate to 834th Air Division, organized on 25 October 1966 at Tan Son Nhut AB in the suburbs of Saigon, and responsible to the Seventh Air Force for tactical airlift within South Vietnam. ALCC functioned countrywide through local airlift control elements, liaison officers, field mission commanders and mobile combat control teams. ALCC also controlled the C-130s that were rotated into South Vietnam on one- and two-week cycles from the 315th Air Division in Japan.

By the summer of 1966 PACAF's permanently assigned C-130 strength stood at twelve squadrons, and this reached a peak of fifteen units early in 1968 with three deployed TAC squadrons on TDY tours.

Thus in February 1968 a total of ninety-six C-130s were stationed in Vietnam: the huge port complex at Cam Ranh Bay was home to fifty-one C-130As and -Es; Tan son Nhut accommodated twenty-seven C-130Bs; Tuy Hoa had ten C-130Es; and Nha Trang, eight C-130Es. By the end of 1971 only five C-130 squadrons remained in the Pacific, although the VNAF airlift force operated two squadrons. Two squadrons were equipped with C-130As just before the 1973 ceasefire.

To Airlift or Paradrop?

At first the US Army and the USAF held opposite views on how best to deploy troops to the combat zones. The Army considered that air mobile operations using helicopters to deploy troops was a more efficient method than the paratroop landing method initially favoured by the Air Force; moreover the USAF were convinced that fixed-wing air-landed operations would deploy more troops to a given area than a paradrop ever would. From then on, airlift aircraft were used to deposit troops, cargo, equipment and supplies, except of course on a larger scale than the Army's air mobile helicopter force, which it complemented. In the assault role the Hercules was almost as

versatile as the air mobile, since the one hundred rudimentary landing strips capable of accommodating C-130s rarely proved an obstacle to the aircraft's excellent short field performance.

In 1965 two US Army paratroop brigades were held in Vietnam as a central reserve force quickly available for offensive or reaction operations. In August 1965 the 173rd Airborne Brigade was airlifted from Bien Hoa to Pleiku in 150 Hercules flights. During Operation *New Life-65*, which began on 21 November 1965, the 173rd made a helicopter assault into an improvised airstrip 40 miles (64km) east of Bien Hoa; seventy-one C-130s arrived over the next thirty-six hours to resupply them, the first landing within an hour of the initial assault. Meanwhile for twenty-nine days, beginning on 29 October, the C-130s kept the 1st Cavalry Division supplied during operations against Piel Me camp south of Pleiku. Using a rough airstrip at Catecka Tea Plantation, near the battle area, the C-130s delivered, on average, 180 tons of supplies and munitions per day.

During the following spring and summer, 1966, the 1st Brigade, 101st Airborne Division, was transported on five occasions by the C-130s; each deployment involved 200 Hercules lifts, and each operation was mainly resupplied by air. Operation *Birmingham* was a four-week air deployment into Tay Ninh province beginning on 24 April, in which the C-130s flew fifty-six sorties into the 4,600ft (1,400m) airstrip, delivering supplies and munitions around the clock. (At the same time they also supplied the airborne brigade at Nhon Co.) By the time *Birmingham* ended on 17 May, the C-130s and C-123s had flown almost 1,000 sorties and delivered nearly 10,000 tons of cargo for the 1st Cavalry Division.

The USMC also played a part in airlift operations. By July 1966 the road network north of Da Nang was in a state of disrepair – though in any event, Communist activity had made transport by convoy extremely hazardous, while port facilities and airfields near the DMZ were poor. Therefore the only way to resupply the marines in-country was by air. USMC KC-130Fs, backed up by USAF Hercules, flew more than 250 lifts into a red dirt strip at Dong Ha. Further C-130 flights to the area delivered large quantities of materials and PSP steel matting, and the airstrip was later resurfaced; a second all-weather strip was opened at Quang Tri.

Paratroops of the 1st brigade, 101st US Airborne Division pictured during the airlift from Kontum to Phan Rang, South Vietnam. During the spring and summer of 1966, the 1st Brigade, 101st Airborne Division, was transported on five occasions by the C-130s. Each deployment involved 200 Hercules lifts and each operation was mainly resupplied by air. C-130B (58-0752/3551) in the 463rd TCW, in the background, survived the horrors of the war in south-east Asia and was modified to WC-130B; later it reverted to C-130B, and finally was sold to the Chilean Air Force in 1992. USAF

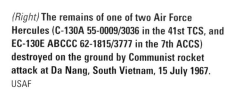

(Right) The remains of one of two Air Force Hercules (C-130A 55-0009/3036 in the 41st TCS, and EC-130E ABCCC 62-1815/3777 in the 7th ACCS) destroyed on the ground by Communist rocket attack at Da Nang, South Vietnam, 15 July 1967. USAF

Communist shelling and mortar attacks at Dak To, South Vietnam on 15 November 1967 destroyed a 1,300-ton ammunition dump and two parked C-130Es (62-1865 (3829) and 63-7827 (3904)) in the 776th TAS. USAF

ammunition dump and two parked C-130Es (62-1865 and 63-7827) from the 776th TAS. Capt Joseph K. Glenn and Sgt Joseph F. Mack courageously taxied a third Hercules from the inferno, and they were awarded the Silver Star and Distinguished Flying Cross for their actions.

Delivery Systems

Not all Hercules missions in Vietnam involved conventional or assault landings to unload the aircraft on the ground; frequently, C-130s parachuted their loads or made use of special delivery techniques. There was the Ground Proximity Extraction System (GPES), in which the loads were pulled out of the aft loading ramp as the aircraft flew a few feet above the ground, by means of a trailing hook which engaged with a cable set up by troops in the field. There was also the Low Altitude Parachute Extraction System (LAPES), in which palletized and shock-proofed loads equipped with large parachutes were simply 'sucked out' from the open hold while the aircraft was flying a few feet from the ground. This method permitted very large items such as tanks and other armoured vehicles to be carried, and for them to be deposited accurately to units in the actual combat zone. C-130s also made use of the Container Delivery System (CDS), a highly accurate method by which loads could be parachuted from as low as 600ft (183m); and of two blind-drop methods, the Adverse Weather Aerial Delivery System (AWADS) which relies heavily on self-contained dual-frequency airborne radar, and another method which relies on the guidance of ground-based radar.

The only major US combat parachute assault of the war took place on 22 February 1967, at the start of Operation *Junction City* when twenty-two US battalions and four ARVN battalions were airdropped in Tay Ninh and bordering provinces. Thirteen Hercules carried 846 paratroopers of the 173rd Airborne Brigade from Bien Hoa and dropped them in the drop zone at Katum near the border with Cambodia. Almost thirty minutes later, ten C-130s dropped the brigade's equipment, returning in the early afternoon to carry out further cargo drops; five C-130s were hit, but they suffered no serious damage. Next day thirty-eight Hercules flew resupply sorties, and these continued for the next five days, during which daily drops averaged 100 tons. By late March, during the final stages of the operation, the C-130s carried out airdrops to a 'floating brigade', using drop-zone locations which the ground unit provided by radio. By the time *Junction City* finished, some 1,700 tons of supplies and munitions had been airdropped by the Hercules.

On four other occasions during 1967–68 small teams of US advisers from the 5th Special Forces Group were parachuted in, along with 300 to 500 Vietnamese

paratroopers. Each C-130 could carry eighty fully-equipped paratroops, who were dropped in two forty-man sticks. In November 1967, C-130s lifted the 173rd Airborne Brigade to Dak To in 250 sorties; they also kept them supplied with more than 5,000 tons of cargo, deposited on the 4,200ft (1,280m) asphalt strip during the three weeks of heavy fighting that ensued. Communist shelling and mortar attacks on 15 November destroyed a 1,300-ton

Delivery of supply pallets from C-130E 62-1806, 776th TAS, 314th TAW, as it continues its ground roll. Col Walt Evans USAF

A 317th TAW C-130E (70-1263/4415) performing a **LAPES** delivery of a Sheridan M551 armoured reconnaissance airborne assault vehicle. The rigged weight of the **AR/AAV** with basic load, fuel and crew equipment is approximately 40,000lb (18,144kg). Delivery of this same load by low-velocity airdrop would require an altitude of 1,500ft (457m) to deploy the eight 100ft (30.48m)-diameter canopy parachutes needed to decelerate the load for impact velocity. Lockheed

Low Altitude Parachute Extraction System (LAPES).
The LAPES technique is characterized by very low flight altitude (ramp height not to exceed 10ft or 3.05m) whereby the load(s) are precisely extracted by vented parachutes which also decelerate the load as it slides on the ground after extraction. The LAPES technique uses a narrow linear extraction zone rather than an open, wider drop zone which is used for low velocity airdrop.

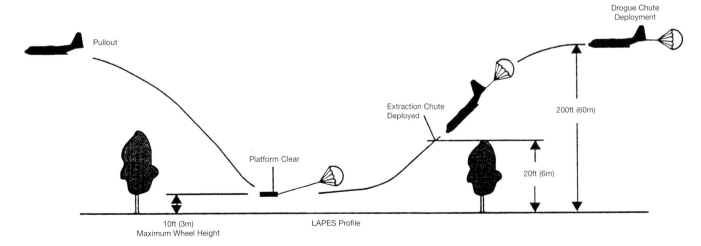

Khe Sanh

For three months in 1968 transports were called upon to keep the remote outpost at Khe Sanh supplied, and in fulfilling this requirement the Hercules made one of its most famous contributions in south-east Asia. Located 10 miles (16km) from the Laotian border and 16 miles (26km) south of the DMZ, Khe Sanh was to become one of the Vietnam War's most controversial battles. Manned initially in 1962 by the US Army, it had become, in 1967, a major Marine Corps base from which search-and-destroy operations were mounted to control Communist infiltrations. Late in 1967 a prolonged Hercules airdrop sup-

French had nowhere near the air support that was available to the defenders of Khe Sanh, and this had resulted in its loss. Furthermore, the loss of Dien Bien Phu had led directly to total French defeat in Indo-China – so if, militarily, history was not to be repeated, then the Marines had to be kept supplied. Operation *Niagara* involved a series of air strikes, together with a planned succession of resupply flights, and was put into effect to keep the beleaguered 'grunts' in business during the long siege.

The NVA first attacked in the pre-dawn hours of 21 January. Eight days later, a thirty-six hour ceasefire for the *Tet* religious holiday began – but NVA and Viet Cong

First operating independently, marine combat aircraft, transports and helicopters, with effective support by Navy and Air Force aircraft (including B-52s), mounted a major effort to help repel the Communist assault; during *Niagara*, some 100,000 tons of bombs were dropped by all US aircraft. VMGR-152 operated four KC-130Fs out of Da Nang AB, together with a single aircraft detached from VMGR-352, primarily to refuel USN and USMC combat aircraft and to fly flare-dropping sorties. On 10 February the USMC lost the first C-130 in the operation when KC-130F BuNo. 149813 was shot down: it crash-landed at Khe Sanh and had to be written off. On 8 March all Marine aircraft and their air control system

A C-130E comes in for a landing in January 1968 at the airstrip at Dongha combat base, South Vietnam, where men of US Naval Construction Battalion Maintenance Unit 301 are repairing the runway. USN

ported operations and airstrip construction at Khe Sanh. By January 1968 some 6,000 marines were holed up at Khe Sanh, and they were entirely dependent on resupply by air. The situation bore comparison to the Viet Minh's three-month siege of Dien Bien Phu in the war with France from 1946–54. Dien Bien Phu had been defended by 16,000 troops, but the

activity almost immediately brought it to an end. On the 31st, just two days before the *Tet* offensive, the Communists launched massive ground attacks throughout South Vietnam. Many cities were attacked, including Hue, which was overrun. NVA troops stormed the A Shau valley, and renewed their attack on the American outpost at Khe Sanh.

came under the command of Gen William W. Momyer, USAF. For seventy-one days, during which the weather was nearly always bad and the fighting intensive, the transports and helicopters flew in supplies from Da Nang – only thirty minutes' flying time away – to Khe Sanh, and brought out casualties (when the siege was lifted on 6 April, American losses included 200 dead and

1,600 wounded). Between 21 January and 8 April the Air Force transports delivered 12,400 tons of cargo to Khe Sanh. A staggering 92 per cent of the total tonnage lifted was carried by the Hercules in 496 drops and 67 extractions, delivering 3,558 tons of cargo, and depositing another 7,826 tons in 273 landings.

When the runway at Khe Sanh was weathered in, the C-130s, C-123s and C-7s made aerial drops of cargo with the help of ground-controlled radar-directed approaches to the drop zones. Potentially the transports were an easy target for Communist small-arms fire, Triple-A and shoulder-launched missiles, so normal approach procedures were often abandoned in favour of what became known as the 'Khe Sanh approach'. In this, each in-bound transport remained at height as long as it could, then the pilot put the nose down into a near-vertical dive and flared out to land on the runway at the last possible moment. Thanks almost entirely to the extensive airborne resupply, and the huge volume of tactical and strategic support, the garrison held out. Flying 1,128 missions between 21 January and 8 April, the USAF C-130s (who flew 74 per cent of these), the C-123s (24 per cent) and the C-7s (1 per cent) delivered 12,430 tons of cargo to Khe Sanh. (The only other recorded loss of a Hercules was just after the Khe Sanh operation, on 13 April, when 61-0967, a TAC C-130B in the 774th Tactical Airlift Squadron, crashed after suffering an engine failure.)

The lifting of the Khe Sanh siege was a victory for the Americans and was due almost entirely to the massive air effort. In contrast, the *Tet* offensive was a tactical disaster for the Communists; Khe Sanh on its own cost the NVA and Viet Cong an estimated 10,000 casualties.

The propaganda effect of the Khe Sanh siege was far greater than they could have ever imagined. The press and television reportage accorded the Communists a strength they did not have, fanning the flames of the anti-war lobby in the US and causing public opinion to turn against the

All hands to the pump. South Vietnamese assist with construction at an airbase in South Vietnam. USAF

continued prosecution of the war. It led, in March 1968, to the cessation of all bombing north of the 20th Parallel, a move that was meant to be a sign of conciliation but one which was interpreted as weakness by the Communists. As a result, only stalemate was achieved and the war dragged on.

Airlift and Evacuation Continues

Two other airlift operations were notable in 1968: the first was Operation *Delaware/Lam Son 216*, the air invasion of the A Shau valley in April 1968. Despite bad weather and Communist groundfire, the Hercules flew daily airdrops to the 1st Cavalry Division (Airmobile), the 101st Airborne Division, and ARVN units at A Luoi. Ground radar was unavailable so the Hercules' crews had to navigate up the cloud-filled valley using their radar and doppler equipment, breaking out of the

overcast just before visual release of their cargo. For nine days, beginning on the 26 April, the C-130s flew 165 sorties, dropping 2,300 tons, most of it ammunition. Such was the urgency that the C-130s continued to fly during one period when the weather was so bad that it grounded even the helicopters. C-130B 60-0298 in the 773rd TAS was lost on the first day when it was hit by NVA fire and crashed trying to land at A Shau. Four other C-130s received major battle damage during the operation. The cavalry division commander described the Hercules effort as 'one of the most magnificent displays of airmanship that I have ever seen.' A rebuilt A Luoi airstrip received its first transport aircraft on 2 May, and before heavy rains turned it to mud on the 11th, USAF Caribous, C-123s and C-130s made 113 landings, more than half by the Hercules.

Equally spectacular was the evacuation of the US and ARVN at the Kham Duc mountain post on 12 May by helicopters and transport aircraft. Air strikes went ahead as the first C-130 landed during the morning: it received heavy battle damage and left hurriedly, carrying only three soldiers, fuel streaming from holes and tyres ripped to shreds. Three more C-130s tried again in the afternoon: of these, Communist fire destroyed C-130B 60-0297 in the 773rd TAS after it took off with more than 100 civilian passengers on board; C-130A 65-0548 in the 21st TAS was crippled in landing and was abandoned; and only the third C-130 made a successful landing and evacuation. It was not until late in the afternoon that three C-130s succeeded in evacuating the last of the garrison. Of 1,500 survivors at Kham Duc, the Air Force succeeded in bringing out more than 500, almost all of them just before the outpost was overrun.

During 1969–71, massive air transport activity supported US and ARVN incursions into Cambodia and southern Laos. C-130s made ammunition drops to US forces near O Rang, and Operation *Lam Son 719* was preceded by 250 C-130 sorties lifting an ARVN airborne division and

A C-130 drops supplies to US Marines at Khe Sanh in April 1968. USAF

other Vietnamese forces from Saigon to Dong Ha and Quang Tri. Over a seven-week period the Hercules lifted more than 14,000 tons of cargo to a reconstructed logistics base at Khe Sanh (which had been abandoned on 23 June 1968).

In 1972, the Communist spring offensive resulted in more Air Force supply operations being mounted during April and May, to isolated pockets at Kontum and An Loc. Day operations to Kontum ceased abruptly on 17 May after enemy fire damaged several C-130s, burned two VNAF C-123s, and destroyed a C-130E (63-7798) in the 374th TAW; the latter was hit by a missile while taking off. Hercules operations resumed exclusively at night on 18/19 May, with seventeen C-130s running the gauntlet of enemy fire to carry out successful deliveries. Resupply continued nightly under cover of allied gunships, although in one instance on 23 May, C-130E 62-1854 *Quan Loi*

Queen delayed its departure past dawn and was destroyed by a missile on the ground. Two days later the Communists seized a part of the runway, closing the airfield to landings except by helicopters, and it wasn't until the 28th that the Hercules could resume airdrops overhead. More than 2,000 tons were dropped in 130 C-130 sorties before the Hercules could resume night landings on 8 June.

Meanwhile daylight supply operations to 20,000 defenders and refugees at An Loc had cost three C-130s by 3 May. Beginning on 18 April, the first four C-130s successfully parachuted supplies, but each received battle damage; a fifth, C-130E 63-7775 in the 374th TAW, was hit west of An Loc and crash-landed into a swamp near Lai Khe. Altitudes were swiftly increased to above 6,000ft (1,800m), dropping with ground-radar guidance. However, 'high altitude, low-opening' parachute techniques proved

unsuccessful because numerous chutes failed – in part because they had been incorrectly packed by Vietnamese packers. The C-130 crews had no option but to resume the more deadly low-level conventional airdrops; and inevitably the aircraft received hits. Finally, on 25/26 April, the Air Force switched to resupply at night. Sadly these operations got off to a bad start straight away, with the loss of a C-130E-1 (64-0508, in the 318th SOS). Light signals used on the ground failed to guide the C-130s in and many bundles of supplies missed their mark, some falling into Communist hands. Things went from bad to worse on 2/3 May when the C-130s failed to make a single successful delivery, and the following night, C-130E 62-1797 in the 374th TAW was shot down. This brought night operations to an end. On 5 May, high-altitude daylight drops were resumed with loads attached to parachutes rigged properly, and

Supplies dropped by C-130s drift towards men of the 1st Cavalry Division (Airmobile), 101st Airborne Division, in the A Shau valley in April 1968. For nine days, beginning on 26 April, the C-130s flew 165 sorties and dropped 2.300 tons, most of it ammunition; one Hercules was lost to NVA groundfire, and four others received major battle damage. US Army

only one of the twenty-four bundles dropped fell into enemy hands. As from 8 May, when the An Loc garrison recovered 65 of the 88 tons dropped, things improved, and by the end of the siege, on 18 June, some 7,600 tons had been dropped by the C-130s in more than 600 sorties.

As well as being routine on airlift and evacuation operations, C-130s, as we shall now see, were also put to varied use on flare-dropping operations, and for four very different types of bombing mission.

Lamplighter and Blind Bat

Starting in January 1965, C-130As and crews drawn from the squadrons at Naha, Okinawa, were attached to the 6315th Operations Group (TAC) control for use as flareships in south-east Asia. Operating from Da Nang, the flare-dropping C-130A Hercules and their crews were used mostly for the interdiction of the Viet Cong infiltration routes through Laos. The C-130As were designed to operate in conjunction

with the 'fast movers' (fighter-bombers) such as the F-4 Phantom, in nightstrikes against VC convoys using the Ho Chi Minh trail. Two code-names accompanied the start of the flare-dropping project. Operations which were carried out over the 'Barrel Roll' interdiction area in northern Laos were termed *Lamplighter*, while those flown against targets in the 'Steel Tiger' and 'Tiger Hound' areas of southern Laos were known as *Blind Bat*. (Eventually the two operational areas in Laos were merged into one, and *Blind Bat* was normally used to describe flare-dropping missions generally.)

At peak strength, the *Blind Bat* project numbered six C-130As and twelve crews, mainly derived from the 41st Troop Carrier Squadron. The first *Blind Bat* loss occurred on 24 April 1965 (incidentally the first C-130 loss in Vietnam) when 57-0475 and its 817th TCS crew crashed at Korat, Thailand, after the aircraft hit a mountain during a go-around in bad weather. Two more 817th TCS C-130As were lost in a mortar attack on Da Nang on 1 July and on 21 December, 56-0515 was shot down on approach to Tuy Hoa, South Vietnam. In March 1966 the *Blind Bat* project relocated to Ubon, Thailand, and that same year the 6315th Operations Group control was replaced by the 374th Troop Carrier Wing, later designated a Tactical Airlift Wing. The 41st TAS lost two more *Blind Bat* C-130As to enemy action over Laos in 1968–69: on 22 May 1968, 56-0477 was shot down, and on 24 November 1969, 56-0533 was shot down at Ban Salou. A third *Blind Bat* C-130A, 56-0499, crashed on a three-engine take-off from Bu Dop, South Vietnam, on 13 December 1969. The flare-dropping missions continued until 15 June 1970, when AC-130 hunter-killer gunships took over: with electronic detection and image-intensifying night observation equipment, and a 1.5 million candlepower searchlight, they were by now better equipped than the *Blind Bats* for the task of identifying and destroying enemy troop and transport convoys using the Ho Chi Minh Trail.

Carolina Moon

In May 1966 meanwhile, the Hercules was employed in an operation to destroy the giant Ham Rong ('Dragon's Jaw') road and rail bridge over the Song Ma River, 3 miles (5km) north of Thanh Hoa, the capital of Annam Province, in North Vietnam's

bloody 'Iron Triangle' (Haiphong, Hanoi and Thanh Hoa). The 540ft (165m) long, 56ft (17m) wide, Chinese-engineered bridge, which stood 50ft (15m) above the river, was a replacement for the original French-built bridge destroyed by the Viet Minh in 1945, blown up by simply loading two locomotives with explosives and running them together in the middle of the bridge. It had first captured the attention of the US planners in March 1965 when the decision to interdict the North Vietnamese rail system south of the 20th Parallel led immediately to the 3 April strike against the bridge. This, and the repeated strikes by USAF and USN fighter-bombers, ended in failure, and with the loss of sixteen USAF pilots alone.

In May 1966 the Air Force decided to try mass-focusing the energy of certain high explosive weapons against the stubborn structure, an innovative concept. Operation *Carolina Moon* used two specially modified C-130E aircraft in the 314th Troop Carrier Wing to drop the weapon, a rather large, pancake-shaped bomb 8ft (2.4m) in diameter, 2.5ft (75cm) thick and weighing 5,000lb (2,270kg). The C-130s would fly below 500ft to evade radar along a 43-mile (69km) route – which meant they would be vulnerable to enemy attack for about seventeen minutes – and drop the bombs, which would float down the Song Ma River until they passed under the Dragon's Jaw, where sensors in the bombs would detect the metal of the bridge structure and cause them to detonate.

Because the slow-moving C-130Es would need protection, F-4C Phantoms from the 8th Tactical Fighter Wing at Ubon, Thailand, would fly a diversionary attack to the south, using flares and bombs on the highway just before the C-130E was to drop its ordnance. The F-4Cs were to enter their target area at 300ft (90m), attack at 50ft (15m) and pull off the target back to 300ft for subsequent attacks. Additionally, an EB-66 was tasked to jam the radar in the area during the attack period.

The first C-130E was to be flown by Maj Richard T. Renners, and the second by Maj Thomas F. Case, 62nd Troop Carrier Squadron, both of whom had been through extensive training for this mission at the Tactical Air Warfare Center at Eglin AFB, Florida; they had been deployed to Vietnam only two weeks before. Ten mass-focus weapons were provided, allowing for a second mission should the first fail to accomplish the desired results. Last-minute changes to coincide with up-to-date intelligence included one that would be very significant. Renners felt that the aircraft was tough enough to survive moderate AAA hits and gain enough altitude should bail-out be necessary. Case agreed that the aircraft could take hits, but considered that the low-level flight would preclude a controlled bail-out. In view of these conflicting philosophies, and the fact that either parachutes or flak vests could be worn, but not both, Renners decided that his crew would wear parachutes and stack their flak vests on the floor of the aircraft, whereas Case decided that his crew would only wear flak vests and store the parachutes.

On the night of 30 May, Renners and his crew, including navigators Capt Norman G. Clanton and 1/Lt William 'Rocky' Edmondson, departed Da Nang at 00.25 hours and headed north under radio silence. Although the Hercules met no resistance at the beginning of its approach, heavy – though fortunately, inaccurate – ground fire was encountered after it was too late to turn back. The five weapons were dropped successfully in the river and Renners made for the safety of the Gulf of Tonkin. The operation had gone flawlessly, and the Hercules was safe; furthermore, although the diversionary attack had drawn fire, both F-4s returned to Thailand unscathed. Unfortunately the excitement of the crew was short-lived, because reconnaissance photos taken at dawn showed that there was no noticeable damage to the bridge, nor was any trace of the bombs found. A second mission was planned for the night of 31 May.

The plan for Maj Case's crew was basically the same, with the exception of a minor time change and a slight modification to the flight route. A crew change was made when Case asked 1st Lt Edmondson, the navigator from the previous night's mission, to go along on this one because of his experience gained on the first 'pancake bomb' mission. C-130E 64-0511 departed Da Nang at 01.10 hours, and the two F-4 Phantoms again flew as a diversion for the Hercules strike. One of the backseaters was Col Dayton W. Ragland, a crack US fighter pilot during the Korean War and the veteran of many missions in 'MiG Alley'. Having flown ninety-seven combat missions in Vietnam, Ragland was about ready to be rotated back to the US, but agreed to fly in the back seat of one of the F-4s piloted by 1st Lt Ned R. Herrold, to give the younger

man more combat flight time while he operated the sophisticated technical navigational and bombing equipment.

The two Phantoms left Thailand and headed for the area south of the Dragon, flying at times only 50ft (15m) above the ground. At about two minutes prior to the scheduled C-130 drop time, the F-4Cs were in the midst of creating the diversion when crew members saw AA fire and a large groundflash in the vicinity of the bridge – and Maj Case and his crew were never seen or heard from again. During the F-4C attack, Herrold and Ragland's jet was hit: on its final pass the damaged Phantom did not pull up, but went out to sea, continuing nearly five miles (8km) off shore before exploding. The two crew may have ejected before the explosion because a search-and-rescue aircraft discovered a dinghy in the water the following day. No trace of 64-0511 or its crew could be found. In late 1986 the remains of Case and two of his crew were returned to the US. Herrold and Ragland are among the 2,303 Americans still listed as 'unaccounted for' in south-east Asia.

Almost 700 sorties were flown against the bridge, at a cost of 104 crewmen shot down over an area 75 square miles (194 sq km) around the Dragon. In March 1967 the US Navy attacked the charmed bridge with new 'Wall-eye' missiles but failed to knock out the structure despite three direct hits. The spans were finally brought down on 13 May 1972 by laser-guided 'smart' bombs dropped by F-4Ds of the 8th TFW. Unfortunately, by then the Communists had built several other back-up routes around the bridge, and so the flow of supplies across the Ma River was not seriously affected.

Commando Vault

From 1968, under Project *Commando Vault*, C-130s were used to drop 5-ton M-121 and 7.5-ton BLU-82 weapons to blast out helicopter landing zones in jungle areas, or to demolish enemy vehicle parks and caches. Air Force Systems Command and the US Army co-operated closely to develop a method whereby large bombs could be dropped from both the C-130 and the US Army CH-54 Tarhe helicopters. The first tests involved dropping a 10,000lb (4,500kg) M-121 bomb from both types of aircraft, and these proved so successful that late in 1968 operational deployment in south-east Asia took place, the Hercules

C-130B 61-0950 (3626) of TAC unloading a tank in Vietnam. This aircraft was finally retired from the Air Force in 1994, and was sold to Romania in 1996. USAF

'bomber' being assigned to the 463rd Tactical Airlift Wing. In Vietnam, approach to the designated release point was made easier by using signals from the MSQ-77 ground radar sites. The Hercules could carry two palletized weapons in the hold, and given that a single M-121 bomb was capable of clearing an area about 200ft (60m) in diameter, more than enough for a helicopter to land safely, the C-130A and C-130E Hercules therefore had the advantage over the C-54 in Vietnam, being able to create two clearings per mission and over greater distances. Invariably, Hercules bomb delivery was made by the parachute extraction method described earlier, usually from about 7,000ft (2,100m); stabilizing parachutes were deployed to lower the weapons to the ground.

After a lull in operations during the winter months, the 463rd TAW resumed *Commando Vault* operations in March 1969. In 1970 the 15,000lb (6,804kg) BLU-82 bomb appeared; this was capable of clearing an area about 260ft (80m) in diameter, and was first dropped operationally from a Hercules on 23 March 1970. 'Big Blue' as it was called, was dropped using a delivery technique similar to that used to unleash the M-120, though a 'daisy cutter' fuse-extending rod ensured that the block-buster detonated at a

RAAF C-130A A97-212 57-0505/3212) returning from Vietnam in 1971. During the Vietnam War the 86th Wing (Airlift Group), RAAF, used Hercules extensively between Australia and Vietnam, for carrying war material and mail, as well as for medical evacuation. No. 36 Squadron operated twelve C-130As, and No. 37 Squadron flew twelve C-130Es from 1966. RAAF

height of 4ft (1.2m) above the ground. Late in 1971 the 374th Tactical Airlift Wing at Tan Son Nhut assumed direction of *Commando Vault* operations, and not surprisingly perhaps, they were extended to include troop and vehicle concentrations in south-east Asia. These accounted for many of the 600 weapons dropped (about two-thirds of which were 'Big Blues') in Vietnam, Laos and Cambodia, before the Vietnamese ceasefire in 1973. (In 1991 during *Desert Storm*, BLU-82B 'Big Blues' were used by MC-130Es of Special Operations Command against Iraqi troop concentrations and for mine clearing, with devastating effect.

Finale in Vietnam

After the C-7 Caribou and C-123 Provider had been phased out of service by the USAF, the Hercules units remained the only Air Force tactical transports in south-east Asia, and these operated from Thailand during the final months of the war From July 1965–November 1972, the Hercules flew no fewer than 708,087 sorties in Vietnam, with peak monthly operations being recorded in May 1968 when in-country Hercules flew some 14,392 sorties. US bombing of North Vietnam had resumed with a vengeance on 10 May 1972, with *Linebacker I* raids aimed at the enemy's road

and rail system to prevent supplies reaching the Communists operating in South Vietnam. *Linebacker II* operations began on 18 December 1972 and lasted until the 29th. These were the most effective strikes against enemy defences in the whole war, and they ultimately persuaded the Hanoi government to seek an end to hostilities and to conclude a peace treaty. Negotiations in Paris ended with the signing of a peace agreement on 23 January 1973, and all air operations ceased four days later; this brought to an end one of the most horrific wars in history. In its course 58,022 Americans died and it brought America itself worldwide condemnation for its role in

C-130B-IIs 59-1525 (3561) *(left)* in the 7406th Combat Support Squadron, and RC-130B 59-1526 (3563) *(right)*, in the 556th Reconnaissance Squadron, both from 347th Tactical Fighter Wing, at Cam Ranh Bay in the Spring of 1971. 59-1526, which was transferred to the 7406th CSS shortly afterwards, was retired from the Air Force in March 1992 and was sold to Argentina in November 1994 where it continues to serve in 1 ET/1 Grupo as TC-57. Lt Col Walt Evans USAF

(Above) C-130A 56-0521 (3129), pictured in 322nd Air Division markings in the early sixties was transferred to the South Vietnamese Air Force in 1973; it was destroyed on the ground at Song Be, South Vietnam, on 18 December 1974. MAP

south-east Asia. A total of 126 tactical airlift aircraft were lost during the war, fifty-five of them Hercules.

Although all US ground forces were withdrawn from South Vietnam, air-raids into neighbouring Cambodia and Laos continued until August 1973. In the spring of 1973 the C-130s switched their full attention to the airlift of supplies to Cambodia, with the last war-related sorties being undertaken in 1975 by an aircraft flown by civilian crews of Birdair Inc., a contract operator to which the USAF gave equipment and technical assistance. Then both Cambodia and Laos fell to the Communists, and early in 1975 the North turned its attentions to the final take-over of South Vietnam. Inevitably the South, now without US military support, collapsed under the full might of the Communists' spring offensive. Indeed the onslaught was so rapid and so intensive that by March, the original *Talon Vise* contingency plan to evacuate US dependents and non-essential personnel was abandoned, and beginning on 1 April, *Frequent Wind* began the wholesale evacuation of all US forces left in Vietnam.

C-130s of Tactical Airlift Command joined C-141As and C-5A Galaxies of the

US Army forces await boarding of 314th TAW C-130s; the nearest aircraft is 62-1859 (3823) in the 345th TAS. Col Walt Evans USAF

Military Airlift Command (MAC) in a mass exodus of US and Vietnamese military and civilians fleeing South Vietnam before the country was completely overwhelmed. (C-5 flights were withdrawn following a tragic crash of a Galaxy, on 4 April, which claimed 155 lives.) After 20 April the situation became even more critical, and safe operating loads were ignored so that transports could take off from Saigon, now completely surrounded by Communist troops, in grossly overloaded condition. C-130s departed carrying between 180 and even 260 evacuees on board, while a VNAF C-130 is reported to have fled loaded with 452 people. By 27 April the danger from Communist small arms, Triple-A and shoulder-fired ground-to-air missiles had become too great for most aircraft and all C-141A flights were suspended. The Hercules, however, carried on, flying right around the clock until the early hours of 29 April when heavy and accurate Communist rocket fire at Tan Son Nhut forced even these to cease operations.

The withdrawal from Vietnam. 'Grunts' of the US 3rd Marine Division embarking on KC-130F
transport/tanker BuNo. 150687 (3734) of VMGR-152 at MCAS Futema, Okinawa, en route home to the US late
in 1974. S/Sgt Mennillo, USMC

From 1–29 April 1975, a total of 50,493 people had been airlifted during the course of 375 C-130, C-141 and other aircraft sorties. On 12 April the US Embassy in Saigon was evacuated, and 287 staff were flown to US carriers offshore. On 29 April, 900 Americans were airlifted by the US Navy to five carriers. Next day, Saigon was in Communist hands and the South was under control of North Vietnam. Six C-130s were among the ninety aircraft flown out of the country to Thailand by VNAF personnel, but about 1,100 aircraft, including twenty-three C-130As in the 435th and 437th Squadrons, fell into Communist hands before the ink was dry on the surrender document issued to the Republic of Vietnam's President Doung Van Minh.

Ex-374th TCW C-130A 55-0045 (3072) which was transferred to the South Vietnamese Air Force in November
1972; here it is pictured at Seletar, Singapore on 7 February 1974. This aircraft was written off in April 1975
with the fall of South Vietnam. W.F. Wilson MCE, via Frank Mason

CHAPTER FOUR

World Military Users

Algeria The Al Quwwat Ali Jawwiya al Jaza'eriya (previously Force Aérienne Algérienne) received two C-130H-30 (CT) Combat Talons in July and August 1981. Ten C-130Hs and five C-130H-30 (CT)s were delivered between 1982–84, and an eighth C-130H-30 (CT) was delivered in November 1990. The ten C-130Hs and eight C-130H-30 (CT)s are shared between 31, 32, 33 and 35 Escadrilles.

Argentina Three C-130Es were delivered to the Fuerza Aérea Argentina in 1968. However, TC-62 was lost on 28 August 1975 when a bomb exploded by the side of the runway during take-off from Tucuman; and during the Falklands War in 1982 one C-130E was shot down by a Sea Harrier on 1 June – this was replaced by a former Lockheed L-100-30 demonstrator in December 1982. Five C-130Hs were received between 1971 and 1975, one of which – TC-68 – was used as a bomber in the Falklands War, and two KC-130H tankers in 1979. Five ex-

TC-65 of 1 Escuadron, 1 Brigada Aérea, one of five C-130Hs received by the Fuerza Aérea Argentina, 1971–75, and based at BAM El Palomar, Buenos Aires. MAP

USAF C-130Bs were delivered to the FAA between 1992 and 1994. The 1 Esquadron de Transport, Grupo 1 de Transporte Aero at BAM E1 Palomar, Buenos Aires, is the FAA Hercules operator.

Australia The Royal Australian Air Force was the first overseas customer for the Hercules, buying twelve C-130A-50-LMs in 1958 to serve with No. 36 Squadron at Richmond, New South Wales. Twelve C-130Es were delivered from 1966 for service with No. 37 Squadron, also at Richmond, part of the 86th Wing (Airlift Group). During the Vietnam War the twenty-four aircraft were used between Australia and

C-130E A97-168, one of twelve delivered from 1966 for service with No. 37 Squadron, 86th Wing (Airlift Group), RAAF, at Richmond, NSW, pictured at Kai Tak, Hong Kong, in 1991. Gary Madgwick/The Aviation Workshop

C-130H A97-011 (4791) of No. 36 Squadron, RAAF, which was fitted with MAFFS (Modularized Airborne Fire-fighting System) in 1983, discharging its load of fire-retardant slurry on a bushfire in Australia. Lockheed

Vietnam, for carrying war material and mail, as well as for medical evacuation. No. 36 Squadron's twelve C-130As were withdrawn from use in 1978 and replaced by twelve C-130Hs. A handful of the As

returned to service briefly in 1986, and one was sold to the French government (Securité Civil) for Chad. No. 37 Squadron's C-130Es are tasked with long-range transport duties, and No. 36 is the dedicated tactical

unit. Some of the latter's aircraft can be fitted with MAFFS (Modularized Airborne Fire-Fighting System). The RAAF currently has twelve C-130J-30 aircraft on order for No. 37 Squadron.

Bahrain C-130B. No further details.

Belgium The Force Aérienne Belge operates twelve C-130Hs, delivered in 1972 and 1973. They are flown by the 20 Smaldeel (Squadron), Groupement de Transport/No. 15 Wing, at Brussels-Melsbroek. These aircraft are used for United Nations operations and famine relief duties with the Red Cross in Ethiopia and the Sudan, and may be seen in overall white or specially marked finishes. The C-130s have also been involved in the Open Skies treaty verification programme.

Bolivia The Fuerza Aérea Boliviana's (FAB) Grupo Aereo de Transporte 71, based at BA General Walter Arze, La Paz, is operated on a peacetime basis as an internal domestic airline known as Transporte Aereo Boliviano (TAB). However, it doubles as the main tactical support element of the

---

VLAGES

The FAB has played a key role in dropping food in Ethiopia. Having already experimented with such drops without parachutes at low level in 1973–74 during another Sahel country's drought period, the FAB refined its VLAGES (Very Low Altitude Gravity Extraction System) food-drop technique in Ethiopia in 1985–86. A total of 677 live food drops was made at Mehoni (near Maychew) and Sekota (in Wollo Province). The overall success rate was 96.7 per cent, but during the last drop months, an average loss of less than 2 per cent was recorded due to further refinements in bagging procedures and drop techniques.

Grain is put into 25 or 50kg (55 or 110lb) nylon bags, these are then put into bags of 90cm (35in) in size, which in turn are put into two outer bags of 120cm (47in). When the bags strike the ground, the inner bags generally tend to burst and the contents spread into the larger middle bag; should the middle bag also split, the outer bag will, in most cases, retain the grain. After improving the flying and re-bagging techniques,

post-impact damage was reduced in many cases to zero or almost zero losses.

When approaching the drop zone, the speed of the airdrop is 125 knots and the altitude 50ft (15m) radar altimeter. At that moment the nose attitude is higher. At the 'Green On' given by the navigator, the retriever will tighten the cable and the knife will cut the straps holding the load. The load starts moving. When the pallets move towards the ramp, the straps running along the tight cables will cut the D ring of the pallets. Bags leave the pallet and fall separately on the ground.

The Belgian Air Force Hercules' have airdropped food using the VLAGES technique in southern Sudan, flying from Lokichokio in northern Kenya. Although the technique had to be slightly modified again – because of the terrain at the drop zones the delivery altitude had to be changed from 70 to 60ft agl – the results stayed as successful as before, with an average of only about 2 per cent loss rates. Drop loads range from 12 to 16 tons, in a single pallet row, single passage airdrop.

country's military forces, in which role it is known as the Transporte Aereo Militar (TAM). Of the eleven ex-USAF C-130As and C-130Bs delivered to FAB as from October 1988, only two C-130Bs remain in service. Five C-130A/Bs were withdrawn from use, and two were lost in crashes in 1989 and 1994. Two new-build C-130Hs were acquired in 1977, and one L-100-30 in 1979. Of these, C-130H TAM-90/CP-1375 crashed into the water after a night take-off from Panama-Tacumen on 28 September 1979, and L-100-30 TAM 92 was shot down near Malanje, Angola, on 16 March 1991 while on lease to Transafrik.

Brazil Since 1965 the Forca Aérea Brasileria has operated nineteen C-130s (eleven

(Above) The Force Aérienne Belge operates twelve C-130Hs (CH-0I, delivered in Jue 1972, pictured) which were delivered in 1972 and 1973. They are flown by the 20 Smaldeel (Squadron), Groupement de Transport, No. 15 Wing, at Brussels-Melsbroek. The camouflage scheme was replaced with grey in January 1991. FAB

(Below) C-130E 2457 (4290) of the 1st Esquadrao. 1st Transport Group 'Coral' of the Forca Aérea Brasileria which crashed on approach in fog to Santa maria AB, Brazil, on 24 June 1985. Five of the eleven C-130Es delivered in March 1967 remain in service at Rio de Janeiro, being flown by the 1st Esquadrao at Galeao Airport, and the 2nd Esquadrao, 1st Tactical Transport Group 'Gordo', at Campos dos Afonsos. Lockheed

C-130Es, seven C-130Hs, and one KC-130H) at various times. C-130E 4093 crashed on landing with high sink rate on 26 October 1966, and C-130E 4091 was written off on 21 December 1969 at Recife. One C-130E has been put into storage, another (4290) crashed on approach in fog to Santa Maria AB, Brazil on 24 June 1985, and 4293 was destroyed at Formosa, 60km (37 miles) north-east of Brasilia on 14 October 1994 when the ammunition load caught fire in the air. Five Es, six C-130Hs (C-130H 4998 having crashed into the sea on approach to Fernando de Noronha Island, Brazil, on 14 December 1987) and the KC-130H remain in service. These are flown by the 1st Esquadrao, of the 1st Transport Group 'Coral' at Galeao Airport, Rio de Janeiro, and the 2nd Esquadrao, 1st Tactical Transport Group 'Gordo', at Campos dos Afonsos, Rio de Janeiro. The C-130Hs are tasked with serving the Army's 1st Parachute Division. Ski-equipped aircraft also support the Brazilian mission in Antarctica.

Cameroon Two C-130Hs and one C-130H-30 (4933/TJX-AE, later TJX-CE) have been flown by the l'Armée de l'Air du Cameroon. The aircraft were delivered in August and September 1977 and, based at Douala, have been used in support of counter-insurgency (COIN) operations from Batouri, Garoua and Yaounde, and also for civilian passenger purposes. C-130H 4747 (TJX-AC) burned on the ground at Marseilles in December 1989, and in 1997 was to be shipped to Bordeaux for repairs.

Canada Four C-130Bs were received in October–November 1960 and issued to No. 435 Squadron RCAF. Aircraft 10304 was lost in April 1966 when the forward cargo door opened in flight, striking the port inner propeller which threw it over the fuselage, severing the tail control cables before striking both the starboard propellers. The aircraft belly-landed in a wheat field in Saskatchewan. The three surviving C-130Bs were returned to Lockheed in 1967, and these were acquired in 1969 by the Columbian Air Force (two were later lost). Meanwhile, twenty-four C-130Es had been delivered to the RCAF. These were followed by fourteen C-130H models, diverted from the USAF's 1973 Appropriations for Tactical Air Command, and delivered between October 1974 and February 1975.

During the period 1967 to 1993, five C-130Es have been lost, as have three C-130Hs in No. 435 Squadron (two of which were involved in a mid-air collision on 29 March 1985). One of the C-130Es, and one of the C-130Hs were lost in accidents involving LAPES operations.

TJ-XAD (4752), one of two C-130Hs delivered to the l'Armée de l'Air du Cameroon in 1977 (TJX-AC burned on the ground at Marseilles in December 1989). Lockheed

The current Canadian Armed Forces' transport fleet consists of twenty-six Es and Hs – in 1996 two L-100-30 aircraft (5320, and 5307) were modified to C-130H-30 – locally designated as CC-130s; they serve with the following squadrons on strategic and tactical transport, search-and-rescue, and training duties: No. 413 Transport and Rescue, Greenwood, Nova Scotia; No. 418 (Air Reserve) Transport and Rescue, Namao; No. 424 Transport and Rescue, Trenton, Ontario; No. 426 Transport Training, Trenton (no aircraft permanently assigned: it also operates CC-130s for the tactical Air Lift School and Transport Operational Test and Evaluation Facility); No. 429 Transport, Trenton; No. 435 Transport and Tanker, Namao; No. 436 Transport; No. 437 Transport and Tanker, Trenton.

Chad This former French colony's Hercules fleet has been gradually built up as from

(Above) **Four C-130Bs were received by the Royal Canadian Air Force in October–November 1960 and issued to No. 435 Squadron. 10304 (3590) was lost on 15 April 1966 when the forward cargo door opened in flight, striking the port inner propeller, which threw it over the fuselage, severing the tail-control cables before striking both the starboard propellers. The aircraft belly-landed in a wheatfield in Saskatchewan. The three surviving C-130Bs were returned to Lockheed in 1967, and these were acquired in 1969 by the Columbian Air Force (two were later lost).** Lockheed

The RCAF received fourteen C-130H models between October 1974 and February 1975. During 1967–93 three C-130Hs in No. 435 Squadron were lost, including 130329 (4553), which crashed near CFB Mamao during a LAPES approach after the load jammed. Lockheed

1983 when the country became involved in a full-scale war with its northern neighbour Libya; at the time of writing it has reached a peak of seven aircraft. C-130A (3208, A97-208) formerly of the RAAF, was obtained by France's Sécurité Civile in November 1983. Four ex-USAF C-130As were acquired during the 1980s, though two of these were lost in crashes in 1986 and 1987, and two more were sold in 1991. Two new-build models, a

C-130H and a C-130H-30, were acquired in 1988 and 1989 respectively. These, and the surviving C-130A, remain in service with the Force Aérienne Tchadienne.

Chile The Fuerza Aérea de Chile currently operates C-130s with Grupo de Aviaçon 10 at Santiago-Merino Benitez. The fleet consists of two C-130Hs which were delivered in 1972 and 1973, and four ex-USAF C-

130Bs acquired in 1992, the latter retaining their former 'European One' camouflage.

Colombia In 1969 the Fuerza Aérea Colombiana bought three ex-RCAF C-130Bs which had been returned to Lockheed in 1967. Two of these were subsequently lost, in August 1969 and October 1982. Eight ex-C-130Bs were also required, and of these, five remain in service. Two new-build C-

C-130B 1003 (3572), one of three ex-RCAF C-130Bs which were returned to Lockheed in 1967 and bought in 1969 by Columbia for the Fuerza Aérea Colombian. 1003 was ditched 220 miles (350km) east of Cape May, New Jersey, on 16 October 1982, after the navigational system collapsed and the aircraft ran out of fuel. It floated for fifty-six hours. MAP

The Fuerza Aérea de Chile received two C-130Hs, in 1972 and 1973. The second aircraft, 996 (4496) of Grupo de Aviaçon 10 at Santiago-Merino Benitez, is pictured at Greenham Common in 1979. MAP

C-130H B-679, the second of three purchased for the Kongelige Danske Flyvevaabnet (Royal Danish Air Force, RDAF) between April and July 1975. The original overall dark green finish was later replaced with a subdued grey, and in July 1988 wing-tip ECM/ESM pods were fitted. RDAF

C-130H FAE-812 of the Fuerza Aérea Ecuatoriana (FAE), delivered to Ecuador in April 1979 as a replacement for FAE 748 which crashed into the Pichincha Mountains, 12 July 1978. MAP

130Hs were delivered in 1983. The FAC Hercules' are operated by the Escuadron de Transporte at Eldorado Airport, Bogata.

Denmark The Kongelige Danske Flyve-vaabnet's (Royal Danish Air Force, RDAF) Escadrille 721 of the Flyvertaktisk Kommando (Tactical Air Command) at Vaer-lose uses three C-130Hs to provide support for the Danish Air Force and Army since delivery during the months April–July 1975. Originally finished in overall dark green, they are now painted in a subdued grey finish and have been equipped with wing-tip ECM/ESM pods.

Ecuador The Fuerza Aérea Ecuatoriana's (FAE) small Hercules fleet serves with Ala de Transporte II at Quito-Mariscal Sucre. Four ex-USAF C-130Bs were obtained in the 1970s; these were joined by three new-build C-130Hs, the first two being delivered for service with Escuadrilla 11 in July and August 1977. The second of these (4748) was lost when it crashed into the Pinchincha Mountains in Ecuador on 12 July 1978 (4812, a replacement, was delivered in April 1979). The first (4743), also crashed into a mountain, 15km (9miles) from Marisal Sucre airport near Quito on 29 April 1982, during a go-around after a missed approach. An L-100-30 was obtained in July 1981.

Egypt The Al Quwwat Ali Jawwiya Ilmisriya (the Air Force of the Republic of Egypt, EAF) received twenty-three C-130Hs between 1976 and 1982 and three C-130H-30s in 1990. The first six C-130Hs were diverted from the USAF's 1976 Appropriations and were delivered during December 1976 and January 1977. The first C-130H delivered (SU-BAA/4707) was written off after it had its nose burned out during Egypt's commando-style assault against terrorist hijackers who had taken a number of Egyptian nationals hostage at Larnaca airport, Cyprus, on 19 February 1978. A second C-130H (SU-BAH, which was carrying a cargo of ammunition) was lost when it hit the ground after take-off from Cairo-West on 29 May 1981. Two of the C-130Hs are

C-130H SU-BAK (4797) was delivered to the Al Quwwat Ali Jawwiya Ilmisriya (the Air Force of the Republic of Egypt, EAF) in November 1978; it was one of twenty-three C-130Hs delivered between 1976 and 1982. MAP

C-139H 750 (4729) was one of four C-130Hs acquired by the Ellinki Aéroporia (Royal Hellenic Air Force) and delivered in April 1974 for service with 356 Mira (Squadron). This aircraft hit a mountain on approach to Tanagra air base on 20 December 1997 whilst searching for a crashed Ukranian airliner near Athens. MAP

now configured as VC-130H VIP transports, and two serve as ECM/ELINT platforms or airborne command posts. The other twenty serve in the transport role.

France The Armée de l'Air has five C-130Hs (including two ex-Zaire Air Force machines which were impounded in February 1982 at Milan-Malpensa), and nine C-130H-30s that were delivered between 1987 and March 1991. All are flown by the Escadron de Transport 2/61 at Orléans-Bricy, and became a familiar sight on television news reports from the former Yugoslavia at the height of the UN and NATO peacekeeping missions there.

Gabon The Force Aérienne Gabonaise has just three Hercules (an L-100-30 was sold in 1989): a C-130H, an L-100-20, and an L-100-30 (the presidential aircraft), operated by the Escadrille de Transport at Libreville-Leon M'Ba Airport.

Greece Four C-130Hs were acquired by the Ellinki Aéroporia (Royal Hellenic Air Force) and delivered between September 1975 and June 1976 for service with 356 Mira (Squadron), 112 Pterix, of Air Matériel Command. Greece withdrew from NATO following Turkey's invasion of Cyprus, and it was not until 1977 that the US export of arms was resumed when eight C-130Hs, diverted from the 1975 USAF Appropriations, were sold to the RHAF. C-130H 4724 crashed into Mount Billiuras during its landing approach to Nea Anchialos on 5 February 1991, and 4729 hit a mountain on approach to Tanagra air base on 20 December 1997 whilst searching for a crashed Ukranian airliner near Athens. One of the C-130Hs was withdrawn from use in 1997. Meanwhile, in 1992, five ex-USAF C-130Bs were acquired to supplement the Hercules fleet. The fourteen C-130Hs that remain in service continue to be flown by 356 Mira at Eleusis. Some are equipped for fire-fighting missions with the MAFFS system, and a few are modified for electronic surveillance duties.

Honduras During 1986–89 the Fuerza Aérea Hondurena received an ex-USAF C-130D (57-0487) and four ex-USAF C-130As. The C-130D crashed near Wampusirpi, Honduras on 14 August 1986, while one of the C-130As was withdrawn in 1991. The Escadrilla de Transporte currently operates the three remaining C-130As at Tocontin Airport, Tegucigalpa.

Indonesia In 1958–59 the Angkatan Udara Republik Indonesia received ten C-130Bs diverted from Tactical Air Command's production allocation for that year, and these entered service with No. 31 Squadron at Jarkarta-Halim, Java. T-1307 was lost on 3 September 1964 when it crashed in Malaya, and T-1306 was lost a year later, on 21 September 1965, when it was believed to have been 'frightened down' by an RAF Javelin. Two C-130Bs were modified to KC-130B. In September 1980, 32 Squadron received the first stretched C-130H-30 (4864) from the production line. C-130H-MP (TNI-AU/4898) crashed into volcano Sibyak on 21 November 1985. Some of the L-100-30 models were leased or sold to Pelita Air Service. The Tantara Nasional Indonesia-Angkatan Udare (TNI-AU) still operates most of the total of twenty-five Hercules it has received. No. 31 Squadron at Jakarta-Halim operates the survivors of the sixteen C-130Bs delivered in 1960 and 1961, 1975, and 1979, and also the L-100-30, while No. 32 Squadron at Malang flies the remaining H and H30 models (TNI-AU/4927 crashed after take-off from Halim-Perdanakasuma, Jakarta, on 5 October 1991).

C-130H-30 A-1321 (4925) was delivered to the Tantara Nasional Indonesia-Angkatan Udare (TNI-AU) in May 1982. No. 32 Squadron at Malans flies the remaining C-130H and C-130H-30 models in the TNI-AU inventory. via Frank Mason

C-130H 5-136 (4439) was delivered to the Imperial Iranian Air Force (IIAF) in December 1971. Based at Shirah, it was renumbered 5-130 in November 1973, and renumbered again in 1976, as 5-8524. MAP

C-130E 5-111 (4153) was one of five C-130Es sold by the Nirou Havai Shahanshahiye Iran (Imperial Iranian Air Force, IIAF) in the mid-1970s to the Pakistan Fiza'ya; it was operated by No. 6 Squadron as 64312/L. MAP

Iran Beginning in 1962, the Nirou Haval Shahanshahiye Iran (Imperial Iranian Air Force, IIAF) took delivery of four C-130Bs, twenty-eight C-130Es, and thirty-two C-130Hs (the last two being delivered in May 1975), making it the third largest user (with sixty-four aircraft) of the Hercules after the US and the RAF. The C-130Bs were used for about four years with No. 5 Air Transport Squadron at Mehrabad before being purchased by Pakistan, pending delivery of seventeen C-130Es in 1965–66 (eight) and 1968 (nine). C-130E 107/4118 was destroyed following a lightning strike on 18 April 1967, and C-130E 5-112/4154 crashed while simulating two-engines out in Shiraz, on 7 April 1969. In 1970–71, eleven more C-130Es were delivered. In the mid-1970s, five C-130Es were subsequently disposed of, again to Pakistan. Four IIAF C-130Hs were modified for covert signal monitoring and electronic reconnaissance along the Iranian border with the Soviet Union, as part of the Ibex ELINT-gathering network; the electronic equipment was installed in pods carried outboard of the outer engines. Following the Islamic revolution, the arms embargo imposed on Iran has taken a toll of the remaining fleet, and only a handful are believed to be still fly-able (since February 1974, seven Iran Air Force C-130s have been lost).

Israel During 1971–72, the Heyl Ha'Avir (Israeli Defence Force/Air Force, IDAF) acquired twelve C-130Es – all recently disposed of by the 313th, 316th and 516th Tactical Airlift Wings, USAF – and gave them dual military/civil registrations to disguise their military purpose. Starting in October 1971 and ending in September 1976, the IDAF took delivery of ten C-130Hs and two KC-130H tankers. After

transport duties. All are thought to be operated currently by No. 131 Squadron from Lod Airport, Tel Aviv. One (4X-FBD) is known to have been lost in a crash at Jebel Halal on 25 November 1975, and others have been placed in storage.

Italy The Aeronautica Militaire Italiana's 50th Gruppo of the 46 Aerobrigata at Pisa-San Giusto continues to fly the Hercules on strategic airlift duties, using twelve C-130Hs from a batch of fourteen delivered in 1972. In June 1978 three were used on fire-fighting duties. 46-10 (4492) was lost

Jordan The Al Quwwat Almalakiya (Royal Jordanian Air Force) initially received four ex-USAF C-130Bs in 1973, followed by four C-130Hs acquired in 1978 and an HC-130H (not confirmed). Two of the C-130B models were sold to Singapore, and the remaining aircraft are flown by No. 3 Squadron from Amman-Ling Abdullah.

Kuwait The Kuwait Air Force originally took delivery of two L-100-20s in 1970; one of these was destroyed on 5 September 1980 when it crashed near Montelimar in southeast France after a lightning strike, and the

The Heyl Ha'Avir (Israeli Defence Force/Air Force, IDAF) acquired twenty-four ex-USAF C-130Es, ten 130Hs and two KC-130H tankers. Ten C-130Hs are still in use on transport duties. All are thought to be operated currently by No. 131 Squadron, from Lod Airport, Tel Aviv. One C-130H is known to have been lost in a crash in 1975, and others have been placed in storage. MAP

the outbreak of the Yom Kippur War in 1973, twelve more ex-USAF C-130Es were delivered. In Operation *Thunderbolt* on 4 July 1976, four took part in a daring rescue: flying over the Red Sea, Ethiopia and Kenya, they flew almost 2,500 miles (4,000km) to Entebbe Airport, Uganda, to mount a daring rescue of 103 hostages, many of them Israelis, held by the Gaza Commando of the Palestine Liberation Force, who threatened to kill them. The C-130Hs landed 245 Israeli commandos, and they freed the majority of the hostages in a brief battle. Seven hijackers, three hostages, one Israeli officer, and at least twenty Ugandan soldiers were killed in the operation. Ten C-130Hs are still in use on

when it flew into Monte Serra 15km (9miles) east of Pisa on 3 March 1977. In 1980, 46-14 was cannibalized for spares (subsequently used for C-130H 46-09) on 23 January 1979 when it jumped its chocks during an engine run-up at Milan-Malpensa and hit a tree. The AMI currently has ten C-130J aircraft on order.

Japan The fifteen C-130Hs of the Koku Jietai (Japan Air Self-Defence Force, JASDF) have been operated since entering service in 1984 by the 401st Hikotai (Squadron) of the 1st Tactical Airlift Group at Komaki AB. Some of the aircraft have been fitted with a locally produced, Naval minelaying system.

other (4412) was sold back to Lockheed – it was used as a high technology testbed (HTTB), and was subsequently lost on 3 February 1993 when it crashed during a high-speed ground-test. Four L-100-30s were acquired from 1983; 4949/KAF322 (N4107F) was hit by groundfire at Kuwait City Airport on 2 August 1990 during the Iraqi invasion and flown to Iraq – where it was hit by a bomb which badly damaged the centre fuselage. It was transported by road to Kuwait in March 1995, but was not repaired. 4951/KAF323, 4953/KAF324 and 4955/KAF325 were evacuated to Saudi Arabia on 2 August 1990 and currently flown by No. 41 Squadron at Kuwait International Airport.

C-130H MM61997 46-11 (4493) of the 46 Aerobrigata at Pisa San Giusto, one of fourteen C-130Hs purchased for the Aeronautica Militaire Italiana. In June 1978 it was one of three MAFFS C-130Hs used on fire-fighting duties. via Frank Mason

Fifteen C-130Hs (95-1082/8907 pictured) are operated by the Koku Jietai Jietai (Japan Air Self-Defence Force, JASDF) in the 401st Hikotai (Squadron) of the 1st Tactical Airlift Group at Komaki AB. Mick Jennings

(Above) The Al Quwwat Ali Jawwiya Almlakiya (Royal Jordanian Air Force) initially received four ex-USAF C-130Bs in 1973, including '140' (60-0304/3612). Two of the C-130Bs were sold to Singapore, although '140' is in storage in Amman. via Frank Mason

(Below) Four L-100-30s were acquired for the Kuwait Air Force. KAF323 (4951) was one of three evacuated to Saudi Arabia on 2 August 1990 during the Iraqi invasion and is currently flown by No. 41 Squadron at Kuwait International Airport. Mick Jennings

C-130H 116 (4401), one of eight delivered to the Libyan Arab Republic Air Force between 1970 and 1971, was destroyed by fire during the Israel hostage rescue mission at Entebbe, Uganda, on 8 April 1979. via Frank Mason

Libya Eight of the sixteen C-130Hs ordered for the Libyan Arab Republic Air Force were received between 1970 and 1971, the others being embargoed in 1973 and placed in storage at Marietta. 4401 was destroyed by fire at Entebbe, Uganda, on 8 April 1979. Seven of the aircraft are thought to still be in service, supplemented by L-100-20s and -30s operated by Libyan Arab Air Cargo. L-100-30 4992 eventually ended up at AFI International Ltd 'for oil exploration in Benin' and was delivered to Libya in May 1985. It was hijacked by a Libyan crew to Egypt in March 1987 and was returned to Libya. L-100-30 (5000) was sold to AFI International Ltd, registered to Benin as TY-BBU (not used) and obtained by Jamahiriya Air Transport, Libya, in May 1985.

Malaysia The Tentar Udara Diraja Malaysia (Royal Malaysian Air Force) has received six C-130Hs (FM2401/6), delivered between 1976 and 1980; of these, FM2403/4674 crashed whilst landing at Sibu, Sarawak, on 25 August 1980, while FM2401/4656 was put into storage in April 1997. It also has three C-130H-MPs, and six C-130H-30s. Nos. 14 and 4 Squadrons at Kuala Lumpur-Subang Fly the four C-130H, and three C-130H-MPs

respectively, in joint maritime and transport duties; the latter are distinguished by an overall light grey finish. No. 20 Squadron operates the six C-130H-30s.

Mexico The Fuerza Aérea Mexicana has received a total of nine ex-USAF C-130As and one RC-130A since 1987 for use by Escuadron Aereo Transporte Pesado 302 at Santa Lucia. The RC-130A was briefly operated under a civil registration on Presidential Flight duties. Four of the C-130As were written off in 1997. An L-100-30 was sold to Protexa in September 1994.

Morocco A total of seventeen C-130H transports were delivered to the Force Aérienne Royal Morocaine (Al Quwwat Ali Jawwiya Almalakiya Marakishiya, Royal Maroc Air Force) in three batches between 1974 and 1981, the last being two C-130Hs (4888 N4162M/CNA-OP and 4892 CNA-OQ) in August 1981 with an SLAR (sideways-looking airborne radar) on the left main undercarriage fairing for use in detecting Polisario infiltrations in the Western Sahara. Two KC-130Hs were also delivered in November–December 1981. Polisario rebels shot down 4537/CNA-OB over the Sahara on 4 December 1976 and 4717/CNA-OH at Guelta Zemmour in

West Sahara on 12 October 1981. Several aircraft at Kenitra were fitted with underwing Chaff and flare pods, two were equipped with an SLAR pod for surveillance work, and 4875/ CNA-OM has been modified to carry MAFFS equipment for locust spraying. Civilian-style registrations are worn, with the aircraft construction number on the fin.

Netherlands The Koninklijke Luchtmacht received the first of two C-130H-30s in 1994 (G273 *Ben Swagerman*, and G2775 *Joop Mulder*), to become the newest European Hercules operator. The aircraft are flown by No. 334 Squadron at Eindhoven as part of the recently expanded transport office.

New Zealand No. 40 Squadron of the Royal New Zealand Air Force at Whenuapai operates five C-130Hs, including the first three production H models which were delivered in April 1965. The squadron's duties include flights to the Antarctic base at McMurdo. The first major operation carried out by the RNZAF C-130Hs was in July 1965 when the three aforementioned C-130Hs (followed by the other two in January 1969) airlifted the NZ Army's No. 161 Artillery battery and its

C-130H FM2401 (4656) was the first of six C-130Hs delivered to the Tentar Udara Diraja Malaysia (Royal Malaysian Air Force) 1976–80 for operation by No. 14 Squadron at Kuala Lumpur-Subang. It is now stored. Lockheed

C-130H CNA-OL (4742) of the Force Aérienne Royal Marocaine comes into land at Mogadishu on 1 March 1993 during Operation Provide Relief. Seventeen C-130Hs were delivered to the Royal Maroc Air Force between 1974 and 81. Author

equipment from New Zealand to Bien Hoa AFB in South Vietnam. Over seven days, 14–21 July, the aircraft carried ninety-six soldiers, five 105mm howitzers, fourteen laden Land Rovers, eight trailers, two water tankers and other equipment – a total of 70 tons. No. 40 Squadron continued regular flights in support of New Zealand's contribution to this war, flying into Saigon and Vung Tau; between 6–19 April 1975 it made three trips between Saigon and Singapore to evacuate New Zealand Embassy staff, refugee children and news media representatives.

Niger The small Escadrille Nationale du Niger (Force Aérienne Niger) took delivery of two C-130Hs (5U-MBD/4829 and 5U-MBH/4831) at Niamey in 1979. 5U-MBD was put into storage during 1986, but was returned to service in 1988. It was lost on 16 April 1997 when, with two engines on fire, it crashed at the village of Sorei on its approach to Niamey.

Nigeria The Federal Nigerian Air Force received six C-130Hs delivered in two batches of three between September 1975 and February 1976; also three 'stretched'

C-130H-30s were acquired in 19855. C-130H 911/4624 crashed after take-off from Lagos, Nigeria, on 26 September 1992 when three engines failed because of contaminated fuel. The eight remaining aircraft are operated from the base at Lagos-Murtala Muhammed.

Norway Six C-130Hs were delivered to the Konelige Norske Lufforsvaret in June and July 1969, and are still flown by Skvadron 335 based at Gardermoen. They are: 68-10952 BW-A *Odin*; 68-10953 BW-B *Tor*; 68-10954 BW-C *Balder*; 68-10955

5U-MBD/4829, the first of two C-130Hs delivered to the small Force Aérienne Niger in 1979, was put into storage during 1986 but was returned to service in 1988. It was lost on 16 April 1997 when, with two engines on fire, it crashed at the village of Sorei on approach to Niamey. via Frank Mason

C-130H 68-10955 BW-D *Fröy*, one of six C-130Hs delivered to the Konelige Norske Lufforsvaret (Royal Norwegian Air Force) in June and July 1969, which are still flown by Skvadron 335 based at Gardermoen. RNoAF

The RNoAF C-130Hs are frequently assigned to tasks on behalf of the United Nations, and are consequently often seen bearing prominent 'UN' titling. 68-10956 Ty is pictured at Sheremetyevo 1 Airport, Moscow, on 14 August 1992. In 1994 this aircraft was marked '30,000 Hours of Flying'. Author

BW-D *Froy*; 68-10956 BW-E *Ty*; and 68-10957 BW-F *Brage*. Frequently assigned to the United Nations, they consequently often bear prominent 'UN' titling.

Oman The Sultan of Oman's Air Force acquired three C-130Hs in 1981 for use by No. 4 Squadron from their base at Muscat-Seen Airport. These remain in service.

Pakistan A mixed force of thirteen Hercules remains in service with No. 35 (Composite) Air Transport Wing of the Pakistan Fiza'ya; this is from a total of thirteen

C-130E 64312/L (4153), one of four ex-Imperial Iran Air Force C-130Es, of No. 35 (Composite) Air Transport Wing of the Pakistan Fiza'ya, pictured in Turkey in 1991. Mick Jennings

C-130Bs (five of which were ex-USAF and four ex-Imperial Iran Air Force), five C-130Es (all ex-IIAF), and two L-100s (bought by the Pakistan government for PIA, but operated by the PAF) delivered at various times. Seven of the twenty aircraft (five C-130Bs, one C-130E and one L-100) were lost or written off between 1965 and 1988. C-130B 62-3494/PAF 23494 crashed on 17 June 1988 after take-off 7km (4 miles) north of Bahawalpur airport, Pakistan, en route to Rawalpindi. President Zia-ul-Haq and many senior officers were killed. The remaining aircraft, which includes the world's last unmodified L-100, are operated mainly by No. 6 Tactical Support Squadron at Chaklala AB, Rawalpindi.

Peru The Fuerza Aérea Peruana (Peruvian Air Force) has operated a total of sixteen Hercules since 1970, having received six ex-USAF C-130Bs, two ex-USAF C-130Ds (both of which were scrapped in August 1993), and eight L-100-20s. Two of the C-130As were converted to tankers, one of which was withdrawn from use in 1997. Only three C-130As remain in service. Of the eight L-100-20s, three were written off in crashes: 4364/FAP394 suffered an engine shutdown on take-off from Tarapoto on 19 February 1978. 4450, delivered to the FAP

in April 1972 and coded 396, made an emergency landing at night with no fuel near San Juan on 24 April 1981 and was written off. 4708, delivered in December 1976, crashed at Puerto Maldonado, southern Peru, on 9 June 1983. The remaining Hercules in the FAP inventory are operated by Escuadron 841, Grupo Aereo de Transporte 8, from Jorge Chavez Airport, Lima.

Philippines The Philippine Air Force acquired an ex-RAAF C-130A (later sold), and seven ex-USAF C-130Bs, four of which were either withdrawn from use

L-100-20 FAP394 (4364), one of eight L-100-20s operated by the Fuerza Aérea Peruana (Peruvian Air Force); it suffered an engine shut-down on take-off from Tarapoto on 19 February 1978. via Frank Mason

The Forca Aérea Portuguesa acquired five C-130Hs in 1977 and 1978, the third of which was 6803, delivered in April 1978. The Esquadra de Transporte 501 at Montijo Air Base operates all of Portugal's C-130 fleet.
Gary Madgwick/The Aviation Workshop

between 1996 and 1997, or were rendered non-operational. L-100 (N1130E), the ex-Lockheed demonstrator, was acquired by the Philippine government in 1973 and issued to the Air Force after long storage in Manila. The Philippine government also acquired four L-100-20s, two of which were for the Air Force. One L-100-20 was withdrawn from use in 1991. Three new-build C-130Hs were acquired in the period 1976–97 and issued to No. 222 Heavy Airlift Squadron at Mactan. The third air-

Romania The Romanian Air Force acquired four ex-USAF C-130Bs, which were delivered from Ogden Air Logistics Center to Romania in 1996–97. No details of unit or base are currently available.

Saudi Arabia The first Hercules of the Al Quwwat Ali Jawwiya Assa'udiya (Royal Saudi Air Force) were nine C-130Es delivered between 1965 and 1968. Losses were 4128/RSAF453, which suffered and engine fire and crashed taking off from

130H for the Saudi royal family, while 4756 and 4754 were lost in crashes on 27 March 1989 and 21 March 1991 respectively. Six L-100-30s were acquired. One (4954) was sold to Sheikh Ibrahim, a Saudi VIP, and the other five (4950, 4952 – configured as a dental clinic – 4956/57, and 4960) were modified for use as airborne hospitals and operated by Saudia. In 1992 and 1993 respectively, 4950/HZ-MS05 and 4957/HZ-MS10 were demodified to L-100-30 designation, and their

C-130H 1619 of No. 16 Squadron, one of thirty-seven C-130Hs purchased by the Royal Saudi Air Force, pictured at Riyadh in 1991. Gary Madgwick/The Aviation Workshop

craft (4761) crashed into Mount Manase 250km (155 miles) south-east of Manila on 15 December 1993 during descent towards Naga airport.

Portugal The Forca Aérea Portuguesa acquired five C-130Hs, delivered from August 1977 through to June 1978. Two were subsequently modified to C-130H-30 configuration. A new-build C-130H-30 was added in October 1991. Esquadra de Transporte 501 at Montijo Air Base Operates all six aircraft, all of which can be equipped with the MAFF system for fire-fighting.

Medina on 14 September 1980, and 4136/RSAF454 which crashed at Le Bourget, Paris, on 1 January 1969. The C-130Es were followed by thirty-seven C-130Hs beginning with two in December 1970, and including eight delivered between October 1991 and March 1992, plus eight KC-130Hs (delivered in 1973–74, 1977, and 1980–81), and two VC-130Hs (delivered in July 1980). One of the KC-130Hs (4872) crashed landing at Riyadh on 24 February 1985. Three of the C-130Hs were modified to hospital aircraft, one was reconfigured as a VC-

hospital equipment was removed. Three C-130H-30s were delivered, the first in 1984 and the other two in 1992; the first of these (4986) being converted to a hospital aircraft and operated by Saudia. The standard transport aircraft are flown by Nos 4 and 16 Squadrons at Jeddah/Prince Abdullah AB. The single VIP-configured L-100-30 and the three VC-130Hs operate from King Faisal AFB, Riyadh, alongside the three C-130H hospital aircraft, and the three medically configured L-100-30s and one medically configured C-130H-30.

Singapore The first Hercules acquired for the Republic of Singapore Air Force were four ex-USAF C-130B models, two of which had also served with the Royal Jordanian Air Force. Delivered in 1977, all were converted to KC-130B transport/ tanker configuration in 1985 and 1986. In 1980 four C-130Hs were delivered, followed by a fifth in 1987, together with a KC-130H (ex-Lockheed tanker demonstrator). All the Hercules serve with No. 122 Squadron at Paya Lebar.

South Africa Seven C-130Bs were delivered to the South African Air Force between 1962 and 1963, for issue to No. 28

South Korea The Republic of Korea received four C-130H-30s in 1987–88, and two batches of four C-130Hs in 1989 and 1990, for service with its Air Transport Wing at Seoul-Kimpo. The first C-130H-30 (N408M/5006) was used at Pope AFB in June/July 1987 to test LAPES etc with 'stretched' aircraft). One aircraft was deployed to serve in the 1991 Gulf War.

Spain The first four C-130Hs were delivered to the Ejército del Aire Español (EdA) in December 1973 and early 1974; initially these were assigned to Escaudron 301 of the Mando Aviacion Tactica (Tactical Air Command) at Valenzuela-

130Hs, and in 1980 by two more KC-130Hs. 5003, a C-130H-30 (TL-10-01) was delivered in 1988. Currently this, and all C-130 transport aircraft, are flown by Escuadrone 311, Ala de Transporte 31, at Zaragoza. The KC-130Hs (TK-10s) are operated by Escuadron 312.

Sudan Six C-130Hs for the Silakh al Jawwiya and known as 'Sudaniya' were delivered to Khartoum between January and May 1978. One Aircraft (4766) has occasionally operated as ST-AHR and ST-AIF in the markings of Sudan Airways. The third aircraft (4769/Sudan AF1102) is the 1,500th Hercules delivered.

C-130B 403 of Air Transport Command, SAAF, delivered to No. 28 Squadron, at Waterkloof, Transvaal, in January 1963. This aircraft is one of seven C-130Bs delivered to South Africa in 1962 and 1963, and all continue to fly to this day. SAAF

Squadron, Air Transport Command, at Waterkloof, Transvaal, which continues to fly these to this day. A UN arms embargo on sales to South Africa meant that no further Hercules were purchased until 1996–97, when three ex-USN C-130Fs were acquired. In 1997–98, two ex-USAF C-130Bs were added. The nineteen L-100-30s operated by Safair Freighter (Pty) Ltd, Johannesburg at various times (only about six remain), have also been available as a reserve airlift asset.

Zaragoza. In Spanish service these were designated T-10s. The first aircraft, 4520/T-10-1, crashed into a mountain in central Gran Canaria while operating from Las Palmas, on 28 May 1980. The third aircraft (4531/T-10-3) had a fortunate escape on 15 November 1988 when it collided with an F-18 near Zaragoza and lost 30ft (9m) of its wing: both aircraft landed safely. In 1976 three KC-130Hs (TK-10s) were delivered; in 1979–80 these were followed by three more C-

Sweden The Svenska Flygvapnet became the first European air force to operate the Hercules, leasing C-130E 64-0546/4039 from Lockheed in February 1965 after the aircraft had been sold back before delivery to the USAF. A second C-130E joined this aircraft in Flygflottilj 7 (F7) Transportglyg-divisionen at Satenäs, and in 1982 both were modified to C-130H configuration. Six additional C-130H models had by then entered service. Designated Tp 84, the aircraft continue to be flown by F7 at Satenäs,

The single C-130H-30 31-01 (TL-10-1) of the Ejército del Aire Español (EdA) delivered in 1988, pictured at
Saragoza in 1995. Currently this and all C-130 transport aircraft are flown by Escuadrone 311, Ala de
Transporte 31, at Zaragoza. Gary Madgwick/The Aviation Workshop

C-130H 1100 (4766), one of six C-130Hs operated by the Silakh Ali Jawwiya as 'Sudaniya', pictured at
Norwich Airport. This aircraft, which was delivered to Sudan in January 1978, has occasionally operated
as ST-AHR and ST-AIF in the markings of Sudan Airways. Ron Green

C-130H (Tp 84) 847 (4887) of the Svenska Flygvapnet (Swedish Air Force), one of six delivered to Flygflottilj 7 at Satenäs, Sweden by 1982, being overhauled by Marshall Engineering at Cambridge. Marshall Aerospace

and have been equipped with flare and chaff dispensers and armoured cockpits.

Taiwan The Republic of China Air Force has received twenty-one C-130Hs, the first twelve having been delivered in 1986. One (5067/Taiwan1310) crashed during an attempted go-round at Taipeh-Sung-Shan in a rainstorm on 10 October 1997. The twenty remaining aircraft (at least one of which is equipped for electronic warfare) are operated by No. 101 Squadron based at Pingtung AB.

Thailand The Royal Thai Air Force received its first three C-130Hs in 1980 under the US Military Assistance Program. A C-130H-30 was delivered in 1983, followed by three more in 1988, and 1990. During 1990–92, three C-130Hs were acquired, one going to Cambodia in 1997. In 1992 also, two more C-130H-30s were acquired, one of which is presumed to be used as a VIP aircraft. Most of the Hercules are flown by No. 601 Squadron, part of No. 6 Wing at Bangkok-Don Muang.

Tunisia Seven ex-USAF C-130Bs were acquired for the Tunisian Air Force, and these were delivered between 1995 and 1998. Meanwhile, two C-130Hs were purchased in 1985: they serve with the Escadrille de Transport et Communication at Bizerte, and wear quasi-civilian markings.

Turkey Under the US Military Assistance Program (MAP), the Turk Hava Kuvvetleri received eight C-130Es 1964–1974 for service with Air Transport Command at Erkilet. 4100/ETI-949 in 131 Squadron crashed

C-130H 60101 (4861) of the Royal Thai Air Force, one of three received in 1980 under the US Military Assistance Program and flown by No. 601 Squadron, part of No. 6 Wing at Bangkok-Don Muang. via Frank Mason

(Below) C-130E ETI-187 (63-13187/4012) of the Turk Hava Kuvvetleri, one of eight C-130Es received in 1964 under the provisions of the Military Assistance Program (MAP). All Turkish Air Force Hercules are operated by 222 Filo at Erkilet/Kayseri AB.
Turkish Air Force

into a mountain during approach to Izmir, Turkey, on 19 October 1968. The Hercules were used to support the 6th Allied Tactical Air Force of NATO Allied Air Forces Southern Europe, and on relief operations. They also took part in the Turkish invasion of Cyprus in 1974, which led to an arms-sale embargo on Turkey. Seven ex-USAF

C-130Bs were delivered to Turkey during 1991–92, one subsequently returning to the US and being sold to Romania. All Turkish Air Force Hercules are operated by No. 222 Squadron at Erkilet/Kayseri.

Uganda L-100-30 (no further details available).

United Arab Emirates The integrated air forces of Abu Dhabi and Dubai comprise the UAE Air Force. Two C-130Hs (4580 and 4584) delivered to Abu Dhabi in March 1975 were sold back to Lockheed in February 1984 (subsequently being acquired by Canada for the CAF) in exchange for two new C-130Hs (4983 and

C-130Hs 1211/N4246M (4580) (right) and 1212/N4247M (4584) (left) of the United Emirates Air Force. These two aircraft were delivered to Abu Dhabi in March 1975 and were sold back to Lockheed in February 1984 (subsequently being acquired by Canada for the CAF) in exchange for two new C-130Hs (N4161T/4983 and N4249Y/4985 respectively). via Frank Mason

C-130H N4249Y/1212 (4985) of the UAE, operated by the Transport Wing of Western Air Command from Bateen AB, Abu Dhabi, along with the other C-130H and two more delivered to Abu Dhabi in 1981.
Mick Jennings

4985 respectively). Two other C-130Hs were delivered to Abu Dhabi in 1981. The four C-130Hs now operate with the Transport Wing of Western Air Command from Bateen AB, Abu Dhabi. An L-100-30 (4834) was delivered to Dubai in 1979, and a C-130H-30 was delivered in 1983. Both fly with the Transport Squadron, Central Air Command, from Minchat AB, Dubai.

United Kingdom Sixty-six C-130K models were ordered for the RAF in 1965. These were 65-13021/13044, 66-8550/8573 and 66-13533/13550, and they were essentially C-130H airframes powered by 4,508 eshp T56-A-15s with some components made by Scottish Aviation, and British electronics. The first aircraft (65-13021/XV176/4169) flew at Marietta, Georgia, on 19 October 1966. Known in service as the Hercules C.Mk.1, it was the first to be delivered, and was assigned to No. 242 OCU at Thorney Island, Hampshire, in April 1967. Final deliveries to the RAF of the C.Mk.1 were made in 1968.

Four aircraft have been lost and twenty-five were provided with in-flight refuelling probes and modified to C.Mk.1P standard. Six more were fitted with the air-refuelling probe and a hose-drum unit in the fuselage, and were designated C.Mk.1K Hercules. XV223 was modified by Lockheed as the prototype of the Hercules C.Mk.3. with the fuselage stretched by 15ft (4.57m) to increase capacity from ninety-two to 129 infantrymen, or from sixty-four to ninety-two paratroops. This aircraft first flew in modified form on 3 December 1979. Twenty-nine C.Mk.1s were stretched by Marshall Engineering, to be brought up to C.Mk.3 standard.

C-130K US Serials/Construction Nos/RAF Serials

65-13021/4169/XV176 to C.Mk.3 and to C.Mk.3P
65-13022/4182/XV177 to C.Mk.3 and to C.Mk.3P
65-13023/4188/XV178 to C.Mk.1P
65-13024/4195/XV179 to C.Mk.1P
65-13025/4196/XV180 stalled on 3-engined t/o Fairford 24 March 69
65-13026/4198/XV181 to C.Mk.1P
65-13027/4199/XV182 to C.Mk.1P
65-13028/4200/XV183 to C.Mk.3 and to C.Mk.3P
65-13029/4201/XV184 to C.Mk.3 and to C.Mk.3P
65-13030/4203/XV185 to C.Mk.1P
65-13031/4204/XV186 to C.Mk.1P
65-13032/4205/XV187 to C.Mk.1P
65-13033/4206/XV188 to C.Mk.3 and to C.Mk.3P
65-13034/4207/XV189 to C.Mk.3 and to C.Mk.3P
65-13035/4210/XV190 to C.Mk.3 and to C.Mk.3P
65-13036/4211/XV191 to C.Mk.1P
65-13037/4212/XV192 to C.Mk.1K
65-13038/4213/XV193 to C.Mk.3 and to C.Mk.3P. Stalled and crashed into a mountainside near Beinn A'Ghlo in Scotland on 27 May 1993.
65-13039/4214/XV194 veered off runway landing at Tromsö, Norway, 12 Sept '72, Scrapped for parts.
65-13040/4216/XV195 to C.Mk.1P
65-13041/4217/XV196 to C.Mk.1P
65-13042/4218/XV197 to C.Mk.3 and to C.Mk.3P
65-13043/4219/XV190 crashed when an engine failed on a three-engined touch-and-go training flight, Colerne, 10 September 1973.
65-13044/4220/XV199 to C.Mk.3 and to C.Mk.3P
66-8550/4223/XV200 to C.Mk.1P.
66-8551/4224/XV201 to C.Mk.1K
66-8552/4226/XV202 to C.Mk.3 and to C.Mk.3P
66-8553/4227/XV203 to C.Mk.1K
66-8554/4228/XV204 to C.Mk.1K
66-8555/4230/XV205 to C.Mk.1P
66-8556/4231/XV206 to C.Mk.1P
66-8557/4232/XV207 to C.Mk.3 and to C.Mk.3P
66-8558/4233/XV208 to W.Mk.2
66-8559/4235/XV209 to C.Mk.3 and to C.Mk.3P
66-8560/4236/XV210 to C.Mk.1P
66-8561/4237/XV211 to C.Mk.1P
66-8562/4238/XV212 to C.Mk.3 and to C.Mk.3P
66-8563/4240/XV213 to C.Mk.1K
66-8564/4241/XV214 to C.Mk.3 and to C.Mk.3P
66-8565/4242/XV215 to C.Mk.1P
66-8566/4243/XV216 crashed in the sea after take-off from Melovia, Italy, on 9 November 1971.

66-8567/4244/XV217 to C.Mk.3 and to C.Mk.3P
66-8568/4245/XV218 to C.Mk.1P
66-8569/4246/XV219 to C.Mk.3 and to C.Mk.3P
66-8570/4247/XV220 to C.Mk.3 and to C.Mk.3P
66-8571/4251/XV221 to C.Mk.3 and to C.Mk.3P
66-8572/4252/XV222 to C.Mk.3 and to C.Mk.3P
66-8573/4253/XV223 to C.Mk.3 and to C.Mk.3P
66-13533/4254/XV290 to C.Mk.3 and to C.Mk.3P
66-13534/4256/XV291 to C.Mk.1P
65-13535/4257/XV292 to C.Mk.1P
65-13536/4258/XV293 to C.Mk.1P
65-13537/4259/XV294 to C.Mk.3 and to C.Mk.3P
65-13538/4261/XV295 to C.Mk.1P
65-13539/4262/XV296 to C.Mk.1K
65-13540/4263/XV297 to C.Mk.1P
65-13541/4264/XV298 to C.Mk.1P

65-13542/4266/XV299 to C.Mk.3 and to C.Mk.3P
65-13543/4267/XV300 to C.Mk.1P
65-13544/4268/XV301 to C.Mk.3 and to C.Mk.3P
65-13545/4270/XV302 to C.Mk.3 and to C.Mk.3P
65-13546/4271/XV303 to C.Mk.3 and to C.Mk.3P
65-13547/4272/XV304 to C.Mk.3 and to C.Mk.3P
65-13548/4273/XV305 to C.Mk.3 and to C.Mk.3P
65-13549/4274/XV306 to C.Mk.1P
65-13550/4275/XV307 to C.Mk.3 and to C.Mk.3P

C.Mk.1Ps, and C.Mk.3Ps remain in RAF service, with: the Lyneham Transport Wing (LTW) (Nos 24, 30, 47, 57, (Reserve) and 70 Squadrons), No. 1312 Flight, Falklands Islands, and No. 1 Parachute Training School (including the RAF Falcons Parachute Display Team) at Brize Norton. Twenty-five of these are to be replaced by C-130Js/-30s.

RAF C-130J/C-130J-30/ Construction Nos/Service Allocations

Model		C/n	Serial No.
382V-49F	C-130J-30	5408	N130JA/ZH865*
382V-49F	C-130J-30	5414	N130JE/ZH866
382V-49F	C-130J-30	5416	N130JJ/ZH867
382V-01J	C-130J-30	5443	ZH868
382V-01J	C-130J-30	5444	ZH869
382V-01J	C-130J-30	5445	ZH870
382V-05J	C-130J-30	5446	ZH871
382V-05J	C-130J-30	5456	ZH872
382V-05J	C-130J-30	5457	ZH873
382V-05J	C-130J-30	5458	ZH874
382V-05J	C-130J-30	5459	ZH875
382V-05J	C-130J-30	5460	ZH876
382V-05J	C-130J-30	5461	ZH877
382V-05J	C-130J-30	5462	ZH878
382V-05J	C-130J-30	5463	ZH879
382V-05J	C-130J-30	5459	ZH875
382V-06J	C-130J	5478	ZH880
382V-06J	C-130J	5479	ZH881
382V-06J	C-130J	5480	ZH882
382V-06J	C-130J	5481	ZH883
382V-06J	C-130J	5482	ZH884
382V-06J	C-130J	5483	ZH885
382V-06J	C-130J	5484	ZH886
382V-06J	C-130J	5485	ZH887
382V-06J	C-130J	5500	ZH888
382V-06J	C-130J-30	5503	ZH889

* (C.4/C-130J prototype)

Following the Falklands War in 1982, Marshalls fitted an in-flight air-refuelling probe to twenty-five aircraft, which became C.Mk.1Ps. Beginning in 1986, they also began fitting in-flight refuelling probes to the thirty C.Mk.3s to convert them to C.Mk.3P configuration. Starting in 1987, C.Mk.1Ps and C.Mk.1Ks began receiving AN/ALQ 157 IR jamming equipment and chaff/flare dispensers. At least five C.Mk.1Ps were fitted with Racal 'Orange Blossom' ESM pods beneath their wing-tips to give some degree of surveillance capability.

United States of America

USAF: The original user of the Hercules in December 1956, the USAF has now retired all its earlier A and B models, and currently has a total of 201 C-130E, C-130H and H-30 transports in its inventory, which serve with eleven Airlift squadrons, as follows:

Air Combat Command (ACC)
52nd AS, 71st RQS, 347th Wing, Moody AFB, GA (C-130EHC-130P).
41 ECS, 42 ACCS, 43 ECS, 355th Wing, Davis-Monthan AFB, AZ (EC-130E/H).

Air Mobility Command (AMC)
2nd ALS, 43rd ALW, Pope AFB, NC (C-130E AWADS)
41st ALS, 43rd ALW, Pope AFB, NC (C-130E AWADS).

US Air Force Europe (USAFE)
3rd Air Force:
37th AS, 86th AW, Ramstein AB, Germany (C-130E, equipped with AWADS (Adverse Weather Aerial Delivery Systems).

US Air Force Special Operations Command
16th SOW, Hurlburt Field, FL (MC-130E, MC-130H), AC-130H, AC-130U, MC-130P, C-130E)
352nd SOG, RAF Mildenhall, UK (MC-130, MC-130N)
353rd SOG, Kadena AB, Okinawa, Japan (MC-130H/P).

US Pacific Air Forces (PACAF)
5th AF, 36th ALS, 374th ALW, Yokota AB, Japan (C-130E/H)
11th AF, 517th ALS, 3rd Wing, Elmendorf AFB, AK (C-130H).

US Air Education and Training Command (AETC)
550 SOS, 19th AF, 58th SOW, Kirtland AFB, NM, (MC-130H, MC-130P, C-130H)
53rd ALS & 62nd ALS, 314th ALW, Little Rock AFB, AR (C-130)
AFMC (Air Force Materiel CMD).

US Air Force Reserve Command (AFRes)
AFRes maintains 111 transport C-130s – thirty-six E models and seventy-five Hs – in support of the active-duty fleet, dispersed among the following air forces:

10th Air Force (ACC):
711th SOS, 919th SOW, Duke Field FL (MC-130E)
5th SOS, 919th SOW, Duke Field FL (MC-130P)

22nd Air Force (AMC):
53rd Weather Recon Sqn, Keesler AFB, MS (WC-130H)
700th ALS, 94th ALW, Dobbins ARB, GA (C-130H)
731st ALS, 302nd ALW, Peterson ARB, CO (C-130H), the only AFRes unit trained and equipped with the Modular Airborne Firefighting Systems (MAFFS)
815th ALSS, 403rd ALW, Keesler AFB, MS (C-130E) (the 'Flying Jennies') were a weather reconnaissance squadron, 1975–1993, when they reverted back to airlift duties)
95th ALS, 440th ALW, General Mitchell IAP/ARS, WI (C-130H)

357th ALS, 908th ALW, Maxwell AFB, AL (C-130H)
757th ALS, 910th ALW, Youngstown-Warren Regional Airport/ARS, OH (C-130H)
773rd ALS, 910th ALW, Youngstown Warren Regional Airport, OH (C-130H), (the only unit in the Air Force capable of aerial spray operations, taken over from the active-duty force in 1973)
758th ALS, 911th ALW, Pittsburgh IAP/ARS, PA (C-130H)
327th ALS, 913th ALW, Willow Grove ARS, PA (C-130E)
328th ALS, 914th ALW, Niagara Falls IAP/ARS, NY (C-130H)
96th ALS, 934th ALW, Minneapolis-St Paul IAP/ARS, MN (C-130E).

US Air National Guard (ANG)
The ANG has about 200 C-130 transports assigned to the following commands/Airlift wings:

Air Mobility Command (AMC)
139th ALS, 109th ALW, Schenectady County Airport, NY (C-130H)
105th ALS, 118th ALW, Nashville Airport, TN (C-130H)
165th ALS, 123rd ALW, Louisville IAP/AGS, KY (C-130H)
130th ALS, 130th ALW, Yeager Airport, WV (C-130H)
109th ALS, 133rd ALW, Minneapolis-St

C-130B MAFFS-equipped (modular Airborne Fire-Fighting Airborne System) of the AFRes fighting a forest fire in 1987. A number of these C-130s, each fitted with modularized retardant and compressed air tanks in the cargo hold, and twin nozzles and spraying equipment on the main ramp, were once operated by several AFRes squadrons taken over from the active-duty force in 1973. Now, the C-130H-equipped 910th ALW, 773rd ALS, part of 22nd Air Force (Air Mobility Command) at Youngstown Warren Regional Airport, Ohio, is the only unit in the Air Force capable of aerial spray operations. *Gary Madgwick/The Aviation Workshop*

C-130E 62-1838 (3801) in the 37th TAS, 316th TAW pictured in 1972. This aircraft crashed on 13 May 1995 near Bliss, Idaho, after a fire in the no. 2 engine overheated a turbine spacer. MAP

Paul IAP, MN (C-130H-3)

181st ALS, 136th ALW, NAS, Dallas, TX (C-130H)

185th ALS, 137th ALW, Will Rogers World Airport, OK (C-130H)

180th ALS, 139th ALW, Rosecrans Memorial Airport MO (C-130H)

143rd ALS, 143rd ALW, Quonset State Airport, RI (C-130E)

156th ALS, 145th ALW, Charlotte/Douglas IAP, NC (C-130H)

115th ALS, 146th ALW, Channel Island ANGAB, CA (C-130E)

192nd ALS, 152nd ALW, Reno, NV (C-130E)

187th ALS, 153rd ALW, Cheyenne MAP, WY (C-130H)

158th ALS, 165th ALW, Savannah IAP, GA (C-130H)

142nd ALS, 166th ALW, New Castle County Airport, DE (C-130H)

167th ALS, 167th ALW, Eastern West Virginia Regional Airport/Shepherd Field, WV (C-130H)

164th ALS, 179th ALW, Mansfield Lahm Airport, OH (C-130H)

169th ALS, 182nd ALW, Peoria, IL (C-130E)

154th ALS, 189th ALW, Little Rock AFB, AR (C-130E)*.

* Aircrew CCTU

US Air Combat Command (USACC)

124th Wing+, 189th ALS, Boise Air Terminal, ID (C-130E)

175th Wing+, 135th ALS, Baltimore, MD (C-130H)

+ (A/OA-10A attack wings)

106th Rescue Wing, Francis S. Gabreski IAP, NY

129th Rescue Wing, Moffett Federal Airfield (NASA), CA Pacific Air Forces (USPAC)

204th ALS, 154th ALW, Hickham AFB, HI (C-130H)

144th ALS, 176th ALW, Kulis ANGAB, Anchorage, AK (C-130H)

210th Rescue Squadron, 176th Wing, (HC-130).

USAF Special Operations Command (USSOC)

193rd SOS, 193rd SOW, Harrisburg IAP, PA (EC-130E).

United States Navy (USN)

The USN has only ever operated a small number of dedicated transport Hercules – previously just seven C-130Fs, and currently, eighteen C-130Ts which are assigned to the following US Navy Reserve Squadrons:

VR-53, NAF Washington, Andrews AFB (C-130T)

VR-54, NAS New Orleans, LA (C-130T)

VR-55, NAS Santa Clara, CA

VR-62, NAS Brunswick, ME

Blue Angels NAS Pensacola, FL (TC-130G).

United States Marine Corps (USMC)

VMGR-152 Futenma MCAS, Okinawa (KC-130FR)

VMGR-234 Glenview NAS, IL (KC-130T/T-30)

VMGR-252 Cherry Point MCAS, NC (KC-130F/R)

VMGR-253 Cherry Point MCAS, NC (KC-130F)

VMGR-352 El Toro MCAS, CA (KC-130F/R)

VMGR-452 Stewart Field, NY (KC-130T/T-30).

United States Coast Guard (USCG)

The USCG is a key component of the US Armed Forces, with essential wartime/readiness responsibilities under the US Navy Maritime Defense Zone (MARDEZ). It carries out combat and combat support tasks for the USN (CG district commanders are of USN Rear Admiral rank), which include search and rescue (SAR), port

TC-130G BuNo. 151891 (3878) Fat Albert Airlines, **the 'Blue Angels' support since October 1991, taking off from Midland, Texas, with JATO on 28 September 1996. This aircraft was originally delivered to the USN in December 1964 and was modified to EC-130G. It later became a test bed for EC-130Q equipment, and in 1990 was modified to TC-130G.**
Graham Dinsdale

(Below) **KC-130F BuNo. 149816 (3726) refuelling two F-4 Phantoms of VMFA-232 in the mid-to-late 1980s.**
Lockheed

security, harbour defence, antisubmarine warfare (ASW), logistic support and surveillance interdiction. Apart from SAR, the CG is part of the international ice patrol: in the average year, 200 to 400 icebergs are located and tracked in the 45,000 square miles (116,550sq km) of North Atlantic sealanes patrolled by CG C-130s.

The following rôles are becoming increasingly important for the Hercules: enforcement of immigration and sea traffic laws and treaties (ELT), drug-traffic interdiction, and also marine environmental protection (MEP) – CG Hercules on offshore and port area surveillance detect oil

contamination resulting from offshore drilling operations, tankers, spillage, and other sources. Since 1988, Operation *Bahamas, Turks and Caicos Islands* (OPBAT), a multi-national effort of law enforcement and military agencies, has stemmed the flow of illegal drugs smuggled into the US through the Caribbean; in 1997, a record year for drug seizures, OPBAT netted 12,163lb (5,517kg) of marijuana and more than 2 tons of cocaine.

USCG aircraft are normally funded through the USN Appropriations; the first four Hercules, ordered under the designation R8V-1G (later SC-130B), were

delivered between December 1959 and March 1960. Two more SC-130Bs were delivered from January to March 1961, by which time the aircraft were re-designated HC-130G. Then three more were delivered to the CG in March and April 1962, and another three (now re-designated as HC-130Bs) between December 1962 and February 1963. All were withdrawn from use in the 1980s.

In August 1966 the CG received its first EC-130E (4158, later re-designated HC-130E), and this was used until the mid-1980s. In 1968 three HC-130Hs were delivered, and another nine followed, in

C-130E 10305 was delivered to No. 436 Squadron in the Royal Canadian Air Force in December 1964. Lockheed

C-130K Hercules XV184 was delivered to the RAF in March 1967. Lockheed

(Above) USMC KC-130R BuNo 160014 of VMGR-152 refuelling two F-4 Phantoms. Lockheed

(Right) C.Mk.1P XV206 pictured in Nevada during the 1989 Red Flag exercise in the experimental 'pink' scheme applied that August. Pete Nash

Phantom FGR.2 of No. 23 Squadron from Stanley in the Falklands takes on fuel from a C.Mk.1K during a sortie in December 1982.
Mick Jennings

(Above) **AC-130A 53-3129** The First Lady, **the first production C-130A Hercules, which flew for the first time at Marietta, Georgia, on 7 April 1955. She not only took part in the Vietnam War but was also most certainly the oldest aircraft to take part in Operation** Desert Storm **in 1991.** The First Lady **was presented to the USAF Armament Museum at Eglin AFB in November 1995.** Author

(Right) **The twin 40mm Bofors cannon installation in the rear hold of** The First Lady. Author

(Above) **C-130A (3189) NI33HP (formerly, 57-482)** (nearest camera) **of Hawkins & Powers pictured at Greybull, Wyoming, in August 1989.** Author

(Below) **KC-130F BuNo 149791, the** Blue Angels **support aircraft, pictured at NAS Whidbey Island, Washington, in August 1989.** Author

In December 1991 C-130K XV292 appeared with a large '25' on its tail to celebrate twenty-five years of the Hercules in the RAF. It carried these markings, which included the badges of all the squadrons and units on the sides of the fuselage, for two more years. It is pictured at the Mildenhall Air Fete. Author

(Below) C.1P XV185 and C.1P XV293, the two RAF Hercules used in Operation Vigour, at Moi International Airport, Mombasa, Kenya, 28 February 1993, the day before they flew home to Lyneham. Author

(Bottom) C-130H CNA-OL of the Force Aèrienne Royal Morocaine (Royal Maroc Air Force) taking off from Mogadishu on 1 March 1993 during the Provide Relief operation. Civilian-style registrations are worn with the aircraft construction number, in this case, 4742, on the fin. Author

Pilot 1/Lt Ross Becker and co-pilot 1/Lt Eric L. Meyers, 815th ALS, 403rd ALW, AFRes, their flak jackets on, maintain a close watch as the C-130E wends its way through the steep mountain passes in Bosnia near the end of the flight into Sarajevo, 23 March 1994. Author

(Above) Captains Mike Brignola *(centre, right)* and Darren Maturi *(right, hands behind back)* brief their crew in front of C-130E 64-0529 (4017) in the 41st ALS, 43rd ALW, from Pope AFB, at Rhein-Main just before the 'off' for the night air drop at Bjelimici, Bosnia, 24/25 March 1994. Author

(Left) MC-130H Combat Talon II 88-0193 (5132) Night Rider, one of twenty-five MC-130H Combat Talon IIs built, serves in the 7th SOS, 352nd Special Operations Group at Mildenhall, pictured in 1996. Author

C-130s of the 37th 'Blue Tail Flies' Airlift Squadron, 435th Airlift Wing, 17th AF, at Rhein-Main AFB, Frankfurt, in 1994. USAF

(Above) **TC-130G BuNo 151891 (3878)** Fat Albert Airlines, **the** Blue Angels **support aircraft since October 1991, taking off from NAS Jacksonville, Florida, airshow on 26 October 1996 with JATO.** USN

(Right) **N130JA/ZH865, the C-130J prototype for the RAF, which was rolled out at Marietta, Georgia, on 18 October 1995 and first flew on 5 April 1996.** Lockheed-Martin

C-130J 94-3026 N130JC for Air Combat Command, which was rolled out on 20 October 1995 and which flew for the first time on 6 June 1996. Lockheed-Martin

The C-130J cockpit, equipped with four flat-panel liquid-crystal, head-down colour displays which present all the information needed to fly the aircraft, and one of the two Flight Dynamics holographic head-up displays which permit the pilots to maintain a constant out-of-the-window view while monitoring all the data necessary to control the aircraft. Lockheed-Martin

(Above) Over a very foggy Lincolnshire on 22 September 1998 C-130K XV290 (4254) of LXX Squadron, flown by Sqn Ldr Dave Fry, was on hand when the Battle of Britain Memorial Flight (BBMF) put up the first ever formation of all five Spitfires, which were led by Sqn Ldr Paul Day AFC. Author

(Below) C-130E 63-13187 (4012) 'ETI-187' pictured at the 1998 Air Fete at RAF Mildenhall, was delivered under the US Military Assistance Program (MAP) to the Turk Hava Kuvvetleri in October 1964 and is still in first-line service with the Turkish Air Force. Author

L-100 382-17B (c/n 3946), the Lockheed demonstrator, on its first flight, 20/21 April 1964 (25hr 1min). This aircraft was modified to L-100-20 and first flew in this configuration on 19 April 1968. After operation with US commercial operators, it was used by the Philippine Aerospace Development Corporation (PADC) and the Philippine Air Force. Lockheed via GMS

C-130K/Hercules C.Mk.1. (c/n 4169), which first flew 19 October 1966, and was delivered to the RAF in May 1967. The aircraft was upgraded to C.3 configuration in 1985, and to C.3P in March 1997. Lockheed via GMS

C-130B 58-0712 (c/n 3507), which before delivery was modified to BLC (Boundary Layer Control) test aircraft intended for the proposed C-130C STOL US Army version. Fitted with blown flaps and control surfaces and compressors on the outer wings, it flew for the first time on 8 February 1960. It is still flying today, as N707NA, with NASA Dryden, at Edwards AFB, CA. Lockheed via GMS

L-100 (c/n 4147) N9268R, which was acquired by Delta Airlines in August 1966. This aircraft was modified to L-100-20 in December 1968, and sold to Saturn in September 1973. It is now in storage at Marana, AZ. Lockheed via GMS

1973, 1974 and 1977. One HC-130H (4757) crashed 2.5 miles (4km) south of Attu in the Aleutian Islands on 30 July 1982 while trying to land in bad weather. In 1983 and 1984, eleven HC-130H-7s were received, and between 1985 and 1987 a further eleven HC-130Hs were added. In 1988 one additional HC-130H (5121) was delivered, to CGS Clearwater, Florida, and then modified in 1991 to EC-130V; it was transferred to the USAF in 1993. On 24 January 1992, HC-130H-7 CG1706, based at Kodiak, Alaska, lost a propeller in flight and suffered fuselage and wing damage, but managed to land

safely. Three months later, on 24 April, HC-130H 1452 (67-7183) was attacked by Peruvian Su-22s while on an anti-drug mission and suffered extensive damage; it was repaired, but was consigned to AMARC in 1993. Currently, thirty CG C-130H and H-7 aircraft (the HC-130J version will be introduced in the future) are in the USCG inventory at the following CG stations: Barbers Point, HI (HC-130H); Borinquen, Puerto Rico (HC-130H); Clearwater, FL (HC-130H); Elizabeth City, NC (HC-130H); Kodiak, AK (HC-130H); Sacramento, McClellan AFB, CA (HC-130H).

(Below) **KC-130R BuNo. 160628 (4776) delivered to VMGR-252 at MCAS Cherry Point, North Carolina, in September 1978. Unlike earlier USMC tanker versions such as the KC-130F, the KC-130Rs are not dual-purpose transport and tanker versions.** Mick Jennings

(Bottom) **HC-130B CG1345 (3595), US Coast Guard, pictured at Clearwater in 1978. This aircraft was delivered to Elizabeth City in March 1961 and it went on to serve at San Francisco and Clearwater, before being retired in August 1983. Parts only were transferred to the USAF in October 1990, and in May 1996 the aircraft was sold to Charlotte Aircraft, North Carolina. By April 1997 only the cockpit remained.** via Frank Mason

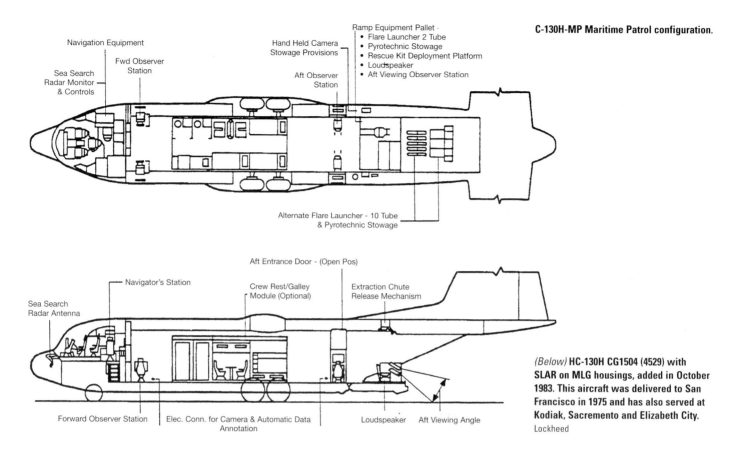

C-130H-MP Maritime Patrol configuration.

Navigation Equipment

Fwd Observer Station

Sea Search Radar Monitor & Controls

Hand Held Camera Stowage Provisions

Aft Observer Station

Ramp Equipment Pallet
- Flare Launcher 2 Tube
- Pyrotechnic Stowage
- Rescue Kit Deployment Platform
- Loudspeaker
- Aft Viewing Observer Station

Alternate Flare Launcher - 10 Tube & Pyrotechnic Stowage

Aft Entrance Door - (Open Pos)

Navigator's Station

Crew Rest/Galley Module (Optional)

Extraction Chute Release Mechanism

Sea Search Radar Antenna

Forward Observer Station

Elec. Conn. for Camera & Automatic Data Annotation

Loudspeaker   Aft Viewing Angle

(Below) **HC-130H CG1504 (4529) with SLAR on MLG housings, added in October 1983. This aircraft was delivered to San Francisco in 1975 and has also served at Kodiak, Sacremento and Elizabeth City.**
Lockheed

98

Cockpit interior of CG HC-130H CG1719 (5107) at Clearwater, March 1998. This aircraft was delivered to Elizabeth City in December 1987, and was transferred to Clearwater in May 1985. Author

(Below) C-130H 4224 (4556), one of two C-130H models delivered to the Fuerza Aérea Venezolana in February 1975 for operation by Escuadron 62 at Maracay-El Libertador. via Frank Mason

Uruguay Between 1992 and 1994 the Fuerza Aérea Uruguaya acquired three ex-USAF C-130Bs, although the last (3541) was never used, and was withdrawn from use in August 1996. The two remaining aircraft are flown by the Regimento Tactico 1 at Montivedeo-Carrasco.

Venezuela The original order intended for the Fuerza Aérea Venezolana and placed in 1969, was for six C-130Hs for service with Escuadron de Transporte 1 at Caracas, four to be delivered in 1970, and two in 1975. Four were delivered to the FAV in 1971 for operation by Escuadron 62 at Maracay-El Libertador, and the other two duly arrived in 1975. However, 4408/FAV7772 *24 de Julio* crashed on night approach to Lajes, Azores, in bad visibility and high winds on 27 August 1976; and 4406/FAV3556 crashed attempting a three-engined take-off from Caracas airport on 4 November 1980. Two further C-130H models were delivered, in December 1978 and 1988, as an attrition replacement for the two crashed aircraft.

Vietnam As part of Operation *Enhance Plus*, thirty-five C-130As were speedily transferred from ANG squadrons in the US and delivered to the Republic of Vietnam Air Force (South Vietnam) in November 1972. By April 1975, when the country was overrun, three C-130As had been lost, nineteen were flown to Thailand, but thirteen were captured in 1975 and entered service with the 918th Regiment, Vietnamese People's Air Force. Some were kept flying by cannibalizing others, and were used as makeshift bombers in the invasion of Kampuchea in 1978. A few may have been given to the former USSR. Attempted sales of surviving airframes in the early 1990s were unsuccessful.

Yemen In August 1979, the Yemen Arab Republic Air Force received two C-130Hs donated by Saudi Arabia; they are currently operated by Yemen Airways.

Zaire Only one (4411/9T-TCA) of the seven C-130Hs which served with the Force Aérien Zairoise remain in service: this is with 191 Escadrille of 19 Wing d'Appui Logistique at N'Djili Airport, Kinshasa. Initially, three C-130Hs were delivered in 1971, then three more in 1975, and the seventh (4736/9T-TCG) in 1977. 4422/9T-TCD crashed at Kisangani, Zaire, on 18 August 1974, but all the rest were used during the war of 1977 which followed the invasion of Shaba by foreign mercenaries. Subsequently, 4569/9T-TCE

C-130H 1160, one of two H models donated to the Yemen Arab Republic Air Force in August 1979 by Saudi Arabia. They are currently operated by Yemen Airways. via Frank Mason

crashed during a three-engined take-off with maximum load from Kindu, Zaire, on 14 September 1980. Then 4736/9T-TCG crashed near Kinshasa, Zaire on 19 April 1990 because a propeller blade broke off.

Finally 4416/9T-TCB and 4588/9T-TCF were impounded at Milan-Malpensa airport in October 1994, the latter going on to serve with the French Armée de l'Air (as did 4589/9T-TCC after 1995).

Zambia Though no Hercules has officially served with the Zambian Air Force, five L-100s have been used by the Zambian government and Zambia Air Cargoes, and possibly by the air force, too.

C-130H 9T-TCB (4416), one of three C-130Hs delivered to the Force Aérien Zaïroise in 1971. This aircraft, and 9T-TCF (4588), were impounded at Milan-Malpensa airport in October 1994. via Frank Mason

CHAPTER FIVE

Air Commandos

The Quiet Professionals

MC-130E-Y Rivet Yank **63-7785 (3852), one of four operating with 8th SOS, 16th SOW, at Hurlburt Field, Florida.** Gary Madgwick/The Aviation Workshop

It is not usually militarily expedient for a commander in the field to have all his eggs in one basket. However, all the USAF, USN and USMC forces trained in air rescue and special operations are combined into one force and are therefore an exception to this rule. Nor is it militarily expedient to mount an operation using available USAF transports, Navy helicopters and USMC tanker aircraft – despite political attempts to the contrary, often using financial savings as a justification. This was proved at huge cost during the final days of the Carter administration when a joint USAF/USMC attempt to rescue US hostages in Iran on 24 April 1980 using Hercules aircraft, and Navy RH-53D helicopters flown by marine pilots, ended in disaster at 'Desert One', Posht-i-Badam, a remote location in Iran. EC-130E (ABCCC) 62-1809 was destroyed in a collision with an RH-53D, and five personnel in the 8th SOS were killed. Largely because of this, and the subsequent acts of terrorism and hostage-taking, it was decided that all forces trained in air rescue and special operations should operate under a specialized,

unified, *USAF* command, with its *own* helicopters and fixed-wing aircraft. And so, on 1 March 1983, the 23rd Air Force was activated at Scott AFB, Illinois. The precursors of this organization's units, the air commando squadrons (from 1968, special operations squadrons), had played an essential covert role during the war in South-east Asia.

Persuaders in the Sky

A requirement for 'airborne radio stations' first occurred during the Dominican Crisis of 1965 when it was found that a broadcast capability was needed, to break into civilian and military radio networks. 'Volant Solo II' was put into effect, and in the summer of 1968 the newly activated 193rd Tactical Electronic Warfare Group, ANG, began receiving EC-121 aircraft at Olmstead Field. Their successful use in South-east Asia during Operation *Commando Buzz*, operating from Thailand from July to December 1970, led to further deployments, with the US Navy and NATO. In 1977 the 'Persuaders in the Sky' took delivery of its first EC-130E, and all the EC-121Es were finally replaced by EC-130Es from March 1979.

Urgent Fury and *Just Cause*

The first test for the new air force came on 25 October 1983 when the 23rd Air Force took part in Operation *Urgent Fury*, the rescue of US citizens from Grenada. During the invasion, AC-130 gunships, and MC-130 and HC-130 tankers, played their part very effectively. The operation even had the services of special EC-130E aircraft to broadcast recorded radio programmes to the residents of Spice Island. In December 1989 and January 1990, 'Volant Solo II' EC-130Es – 'Coronet Solo' – were used during Operation *Just Cause*, the US invasion of Panama, to broadcast misinformation to Panamanian forces. In addition, twenty-one aircraft of the 1st Special Operations Wing, plus the 1720th Special Tactics Group (STGP) and elements of the 9th and 55th Special Operations Squadrons, flew over 400 missions during the operation. Seven of the aircraft were AC-130 gunships from the 16th SOS; three MC-130E 'Combat Talons' were from the 8th SOS, whose motto is 'With the Guts to Try'. The 8th SOS secured the airfield at Rio Hato AB under fire, with two HC-130 refuelling tankers from the 55th SOS supporting them. (These and the MH-53E/J Pave Low and MH-60D Pave Hawk helicopters in the 20th 'Green Hornets', and 55th SOS respectively, were part of Military Airlift Command (MAC).) AC-130s were among the first in action early on the morning of 20 December, destroying the Panamanian Defense Force's Comandancia HQ with devastating fusillades of cannon and machine-gun fire. MC-130E 'Combat Talons' and MH-53E helicopters were used to infiltrate US Navy SEALS (Sea-Air-Land) into Panamanian positions. It was the 23rd Air Force's final operation before its deactivation.

AFSOC Organization and Mission

On 22 May 1990 the 23rd Air Force became the USAF component of the Air Force Special Operations Command (AFSOC), when special forces of each branch of the armed forces came under its central operational control. Headquarters were established at Hurlburt Field, Florida, where special operations personnel have trained since 1942, when they prepared for the Doolittle raid on Tokyo. The new command's directive was to organize, train, equip and educate Air Force special operations forces. AFSOC is the air component of the unified US Special Operations Command. The 720th Special Tactics Group, with its headquarters at Hurlburt Field, has units in the US, Europe and the Pacific. The group has special operations combat control teams and para-rescue forces. AFSOC missions include air traffic control for establishing air-assault landing zones; close air support for strike aircraft and AC-130 'Spectre' gunship missions; establishing casualty collection stations; and providing trauma care for injured personnel.

The 16th Special Operations Wing at Hurlburt Field, and Eglin AFB, Florida, is the oldest and most seasoned unit in AFSOC. It has no less than six special operations squadrons, three of which operate MC-130E 'Combat Talon I' and MC-130P (formerly HC-130N/P) 'Combat Shadow' tankers: the 8th SOS (MC-130E), the 9th SOS (11 MC-130P tankers at Eglin), and the 15th SOS (MC-130H 'Combat Talon II') – while the 4th SOS and 16th SOS operate AC-130H/U gunships, and the 19th SOS operates AC-130s for training. The 7th SOS and the 67th SOS in the 352nd SOG at RAF Mildenhall, Suffolk, operate MC-130H and MC-130P tankers, respectively (alongside the 21st SOS, equipped with the MH-53J 'Pave Low'). In Japan, at Kadena AB, Okinawa, the 1st SOS and the 17th SOS in the 353rd SOG operate MC-130H and five MC-130P tanker aircraft, respectively.

AFSOC currently has seven SOS squadrons operating MC-130E, MC-130H and MC-130P tankers. AETC (Air Education and Training Command, activated 1 July 1993) and AFRes operate MC-130E, MC-130H, and MC-130P Hercules. AETC currently has one SOS squadron – the 550th SOS/58th SQW (19th Air Force), at Kirtland AFB, New Mexico, which operates MC-130H and MC-130Ps and is also the operational base for 'Combat Talon II' training.

The AFRes (activated on 17 February 1997) currently has two SOS squadrons: the 5th SOS/919th SOW, with MC-130P tankers, and the 711th SOS/919th SOW with MC-130E-Y 'Combat Talon I' and C-130E. Both units are based at Duke Field, Eglin AFB, Florida, and come under AFSOC command when the organizations are mobilized, as does ANG's 193rd SOS/193rd SOW and its EC-130E 'Coronet Solo' aircraft at Harrisburg IAP, Pennsylvania: still the only weapon system within the USAF whose mission is to support Psychological Operations (PYSOP) with airborne broadcasting.

EC-130E(RR) 63-7869 in the 193rd SOS, 193rd SOG, Pennsylvania ANG, at Harrisburg IAP, 1995. Gary Madgwick/The Aviation Workshop

Combat Talon and Combat Shadow

Fifteen Special Operations Support (SOS) MC-130E-1 'Combat Talon Is' were produced as either -C Rivet Clamp, -S Rivet Swap, or -Y Rivet Yank aircraft. Ten MC-130E-C 'Clamp' aircraft were fitted with the Fulton STAR recovery system like the one shown. Lockheed

The MC-130H 'Combat Talon II' supplemented, and will eventually replace, the MC-130Es used by the 1st Special Operations Wing for 'Combat Talon' clandestine and special operations. 88-0193 (5132) Night Rider, one of twenty-five MC-130H 'Combat Talon IIs' built, serves in the 7th SOS. 88-0193 received a modified electronic cockpit fit in March 1994. Author

Fourteen C-130Es were modified to MC-130E 'Combat Talon I' configuration and equipped for use in low-level, deep-penetration tactical missions by the 1st and 8th Special Operations Squadrons based respectively in the Pacific and North America. ('Combat Talons' led the raid on the Son Tay prison camp, 20 miles (32km) northwest of Hanoi on 21 November 1970.) Twenty-four MC-130H 'Combat Talon II' aircraft have been acquired. These aircraft, the first of which flew in 1988, started to be delivered in mid-1991; they are fitted with an in-flight refuelling receptacle, have explosion-suppressive fuel tanks, a modified cargo ramp area for the high-speed, low-level aerial delivery system, Emerson Electric AN/APQ-170 precision terrain-following and terrain-avoidance radar, dual radar altimeters, dual INS, and finally provision for a GPS receiver. Some twenty-eight MC-130P 'Combat Shadow'/tanker aircraft are in service with AFSOC for single-ship or formation in-flight refuelling of its 'Pave Low' special operations' helicopters working in a no- to low-threat environment.

MC-130P 'Combat Shadow' tanker, one of five in the 67th SOS, 352nd SOG, at RAF Mildenhall, Suffolk, refuelling a 21st SOS MH-53J 'Pave Low' helicopter. The primary role of the MC-130P is to conduct single-ship or formation in-flight refuelling of Special Operations forces' helicopters in a low-threat to selected medium-threat environment. While the refuelling pods for the USAF and the USMC tankers are basically the same, the aerial refuelling system of the former is integrated into the aircraft's hydraulic and electrical systems, and the aircraft fuel system is utilized to transfer fuel, while the latter's is basically self-contained within the pod and allows 300 gpm flow rate simultaneously from both pods. USAF HC-130 and MC-130P offload capacity is limited to 150 gpm to one helicopter at a time. Author

(Left) MC-130H 'Combat Talon II' 88-0194 Dawg Pound, in the 7th SOS, pictured at the Mildenhall Air Fête, 1998. Like 88-0193, this aircraft entered service at the Rickenbacker ANGB in August 1989, transferring to the 6512th FTS, 15th SOS, and finally the 7th SOS in 1993. Author

The Gunships

AC-130 gunships used by the Command have evolved since November 1965 when the 4th Air Commando Squadron in Vietnam became the first operational unit to use AC-47 gunships. Call-sign 'Spooky' AC-47s and those of the 14th ACS demonstrated such highly effective convoy escort and armed reconnaissance over the Ho Chi Minh Trail, that the US forces looked to another converted transport for its next generation, fixed-wing gunship. At the Wright-Patterson AFB, the Aeronautical Systems Division tested a Convair C-131B transport fitted with a 7.62mm General Electric SUU-11A minigun, while at Eglin AFB, Florida, experiments were conducted with a C-130 and a C-47. AC-47s flew their first sortie on 15 December 1964. 'Puff the Magic Dragon' was retired from the Special Operations Squadrons in 1969.

Two years earlier, on 6 June 1967, the 4950th Test Wing had begun flight-testing a JC-130A (54-1626) modified by Aeronautical Systems Division, Air Force System Command, at Wright-Patterson AFB, Ohio, to 'Gunship II'/'Plain Jane' configuration. 54-1626 was fitted with four port-side-firing General Electric MXU-470 7.62mm GAU-2 miniguns, and four port-side-firing General Electric M-61 20mm Vulcan cannon, to fire obliquely downward. *Vulcan Express*, as the AC-130A Gunship II was named, was equipped also with the 'Starlight Image-Intensifying Night-Observation Scope', AN/AAD-4 SLIR side-looking radar, computerized NASARR F-1551 fire-control system (adapted from the F-104 Starfighter), beacon tracker, DF homing instrumentation, FM radio transceiver, and an inert tank system, while a semi-automatic flare dispenser, and a steerable 1.5 million candlepower AN/AVQ-8 searchlight containing two Xenon arc lights (infra-red and ultra-violet), were mounted on the aft ramp.

The 'Plain Jane' AC-130A Gunship II was despatched to the 711th SOS at Nha Trang, South Vietnam, in September 1967

A pair of AC-130A gunships on the ramp at Ubon RTAFB early in 1970. The nearest aircraft is from the 35th TAS, 374th TAW, normally based at Naha AB, Okinawa while the other is from the 16th SOS, 8th Tactical Fighter Wing, at its home base. Lt Col Walt Evans USAF

(Right) AC-130A gunship letting fly with a burst of fire from one of its two 40mm Bofors cannon. The AC-130A and AC-130E versions carried two 20mm cannon, two 7.62mm miniguns and two 40mm Bofors cannon, ranged along the port side of the fuselage, all slaved to fire-control radar and a range of sophisticated sensors. Lockheed

(Above) **AC-130A 53-3129** The First Lady **shows off her wares. From the left is the AN/APN-59B navigation and moving target indicator in the nose, ASN/ASD-5 'Black Crow' truck ignition sensor dome, AN/ASQ-24A stabilized tracking set (Korad AN/AVQ-18 laser designator and bomb damage assessment camera), and twin 20mm M-61 cannon below the 919th SOW badge. The ports containing two of the original four MXU-470 7.62mm miniguns (just visible below the engine nacelle) have been sealed and the guns deleted (as were the other two miniguns below the wing trailing edge.** Author

Originally, The First Lady **bristled with two GE 20mm M-61 cannon in the two rear gun-ports, later replaced by two 40mm Bofors cannon (shown). The Motorola AN/APQ-133 beacon tracking radar (right) replaced the original NASARR F-151-A fire-control radar adapted from the F-104 Starfighter.** Author

(Above) **This rare insight into the fuselage of 53-3129 shows the twin 40mm Bofors cannon installation in the rear hold.** Author

Cockpit view of 53-3129. Left is the pilot's computerized fire-control system which he fires after receiving 'consent' from his fire-control officer. Note the inscription, 'First Lady 123' in the centre of the control column. Author

for combat evaluation. As might be expected, the complexity of its sophisticated equipment was responsible for many scrubbed missions, but nevertheless, *Vulcan Express* acquitted itself well between 24 September and December 1967. It was later refurbished in the US, and was then sent to Ubon RTAFB (Royal Thai Air Force Base) in February 1968 for additional evaluation along the Ho Chi Minh Trail until early June that year. In mid-June it was transferred to Tan Son Nhut near Saigon, where it took part in operations in the so-called 'in-country' war against Viet Cong insurgents. It returned to the US in November 1968. (The gunship was finally presented to the USAF Museum at Wright-Patterson in October 1997.)

Meanwhile *Project Gunboat*, as it was code-named, went so well that the Pentagon awarded a contract to LTV Electrosystems of Greenville, Texas, for the modification of seven more JC-130As to AC-130A configuration. Delivered from August to December 1968, they differed from the prototype in being fitted with improved systems, including the AN/AAD-4 SLIR (side-looking infra-red) and AN/APQ-136 moving target indicator (MTI) sensors, and AN/AWG-13 analog computer.

53-3129 was the first of this breed. Named *The First Lady*, she was the first production C-130A Hercules and had made her maiden flight at Marietta, Georgia, on 7 April 1955. Her career had almost been cut short when a fuel leak resulted in half the port wing being burned off during its third flight, but the aircraft was repaired and flew again in February 1956. In September 1957 she was modified as a JC-130A and completed tours of duty at the Cambridge Air Research Center, the Air Force Research Center, the Air Force Missile Center, and Temco Division at Major Field in Texas. In December 1961 she was attached to the 6,550th Support Wing (Range). On 31 October 1968, the 16th SOS based at Ubon – call-sign 'Spectre' – was activated, and *First Lady* became its inaugural AC-130A gunship. She was first used for night interdiction and armed reconnaissance missions during *Barrel Roll* operations in Laos. Ubon became the home of the AC-130 gunships for the rest of the war, being used to mount operations in Cambodia until shortly before the ceasefire came into effect on 15 August 1973.

From Ubon, *The First Lady* and her heir-apparents were used at night, mainly on 'out-country' operations in South-east Asia, and in particular on the Ho Chi Minh Trail, on *Commando Hunt* interdiction missions. *The First Lady* was hit in March 1971 by a 37mm shell. Again she was repaired, and she went on to serve the 415th SOTS and, from November 1976 to 1994, the 711th Special Operations Squadron. *The First Lady* was almost certainly the oldest aircraft to take part in Operation *Desert Storm* in 1991. She was presented to the USAF Armament Museum at Eglin AFB in November 1995.)

The other six AC-130A gunships of the 16th SOS also had colourful careers. From January to March 1969, three were used in South-east Asia, on average destroyed 2.7 enemy vehicles per sortie. Up to twelve crew were carried, including three to five gunners. 54-1623 became better known as *Ghost Rider* and ended her career as the gate guardian at Dobbins AFB in April 1997. 54-1625, *War Lord*, was shot down over the Ho Chi Minh Trail on 21 April 1970 with the loss of all except one of the crew. 54-1627 *Gomer Grinder* went on to serve the 415th SOTS and the 711th SOS before retirement in 1976; while 54-1628, *The Exterminator*, finished its career in 1994 with the 711th SOS. 54-1629, which had been the first C-130 with rear-opening nose-gear doors, suffered battle damage over Laos on 24 May 1969 when it was hit by 37mm fire; it crashed-landed at Ubon in Thailand and burned out, and two crew members were killed. 54-1630, which went by the equally colourful name of *Mors de Coelis*, finished its career at *Azrael* in the 711th SOS from 1995 to 1997,

when it was placed in storage at the Air Force Museum. Used in the fighting in South-east Asia, the AC-130As proved very effective, especially against vehicles along the Ho Chi Minh Trail at night. Operations continued until the summer of 1970, by which time it was clear that aircraft with improved all-weather operation and larger-calibre guns were needed.

The surviving AC-130As were therefore withdrawn for refurbishment, and a C-130A (55-0011) was modified to 'Pave Pronto' configuration under the 'Super Chicken' or 'Surprise Package' programme to meet the requirement for improved all-weather capability. It was armed with two 20mm M-61 Vulcan cannon and two 7.62mm miniguns forward, and two M-1 Bofors clip-fed 40mm cannon aft of the wheel fairing. Uprated avionics included AN/ASD-5 'Black Crow' truck ignition sensor, Motorola AN/APQ-133 beacon-tracking radar, an AN/AVQ-18 laser designator/rangefinder and AN/ASQ-24A stabilized tracking set containing ASQ-145 LLLTV (low-light-level television). Tests were conducted in October 1969, and in November, 55-0011, better known as *Night Stalker*, was despatched to South-east Asia. (The aircraft remained on the active USAF inventory until 1995.) 'Surprise Package' lived up to its name, with expectations proving higher than anticipated, and subsequently nine more C-130As were modified to the AC-130A 'Pave Pronto' configuration, with AN/ASQ-24A stabilized tracking set, AN/AVQ-18 laser designator and bomb-damage assessment camera, SUU-42 flare ejection pods, dual AN/ALQ-87 ECM pods under the wings, and some other improvements. The AN/ASD-5 'Black Crow' truck ignition sensor which was not originally included, was reinstated.

In South-east Asia the 'Pave Pronto' AC-130As of the 16th SOS wreaked havoc among enemy convoys at night, and used their AN/AVQ-18 laser designator/rangefinder to mark targets for F-4D Phantoms carrying laser-guided bombs (LGBs). In December 1971, 55-044 *Prometheus* was damaged by a 37mm shell and lost Nos 3 and 4 propellers, but survived, only to be shot down south-east of Tchepone, Laos, on 28 March 1972, reportedly by an SA-2 missile. Less than three months later, on 18 June, 55-043 was shot down in the A Shau valley, a Communist infiltration route south-west of Hue, by an SA-7A heat-seeking, surface-to-air missile.

Commando Lava, Banish Beach and Commando Scarf

Beginning in 1967, the C-130s of the 374th Tactical Airlift Wing flew twenty-eight *Commando Lava* sorties into the A Shau valley to air-drop 120 tons of defoliants so as to deny the NVA and VC forces their entry corridor into South Vietnam. *Commando Lava* was dangerous work, because the C-130s had to drop down to 200ft (60m) in order to release the chemical compound, thus heightening the risk of being knocked out of the sky by SAM missiles. Unfortunately the mud-making operations – first conceived by William H. Sullivan, the US ambassador to Laos – were no more of a hindrance to the Communists than the annual monsoon, and they simply covered over the worst-affected parts of the route with gravel or bamboo matting.

Meanwhile in 1965 in a similar attempt, *Banish Beach* missions were first flown by C-130s in an effort to deprive the Viet Cong of forest sanctuaries by starting forest fires with almost simultaneous drops of fuel drums. There were also *Commando Scarf* bombing missions in which the C-130s carried small XM-41 anti-personnel mines; and in southern Laos, CDU-10 noisemakers were dropped by C-130s as part of the interdiction campaign.

Further Gunship Losses

AC-130A 56-490 *Thor* was shot down 25 miles (40km) north-east of Pakse, Laos, on 21 December 1972. 55-014 *Jaws of Death* survived, ending its career in 1995 and therefore being allocated to the Robins AFB museum in 1996. 55-029 *Midnight Express* was retired in 1994, while 55-040 was retired in 1976. 55-046, better known perhaps as *Proud Warrior*, and which in 1957 had been loaned to the USMC for in-flight refuelling tests, was retired in 1994. 56-469 *Grim Reaper* also survived the horrors of Vietnam, and since 1995 has been used as a ground trainer at the 82nd TRW at Sheppard AFB, Texas. 56-509 *Raids Kill Um Dead* was damaged at An Loc South Vietnam on 23 December 1972; however, it was repaired and later assigned to the 711th SOS. In 1995, and now named *Ultimate End*, this AC-130A finished its days at the Hurlburt Field Memorial Air Park.

AC-130H 69-6573 (4347), which was built as a C-130E, first delivered to the 61st TAS in August 1969, converted to AC-130E gunship configuration in 1970 and assigned to the 16th SOS in 1972. In 1973 the aircraft was modified again, to AC-130H, and after rejoining the 16th SOS went on to serve in the 415th SOS before rejoining the 16th SOS in January 1978. It was given its overall grey scheme in October 1986. To the right is the AN/ASQ-24A stabilized tracking set consisting of a low-light TV, an AN/ASQ-145 laser illuminator and an AN/AVQ-19 laser designator and ranger. The forward fuselage radome (with its associated blast compensator) contains the AN/ASD-5 'Black Crow' ignition sensor, while the ball turret under the nose houses AN/AAQ-117 FLIR. Ron Green

Pave Spectre

Meanwhile in April 1970 the decision was taken to convert two C-130Es to AC-130E prototype gunships. The C-130E's higher gross weight, stronger airframe and increased power offered greater payload and longer loiter time than the original AC-130A gunships. As a result of experience gained in Vietnam, more advanced avionics were fitted, and what was known as 'Pave Aegis' armament configuration was created by installing a 105mm howitzer in place of one of the 40mm cannon in the port parachute door, while retaining the two 20mm cannon forward of the port undercarriage fairing. The howitzer was

later attached to a trainable mounting controlled by AN/APQ-150 beacon-tracking radar.

In February 1971, nine more C-130E conversions, not dissimilar to 'Pave Pronto' AC-130As, were ordered. However, by the time that the first AC-130Es were completed in June and July 1971, they represented such a leap forward in avionics over the earlier 'Pave Pronto' gunships that they became known as 'Pave Spectre I's'. All eleven 'Pave Spectre' AC-130Es served in South-east Asia, entering combat in the spring of 1972 when they helped repulse the Viet Cong offensive. AC-130Es proved most effective tank killers during night operations and on night

interdiction sorties along the notorious Ho Chi Minh Trail.

All AC-130Es – except 69-6571, which was shot down near An Loc, South Vietnam, on 30 March 1972 – were upgraded in June 1973 to AC-130H standard when they were re-engined with T56-A-15 turboprops. The AC-130H also differed from the AC-130E in having its 7.62 miniguns omitted. In 1978 AC-130H aircraft were retrofitted with an in-flight refuelling receptacle and other improvements. Each AC-130H/U is crewed by five officers: pilot, co-pilot, navigator, fire-control officer and electronic warfare officer – and nine enlisted men: flight engineer, low-light TV operator, infra-red detection set

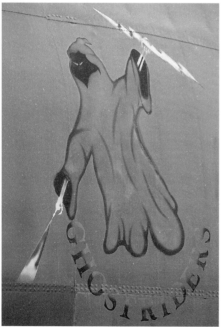

(Above) **The AC-130E (and the AC-130H) retained the AN/ASQ-5 'Black Crow' ignition detector, and the E also retained the twin 40mm Bofors cannon in the rear fuselage; but, as this dramatic photograph shows, the AC-130H introduced a 105mm howitzer in place of one of the two cannon. When fired, this gun momentarily knocks the gunship three degrees off course.** Lockheed

AC-130U Spectre 90-0167 (5262) one of thirteen of the latest Hercules gunships based on the C-130H airframe modified by Rockwell International. All are operated by the 4th SOS 'Ghostriders', 16th SOW, at Hurlburt Field, Florida. Author

operator, five aerial gunners and a load master. At the time of writing, the eight remaining AC-130H gunships are operated by 16 SOS/16 SOW at Hurlburt Field, though these will be progressively replaced by new-build AC-130U gunships.

The 'U-Boat'

In July 1987 Rockwell was awarded a contract to cover the research and development of a new AC-130U Spectre gunship to replace the Special Operation Squadrons' ageing AC-130A. Thirteen new C-130H airframes were procured for the modification, which carries the same armament as the AC-130H except that the trainable GAU-12/U 25mm Gatling gun has replaced the AC-130H's two 20mm cannon. All weapons can be slaved to the Hughes APQ-180 digital

Rare close-up of the single, forward-positioned, 25mm GAU-12/U cannon, which is belt-fed with 3,000 rounds of ammunition. This gun replaces the twin GE M61 20mm cannon arrangement used on all previous AC-130 gunships. Author

rear ramp and starboard forward fuselage side.

Other equipment new to the AC-130U includes a HUD, combined INS, Navstar Global Positioning System (GPS) and Spectra ceramic armour protection, while three underfuselage chaff and flare dispensers (Capable of dispensing 300 chaff bundles and either 90 MJU7 or 180 M206 IR decoy flares), Texas Instruments AN/AAQ-117 FLIR countermeasures, and ITT Avionics AN/ALQ-172 jammer, are all fitted to increase survivability in a low-to-medium-threat environment. Delivery to the 16th SOW began in 1994, at which time the eighteen AC-130Hs were transferred to the AFRes 919th SOW at Duke Field, Florida, whose AC-130As were retired. The AC-130Us or 'U-boats' as they are affectionately known by crews, provide other special operations' roles, including escort, surveillance, and reconnaissance/interdiction in addition to the primary precision fire support mission. All eighteen AC-130Us are operated by the 4th SOS, 16th SOW, at Hurlburt Field, Florida.

Desert Storm

In 1990 the Air Force Reserve's 711th SOS deployed some AC-130As to Turkey for Operation *Proven Force*, the 'second front' for the coming war with Iraq. On 7 January 1991, the joint task force (JTF) was activated at Ramstein AB, Germany, and one of its components, the Special Operations Task Force, was to seek and rescue downed Allied pilots. On 17 January, three EC-130s from the 43rd ECS, 66th ECW, at Sebach AB, Germany, were among the European units that deployed to Incirlik AB, Turkey. Eight AC-130 gunships meanwhile, and six MC-130E 'Combat Talon Is', were deployed to Saudi Arabia for Operation *Desert Storm* missions in the Gulf War, which began on 16 January. (While defending a USMC force under attack by Iraqi forces on 31 January, AC-130H 69-6567 *Spirit 03*, in the 16th SOS, was shot down 68 miles (110km) south-south-east of Kuwait City with the loss of all fourteen crew.)

'Combat Talon Is' of the 8th SOS delivered the 15,000lb (6,800kg) BLU-82/B 'Big Blue' fuel-air explosive bomb, the largest and heaviest conventional bomb in the USAF inventory. On 15 February 'Combat Talons' began dropping BLU-82 'daisy-cutters' on Iraqi minefields as a

fire-control radar, derived from the APQ-70 carried by the F-15E Strike Eagle, AN/AAQ-117 forward-looking infra-red (FLIR) mounted under the port side of the nose, or turret-mounted Bell Aerospace all-light-level TV (ALLTV) in the port main undercarriage sponson, for true adverse weather ground-attack operations. The 'Black Crow' truck-ignition sensor and radome and separate beacon-tracking radar used on earlier gunships were omitted. Observer stations are included on the

Business end of the single 40mm Bofors cannon and 105mm howitzer on board AC-130U Spectre 90-0167. The AN/ASQ-4 'Black Crow' truck ignition sensor and radome, and separate AN/APQ-150 beacon tracking radar (which was located in the space now occupied by the howitzer) used on earlier gunships, have been omitted. Author

(Below) This inside view of the single 105mm howitzer and 40mm Bofors cannon on board AC-130U Spectre 90-0167 contrasts sharply with the earlier photograph of the twin Bofors cannon installation in the rear hold of the AC-130A gunship. Author

prelude to the ground offensive. 'Bombs' containing 16,000,000 leaflets were also dropped by 'Combat Talon' and HC-130N/P aircraft, with messages telling Iraqi soldiers how to surrender to the ground forces; other 'PSYOP' missions dropped leaflets telling Iraqis that more BLU-82s were on the way. EC-130Es helped to psychologically prepare the battlefield for *Desert Storm*, the 193rd SOW being one of the first special operations' units to be sent to the Gulf region. On 22 November, the unit began 'PSYOP' operations, broadcasting the 'Voice of America' into Iraq, Kuwait and Saudi Arabia. A crash modifications programme, lasting several weeks, upgraded the EC-130Es so that the 'Commando Solo' aircraft could broadcast in the local TV format for this region. The 193rd SOG's leaflet drops and broadcast readings from the Koran and testimonials from Iraqi prisoners were instrumental in persuading Iraqi troops to surrender. When surveyed, Iraqi PoWs indicated that PSYOP radio broadcasts reached 58 per cent of the military target audience; of those, 46 per cent indicated that the broadcasts had an influence on their decision to surrender.

Somali Interlude

In June and July 1993 Somalia pushed the war in Bosnia off the world's front pages as American air units fought to prevent General Aideed and his supporters retaking control of Mogadishu. Aideed's fighters were blamed for the killing of twenty-three Pakistani UN peacekeepers on 5 June. AC-130H gunships and Cobra helicopters of a US Army quick-reaction force were used in day and night actions against Aideed and his supporters in Mogadishu. In a one-hour attack on 11/12 June, the

Top view of the single 105mm howitzer and 40mm Bofors cannon on board AC-130U Spectre 90-0167. Author

(Right) S/Sgt Colin Coupens carries out a close inspection of the 25mm GAU-12/U cannon of AC-130U Spectre 90-0167. Author

'Spectre' gunships and Cobra helicopters destroyed Aideed's radio station as American soldiers led attacks on his command headquarters and weapons caches. 'Spectres' attacked ammunition dumps and garages housing 'technicals', close to Aideed's residence. Inevitably there were losses. For instance, in the following year while conducting a routine mission in support of UN forces on 14 March 1994, AC-130H 'Spectre' 69-6576, in the 16th SOS/16th SOW, crashed in the sea 4 miles (7km) south of Malindi, Kenya, after take-off from Mombasa, when a howitzer round exploded in the gun-tube and caused a fire in the left-hand engines. Eight crew members died. Three of the six survivors stayed with the aircraft during the crash-landing while the other three parachuted to safety.

At the time of writing, eight AC-130Hs still serve with the 16th SOS at Hurlburt Field, Florida, although these will be progressively replaced by new-build AC-130U gunships.

'Star Wars' Technology

Perhaps the most dangerous element of AC-130 gunship operations is the relatively low altitude at which the aircraft must operate, exposing themselves to enemy groundfire. Gunpowder technology still limits the effectiveness of the airborne weapons platforms used by the US Special Forces. Lockheed Aircraft Service Company, is exploring some new hypervelocity weapon technologies developed in the Strategic Defence Initiative Organization (SDIO) or 'Star Wars' programme, that promises to increase dramatically the effectiveness of airborne gunships. Craig H. Smyser, principal investigator of advanced weapons systems studies, has written: 'Low projectile velocities mean less energy on target and less accuracy because the slow-moving projectile must spend more time subject to the distorting effects of wind and weather, requiring pilots to fly closer in than might be safe.'

Directed energy devices such as lasers and particle beams are considered not 'mature' enough for tactical applications to gunships, but hypervelocity weapons such as hypercannon, coilguns, electrothermal, light-gas and liquid-propellant guns, developed for the 'Star Wars' applications, could effectively be used aboard gunships of the future. A study has shown that a 4,600hp, turbine-powered, 150mm hypervelocity electro-magnetic rail-gun, and all its support equipment, could be accommodated onboard an AC-130. Hypervelocity guns would enable an AC-130U gunship (and a C-5 for that matter) to operate at stand-off distances at altitudes over 15,000ft (4,500m) — well above the range of 37mm and 57mm AAA fire and IR missiles. Target accuracy remains high because the high projectile velocities of the 'Star Wars' weapons are virtually unaffected by the distorting effects of wind and weather.

This is the future. Then, as now, the part played by the mysterious Hercules of AFSOC may well never be fully told. However, when called upon to deploy specialized airpower, or to deliver special operations, or to conduct psychological and counter-measures operations, as well as a host of other covert activities, Special Operations Command is ready – any time, anywhere.

Nine EC-130E 'Commando Solo' electronic surveillance aircraft of the 193rd SOS/193rd SOW, ANG, helped to psychologically prepare the battlefield for Desert Storm. Gary Madgwick/The Aviation Workshop

CHAPTER SIX

Conflict, *Comfort*, *Relief* and *Hope*

In August 1990 conflict arose in the Persian Gulf after talks between the representatives from Iraq and Kuwait did not resolve grievances over oil pricing. On 2 August President Saddam Hussein of Iraq massed seven divisions, totalling 120,000 troops and 2,000 tanks, along the Iraq/Kuwait border and invaded Kuwait in the early morning hours: on 8 August he announced that Kuwait was the nineteenth province of Iraq. Immediately after the invasion President George Bush had placed a US economic embargo against Iraq and the United Nations Security Council had quickly followed suit. On 7 August, when Saddam

Hussein had refused to remove his troops from Kuwait, President Bush had set the US contingency commitment *Desert Shield* in motion, ordering warplanes and ground forces to Saudi Arabia, saying the country faced the 'imminent threat' of an Iraqi attack. More than 55,000 Air Force personnel would ultimately be despatched to the Gulf, including more than 180 aircraft and 5,400 personnel assigned to USAFE units. During the period 16 to 28 August, fifteen C-130Es from Military Aircraft Command's 37th Tactical Airlift Squadron became the first European-based USAF aircraft deployed to south-west Asia.

The US Central Command HG, which would direct the coalition of allied forces against Iraq under the command of Army General H. Norman Schwarzkopf, immediately set pre-planned preparations in motion. CENTCOM'S function was to co-ordinate US force deployment to the Gulf region to help defend Saudi Arabia and provide security to other Arab states. Lt Gen Charles A. Horner, USAF, the allied coalition's supreme air commander, began co-ordinating all air actions related to the build-up, and within days had established HQ Central Command Air Forces (Forward) in Saudi Arabia. From his HQ, the

USAF C-130s pass burning oil-wells in Kuwait after the Iraqi retreat from the small Arab kingdom. By the time the ceasefire at the end of Operation Desert Storm **had come into effect on 3 March 1991, MAC C-130 transports had, since 10 August 1990, flown 46,500 sorties, and moved more than 209,000 personnel and 300,000 tons of supplies within the theatre.** USAF

air actions which ultimately would bring an end to the war were put into operation.

More than 145 Military Airlift Command (MAC) C-130 Hercules were deployed in support of *Desert Shield* and *Desert Storm*; these aircraft moved units to forward bases once they arrived in theatre. One of their first tasks was to move the 82nd Airborne Division from its staging area to positions near the Kuwait border. In late August 1990, President Bush signed an order authorizing members of the armed

RNZAF (their Hercules deployment is covered elsewhere in this book).

Efforts by the UN Security Council to find a peaceful resolution with Iraq proved futile. On the morning of 15 January 1991, an eleventh-hour appeal by the council for Iraq to withdraw from Kuwait was met with silence, and at twelve noon the deadline for peace had passed. Next day, at approximately 19:00 hours Eastern Standard time, Operation *Desert Storm* began, the allied forces answering Iraq's silence with attacks

Provide Comfort

One of the Gulf War's most immediate consequences was the disintegration of Iraq. Civil unrest erupted among Iraq's Shiite and Kurdish minorities, and Hussein used his military ruthlessly, crushing the uprisings with helicopters and what armour his army had left. In the northern part of the country, 500,000 Kurds made their way to the Turkish and Iranian borders. On 5 April the UN condemned Iraq, and President Bush ordered US European Command to assist Kurds and other refugees in the mountains of northern Iraq. The following day, JTF *Provide Comfort* was formed, and deployed to Incirlik, Turkey, to conduct humanitarian air operations in northern Iraq.

On 7 April, USAF aircraft began dropping food, blankets, clothing, tents and other equipment, while at the same time Iraq was warned not to carry out any kind of activity north of the 36th parallel, where Kurdish refugees had gathered. Eventually, thirteen countries took part in *Provide Comfort* and another thirty were to provide various types of material assistance. By 8 April USAF aircraft had dropped approximately 27 tons of relief supplies to the Kurds; on 9 April, the mission expanded to sustaining the refugee population for thirty days. Two days later *Provide Comfort* took on the additional responsibility of providing temporary settlements for the Kurds. By 6 June the last mountain gap had closed and the refugee population was in the security zone, or 'safe haven'. The UN assumed responsibility for relief operations the following day. The last coalition ground forces let Iraq on 20 July, and *Provide Comfort* ended on 15 July; the emphasis then shifted to preventing a recurrence, with Operation *Provide Comfort II*.

BLU-82/B 15,000lb 'Big Blue' free-fall bomb (shown without P904 fuze), the 'Mother of all Bombs' dropped by the 7th and 8th SOS teams of the 1st Special Operations Wing MC-130E Combat Talon I to clear Iraqi minefields during the Gulf War. Palletized for carriage in the cargo hold, the bomb was simply jettisoned onto the target. Author

forces reserves to be called up for active duty. Throughout the campaign, AFRes and ANG members flew and maintained aircraft, including those used in strategic and tactical airlift operations, as well as tanker support. In addition, a small USMC tanker task force was established using KC-130Fs, KC-130Rs, and KC-130Ts, based at Bahrein and Al Jubail, while the USN operated a few C-130Fs for logistics support, and the EC-130Q in the communications relay role. Finally, it should not be forgotten that Australia, France, Saudi Arabia and South Korea also sent C-130 transports and KC-130 tankers to the Gulf, and that help was sent by the RAF and

by strike aircraft based in Saudi Arabia and Turkey. By the time the ceasefire came into effect on 3 March, MAC C-130 transports had, since 10 August 1990, flown 46,500 sorties and moved more than 209,000 personnel and 300,000 tons of supplies within the theatre. They provided logistical support, medical evacuation of the wounded, and battlefield mobility once the fighting started. (The role played by the Special Operations' AC/EC/MC/HC -130s in the Gulf War is covered in Chapter 5, while the part played by RAF Hercules is covered in Chapter 8.) During the '100-Hour' ground campaign, MAC C-130 transports flew more than 500 sorties a day.

Provide Hope II

In 1992 those USAFE C-130Es based at the relatively small Rhein-Main AFB which shared the city's busy international airport 5 miles (8km) south of Frankfurt, took part in relief operations to the Soviet Union, East and West Africa, and Bosnia. The C-130E element was provided by the 37th 'Blue Tail Flies' Airlift Squadron, 435th Airlift Wing, 17th AF, whose primary mission is the tactical airlift mission within the European theatre. Now based at Ramstein, the 37th Airlift Squadron routinely performs airdrop and air–land missions, delivering equipment, supplies, and personnel 'on target, on time'.

In April 1992 USAFE transports took part in Operation *Provide Hope II*, a long-term effort to aid cities in the former Soviet Union. On the 4 and 5 May 1992, following a 30 April coup in Sierra Leone, a US European Command Joint Special Operations Task Force rescued 438 people from Freetown, Sierra Leone. The 37th ALS contributed nine C-130 sorties, carrying 302 evacuees to Dakar, Senegal. From the 12 August to 9 October, three 435th ALW C-130Es were deployed from Rhein-Main to Luanda, Angola, to be used to relocate government and rebel soldiers during Operation *Provide Transition*, a multi-national UN effort to support democratic elections following the civil war in Angola. The C-130s flew 326 sorties, carrying 8,805 passengers and 265 tons of cargo during the operation.

Provide Promise

On 3 July 1992 the 37th ALS flew the first two C-130s in the first *Provide Promise* mission; these were laden with humanitarian relief supplies from Rhein-Main, their objective the war-torn city of Sarajevo. The flights were not without hazard: on 3 October an Italian Air Force C-130 was hit by a missile 21 miles (34km) west of Sarajevo

and was lost with its four-man crew. and at least two USAF C-130s received small-arms fire at Sarajevo Airport. Undeterred, C-9 Medevac missions began on 2 February 1993; They took place twice a month, and in March the operation expanded to include the airdrop of relief supplies in Bosnia-Herzegovina. On 27 February a USAF Hercules first dropped about a million leaflets in less than forty minutes over eastern Bosnia, telling residents and refugees that the airdropped relief was on its way, and cautioning people of the dangers

of being too close to the drop zone. Night after night Bosnian refugees stood in the open, and waited for the 'parcels from God' to drop.

Provide Relief

On 14 August 1992, the White House, prompted by continuing reports of heavily armed, organized gangs stealing food and famine relief supplies from humanitarian organizations in the famine-ravaged east African state of Somalia, announced that US military transports would support the multi-national UN relief effort. Ten C-130s and 400 personnel were deployed to Moi International Airport, Mombasa, Kenya, in Operation *Provide Relief*, a multi-nation air operation involving the US, Great Britain, Germany, France. Italy, Belgium and Canada, under the leadership of the United Nations in Nairobi. Operation *Provide Relief* began in late August 1992 and continued until the end of February 1993, by which time multi-national efforts

(Left) **Operating from August 1992 to February 1993,** Provide Relief **was a multi-nation air-relief operation in Mombasa, Kenya, involving, at its height, sixteen USAF and USAFE C-130s, with transports from six other nations. It delivered supplies to refugees in neighbouring Somalia, while Operation** Restore Hope **protected the relief efforts.** Author

C-130E of the 711th SOS, 919th SOG from Duke Field, Florida, and C-130H 74-2067 (4678) of the 772nd ALS, 463rd TAW, from Dyess AFB, Abilene, Texas, at Moi International Airport for Operation Provide Relief **in February 1993.** Author

had restored stability to the refugee locations in the country and it was possible to convey supplies over secure land routes from the Somali ports of Mogadishu and Kismaayu directly to the relief locations.

By the end of 1992 clans of opposing beliefs fighting for food, territory and ethnic revenge, had created such a climate of violence in Somalia that *Provide Relief* workers were prevented from providing aid in areas of greatest need. This came to a head on 8 December, and in response, President Bush, implementing Operation *Restore Hope*, sent American troops to protect the relief efforts. At the peak of the operation in January 1993, Joint Task Force *Provide Relief/Restore Hope* included 1,007 Air Force, Marine, Army and Navy personnel as well as flying units from Germany to the UK, three German C-160 Transalls and five Marine KC-130 tankers sharing the ramp space, with occasional C-141s and C-5s. By 25 February 1993 the multi-national unit had flown 1,924 sorties to Somalia and 508 to Kenya, and had carried over 28,000 tonnes of food for international relief organizations who operate feeding centres and clinics for the Somali people in both Kenya and Somalia.

On 28 February Colonel Thomas Samples, CO of the Air Component at Mombasa, and the Dyess crew, made the final US food flight from Mombasa to Mandera loaded with three pallets of powdered milk and bottled water. Other loads during the six-month period had included wheat, beans, rice, maize, various flours, cooking oil and a corn and soya preparation called 'Unimix'. The food used to arrive by ship in Mombasa and was then trucked to the *Provide Relief* operations centre at Moi Airport. 28 February also saw the departure of two ANG C-130s with their support equipment and personnel. Operation *Provide Relief* really made a big difference. The C-130s operated from austere, dusty runways, sometimes littered with rocks and as short as 3,000ft (900m), but without a single accident or mission lost due to a maintenance problem – although several incidents occurred at outlying fields between helicopters and fixed-wing aircraft.

Absolution

'WOC' ('Wing Operations Command') Mombasa, as it was officially called (for Wing Operations Centre), continued to operate as an air component under the JTF

'Absolution'

On 1 March Captain Paul Britton, check pilot Captain Mike P. Brignola, from Westchester, Pennsylvania, and the three-man flight crew boarded the sweltering cabin of the C-130 for an 'Absolution' trooping and supply mission to combat units to Kisaamayu and Mogadishu. Almost at once the cabin and massive hold filled with refreshing icy blasts from the air-conditioning system; cargomasters sealed the rear ramp door, and soldiers and Red Cross girls on board settled down into the rows of sideways-facing seats for the 510-mile (820km) flight up the coast to Mogadishu. Tail-number, souls on board and fuel endurance were relayed to ground control. All around the field were aircraft of every size and type: light aircraft, airliners, southern air Transport L-100 Hercules and a few German and Belgian C-160s and 130s were parked on the apron. An all-white HS 748 of the Royal New Zealand Air Force which had flown in from Auckland, looked like a polar bear in the desert. Highly colourful Kenyan Air Force Puma and Tucano aircraft threaded their way to the ramp, adding to the spectacle. An African Safari Airways DC-8 roared noisily into the air.

The C-130 rumbled along the uneven concrete to the threshold; permission to take off was sought and given. The four massive 4,508-shp Allison T56-A-7 turboprops lifted the C-130H effortlessly into the cloudy sky and the nose-wheel engaged in the well beneath the cockpit with a reassuring thump. Soon the C-130 was on its briefed course at a cruising altitude of 17,000ft (5,200m) at 200–300 knots. Over the Indian Ocean it flew parallel to the lush green coastline of Kenya, then the Murrum red desert floor of Somalia. It was essential that the aircrew gave frequent position reports so as to avoid flying into any conflict, because of the E-2C, King Control had been withdrawn in December. Before entering Somalian airspace, all aircraft gave a position report on 127.45MHz, and loadmasters frequently joined the crew on the flight deck for a quick look or consultation. Down below, the islands of Jofay and Koyaama appeared, and then the navigator pointed into the heat haze past the islands: 'Kismaayu!', he said, above the thundering clamour of the four engines and rushing slipstream.

Captain Britton checked his map, and UHF contact with Kismaayu, call-sign 'Tailpipe Kilo', was established. Bill Murray, the flight engineer, sat like a father confessor immediately behind the two pilots. He smiled, then shouted that the C-130 would be going straight in and turning before landing. Armed battles had taken place in Kismaayu on 22 February between an Aideed backer, warlord Omer Jess, and his rival Hersi, known as 'Morgan', who had taken over the town from the Belgians. At least eleven people had been killed, and Jess's USC/SSDF forces had retreated from the city they had controlled since shortly after the 1991 overthrow by Rebels of Somali dictator Mohammed Siad Aarre.

Britton put the C-130H into a 45-degree descent; it lost altitude rapidly and the altimeter passed through several thousand feet until it read '1'. The young Texan concentrated intensely as he dived for the single paved runway. Up to now the only threat had been a high-

flying stork or crane – birds such as these caused the deaths of two light-aircraft pilots in 1991. Down and down the C-130 plummeted, until finally Captain Britton levelled off and the Hercules zoomed along the runway at a very exciting 150ft (46m) at 260 knots. He was not showing off however: this procedure was designed to scatter any cattle, camels or the odd Somali who might have decided to cross the runway. But none had, and the C-130 whizzed past the control tower and assembled multitude of Cobra helicopters. Captain Britton peeled off to the left at the end of the runway in a beautiful 'fighter' turn and circled for an assault landing. He pulled up within 3,000ft (900m) using the powerful reverse thrust, in doing so producing quadraphonic sound all around the flight deck.

The Hercules' massive four-bladed props were still turning as cargo-masters eased the pallet out – and the C-130 was off again, trundling down the length of the runway in the other direction this time. The pilot's seat was taken now by Captain Brignola. He pointed out a herd of camels to the left – they were not disturbed by the subsequent take-off, which was remarkable, since taking off from rudimentary Somali airstrips in the intense heat with four, let alone two engines, called for strong nerves. Once off safely, and when they had reached 100 nautical miles distance away, contact was made with Mogadishu approach and their intention stated. At 60 nautical miles Mogadishu approach placed the Hercules under positive radar control for a radar service to Mogadishu International. The heart-stopping landing at Kismaayu had been dramatic, but Mogadishu produced an incredible view for an awestruck observer. Dark grey warships were anchored offshore of the war-torn Somali capital. Large breakers pounded the beaches, and sand-coloured Humvees and construction vehicles dotted the landscape inland of the dunes. It looked like a scene from a Normandy beachhead, except that Marines were jogging around the airport perimeter, and handball games were in full swing on the beach.

The C-130 taxied to just in front of the tower, and the troops and supplies were disembarked. A long file of 'grunts' took their place, flopping wearily into the bucket-seats in the cargo hold. A Nigerian C-130 taxied out, returned along the runway at speed, and turned sharply onto 270 degrees, away from the town as machine-gun fire had been reported in the area.

At 05.35 hours Captain Britton followed exactly the same pattern, and the C-130 was off again and climbing away without incident. The faithful Allison turboprops beat a pulsating rhythm, and the tension in the cockpit evaporated with the diminishing heat as the C-130 climbed gradually to 23,000ft (7,000m). The crew settled back as the Hercules droned above the coast at a steady 300 knots. Copies of Stars and Stripes were being read until the sun went down below the right wing and the orange-red instrument lights and green computer CRTs began to light up the pilots' smiling faces. Darkness descended. The stable Hercules headed 'home' and the crew relaxed, knowing that after their exertions, in a few hours they would be enjoying 'field conditions' again at their plush hotel in Mombasa.

Headquarters in Mogadishu, Somalia, moving support supplies, including food and water for the troops, construction items, equipment and personnel throughout Kenya and Somalia. The MAC transport fleet at Mombasa consisted of four C-130Hs of the 463rd TAW, 773rd ALS, from Dyess AFB at Abiline, Texas. The 773rd, which is part of Air Mobility Command, replaced its sister squadron, the 772nd ALS, which redeployed Stateside in the second week of February.

Provide Promise Continues

For the relief operation from Rhein-Main to Bosnia, the 37th ALS were joined by C-130E/H crews on TDY (temporary duty) from the 317th ALW and the 40th ALS, 23rd Wing – both from Pope AFB North Carolina – as well as other stateside-based, active duty AFRes 'mix and match' rather than a 'hard' crew. On 23 March 1994, C-130E, 62-1834, was used for a *Provide Promise* flight (UN Flight 17) to Sarajevo; the aircraft was crewed by AFRes personnel. Pilot and airplane commander 1st Lt Ross Becker, pilot 1st Lt Eric L. Meyers and Captain Thomas D. Mims, navigator, were from the 815th Airlift Squadron, 403rd Wing, at Keesler AFB, Biloxi, MS. S/Sgt Ronald A. Downer, the flight engineer, 327th AS, 403rd Wing, was from Willow Grove Air Reserve Station at Horsham, Pennsylvania. It was Becker's sixteenth mission to Bosnia, Meyers' sixty-seventh, and Mims' twenty-third. S/Sgt Dorothy 'Bobbie' Bach – in the 60th ALW from Travis AFB, the Sat Comm operator at the 'black box' – was flying her 100th air–land/airdrop mission to Sarajevo; she wore a patch commemorating the event on the arm of her flight suit.

Brig Gen James E. Sehorn, director of operations, HQ 14th AF (AFRes) at Dobbins AFB, Georgia, was also on board; he wore the red triangular 'Flying Jennies' badge on his jacket. Gen Sehorn began his air force career in 1963 in primary pilot training. Upon graduation in 1964, he was assigned as an F-100 Super Sabre pilot at RAF Wethersfield, England. He then volunteered for F-105 Thunderchief duty in South-east Asia, and was assigned to Korat Royal Thai AFB, Thailand. He received combat-crew training for the F-100 in 1965 and the F-105 in 1967. Then in December 1967, Gen Sehorn was shot down over South-east Asia while flying a 'Wild Weasel' combat mission, and ended

1/Lt Ross Becker, 815th ALS, 403rd ALW, AFRes at the controls of C-130E 62-1834, a 96th TAS, 934th AG, AFRes aircraft on TDY at Rhein-Main, as it crosses the Alps en route to Sarajevo, 23 March 1994. Author

Pilot 1/Lt Ross Becker and co-pilot 1/Lt Eric L. Meyers, also from the 815th ALS, 403rd ALW, their flak jackets on now, and S/Sgt Ronald A. Downer, flight engineer, 327th ALS, 403rd ALW, maintain a close watch as the C-130E wends its way through the steep mountain passes in Bosnia near the end of the flight into Sarajevo, 23 March 1994. Author

up in the 'Hanoi Slammer', as he describes it. He was released in March 1973.

S/Sgt David A. Caldwell, flying his fortieth mission to Bosnia, and assistant loadmaster senior airman Eric J. Hebb, on his twenty-fifth mission, were from the 758th ALS, 911th ALG, AFRes. Both men came from Pittsburgh. A miner for fifteen years, Dave Caldwell worked in the construction industry during the summer months, between tours of duty; this was his fourth tour in Germany. He did not disguise his delight in being able to make a worthwhile contribution to events in Bosnia by

C-130E 62-1834 taxies in at Split, after flying in from Sarajevo. In front is C-130H 91-1231 (5278) of the 165th AS, 123rd AW, Kentucky ANG from Standiford Field, Louisville, the 2,000th Hercules built. Author

delivering food and medical supplies, his reassuring no-nonsense approach no doubt handed down from his father who served in Patton's 7th Armoured Division in World War II.

UN 17 lifted off from Frankfurt with a take-off load of 23,000lb (10,430kg). Vibration and noise were intense – it was like sitting in a tube train running without wheels. Caldwell and Hebb – brave men – were unseen in the rear of the hold. Tied with green webbing, the bundles of food and medical supplies stacked securely behind the raised ramp looked like goods wagons behind railway buffers.

UN 17 levelled off and headed towards Augsberg, then Innsbruck, Vicenza and Ancona. From the flight deck the snow-covered Alps looked stunning, their black, jagged peaks protruding menacingly through the high cloud layers below. Radio chatter crackled through the headphones: there was mention of 'Magic' (AWACS) and 'egress' speeds out of Sarajevo in the event of an emergency. Gen Sehorn was in discussion with the engineer. After delivering the load to Sarajevo the C-130E would fly on to Split on the Aegean coast in Croatia and deliver more supplies before returning to Sarajevo with another load. This was to be the pattern throughout the day, finishing in a third flight to Sarajevo when the

fuel remaining would determine whether the C-130E would return to Split to refuel or be flown straight home. The general discussed the arrival at Sarajevo with the pilots, querying the predictability of the flight plan – it was long and slow into the Bosnian enclave and he wondered if a fast run in wouldn't be better. Becker explained that the very nature of the mission was its predictability: 'That's the idea, and that's what has been agreed,' he said. The crew had only been together for two weeks, but it did not show: they worked well.

Nearing the war zone, camouflaged flak vests were donned; the crew pressed the front Velcro strip firmly. Flying down high valley walls, the C-130E skirted snow-covered mountain peaks. In front a Hercules toppled over on its left wing and disappeared into the murk for landing as Ross Becker took his turn for Sarajevo Airport. In the distance the long runway appeared: behind it appeared to be a solid mountain wall, and the Hercules a sitting duck for any bored sniper or anti-aircraft gunner. Landing was accomplished without incident, however, though ears ached with the descent and the pressure squeezed the yellow ear-plugs until the pain moved to the cheekbones. It could now be seen that some of the white-walled and orange-roofed houses which had looked so picturesque from high altitude were in

fact burned-out hulks, with blackened openings where windows had once looked onto pleasant vistas. UN17 raced past them, hit the runway perfectly, and taxied to the shattered terminal building. Nearby, a white and blue Ilyushin IL-76 was parked, and a French Air Force Transall taxied in. Evidence of the terrible war was everywhere.

Caldwell said, 'You should have been here in December – it was like the Fourth of July!' White UN trucks and carriers milled around, and forklift drivers wearing blue UN helmets unloaded the pallets; in minutes these were all pushed along the rollers in the floor and out of the Hercules. General Sehorn clambered over the top and helped two soldiers push out the pallets, too!

Take-off for Split was made in sunshine and blue sky, and soon the deep blue waters of the Croatian coast appeared again. Near Split the crew was advised to look out for a Triple A emplacement, fortunately friendly; it tracked every plane in. The C-130E dashed across the built-up area of Split. It was eerie: there were no boats or surfers offshore, and certainly no tourists, and on a road in the distance just two cars could be seen travelling along it. The runway at Split was covered in black tyre marks where a Hercules had burst a tyre but taxied in without problems.

UN17 was loaded and took off again. Climbing away, the mission seemed almost routine now, and but for the flak vests it could almost have been a training flight. Dave Caldwell said that in the event of an emergency the load could be jettisoned in ten seconds. The only drama came on the last flight of the day into Split when 62-1834 sprang a hydraulic leak and had to be left at the Croatian airport. The crew hopped aboard C-130H G-1231 (the 2,000th Hercules) for the flight 'home' to Rhein-Main – at last they could relax. Caldwell got out his hammock and draped it across the width of the Hercules, and soon he was swinging gently to and fro as the aircraft headed back to Germany. The hangar door welcomed the C-130 with appropriate letters: MISSION SUCCESS.

In addition to the air–land missions, as of March 1994 over 2,720 airdrop missions (which had begun on 28 February 1993) had been flown, and over 31,000 bundles had been dropped. The normal method used was the high-velocity Container Delivery System (CDS) in which supplies and equipment were delivered from an aircraft in flight using a stabilizing parachute, approximately 26ft (8m) in diameter when opened. At first two parachutes had been used per bundle, but after well in excess of 25,000 parachutes had been used, and since they could not be recovered, each CDS bundle was fitted with just one 1950s-style, G-12 low-velocity parachute because the manufacturer could produce only fifty a month – enough for just two nights' work. The parachute deploys automatically after exiting the aircraft, and ensures that the bundle remains upright; it cushions the bundle's impact, as does the corrugated honeycomb cardboard base.

Airdrops have to be made from very low altitudes, and as such are vulnerable to small arms' fire and the risk of ground collision in mountainous terrain. In Bosnia,

into 4 × 3½ft cardboard boxes are 'fluttered' onto DZs. The boxes have walls made of three layers of cardboard and self-destruct after leaving the C-130 because the ties holding them together are pulled apart: individual HDRs then scatter into the air and fall to the ground, in much the same way as a leaflet drop. On the night of 23/24 August 1993, USAFE C-130s flew over Mordar and discharged in a 'free fall', 13,440 individual MRE (Meals Ready to Eat) packs weighing approximately 20lb (9kg), in boxes designed to open in mid-air, spreading the packages inside a wide area.

The following account describes a typical high-velocity CDS airdrop mission,

of the Hercules the 43rd Wing maintenance crew were from Pope. Apparently the F-16 had sheared off the right elevator of the C-130 and the crew had ejected. The Hercules crew managed to put down safely.

For this flight, the aircraft commander was Capt. Michael P. Brignola, flying as check pilot for the mission pilot, twenty-seven year-old Captain Darren A. Maturi, an American of Italian extraction from Virginia, Minnesota, who occupied the left seat. Darren had graduated in the top 15 per cent at flying school, and though this qualified him to fly jet fighters, he had chosen transports. He had no regrets, and in the past eighteen months had flown

C-130E 62-1834 is reloaded with supplies at Split, Croatia, for another flight to Sarajevo. Author

drops were often thwarted by bad weather conditions, and the possibility that the DZ could be immediately overrun by unfriendly forces before food could be offloaded from pallets. Worse, in May 1993 six people were killed and eight injured by aid crates parachuted into Goradze and Srebrenica. Moreover, at one DZ, five people were killed in the fight around the parachute, whilst at another, a woman and child lay dead beneath a pallet. Clearly, other methods had to be tried, and to this end the tri-wall aerial delivery system (TRIADS) was first used on 20 March 1993, over Srebrenica: in this method individual HDR packets packed

flown by six Hercules on the night of 24/25 March 1994, to Bjelimici, Bosnia. C-130E 64-0529 – UN call-sign 43 – is from the 43rd Wing at Pope AFB, North Carolina. Those who took part cannot have been greatly encouraged by the fact that the day before, an F-16D had collided with a C-130E of the 2nd ALS at less than 300ft above Pope as both aircraft attempted to land. The F-16 had hurtled into 500 members of the Army's 82nd Airborne Division, Fort Bragg, North Carolina, who were preparing to load onto a C-141 transport for a routine mission. Twenty-three paratroopers had been killed and 100 personnel injured. Inside the rear cargo-hold

drops into Turkey, the Gulf and Angola, as well as to Bosnia; he was also the co-pilot aboard the first Bosnian airdrop mission on 1 March to Cerska, when three C-130s had dropped supplies in a drop zone 1,138 yards (1.040m) wide and 1,935 yards (1,769m) long.

Captain Brignola gathered the flight crew of nine around him outside the Hercules and went through the AAA and SAM avoidance procedures, Chaff dispensers and inert heat-sensitive flares being standard equipment; then everyone climbed aboard. Into the rear fuselage went the loadmasters, S/Sgt David T. Marko from Woburn, Massachusetts;

T/Sgt Mike T. Norton from Chicago, Illinois. T/Sgt Barney 'Joe' Ivy, and AFRes loadmaster from West Memphis, Arkansas also went to gain experience.

On the flight deck all the crew, apart from Sgt Jim A. Carezas, the satellite communications operator, also in charge of oxygen supply, were from the 37th Airlift Squadron; Carezas was from Travis AFB. During a typical airdrop mission the C-130 travels about 1,500 air miles (2,400km), which takes around six hours; and on a typical day, four USAF C-130s would fly to Sarajevo, and twelve would make airdrop missions. The French Air Force sent one C-160D Transall, and the Germans sent two or three on airdrops.

Maturi donned his red-and-white cap with his 'Frank Rules' badge (he's a great Frank Sinatra fan); the cap was a present from Col Harry Andersson, a family friend, who flew F4U Corsairs in the US Marine Corps on Guadalcanal in World War II. Navigator was Capt Mark A. Naumann, from Minnesota. Most navigators appear intense and Mark was no exception, his glasses making him look even more studious as he studied at his small table the large green scope, portable GPS NAVISTAR, maps, and papers marked 'SECRET'. Flight engineer S/Sgt Robert A. Higginbotham, from Mooresville, Indianapolis, sat pensively studying dials and gauges.

The sun dropped behind the far side of the airport as UN43 taxied out. In the lead was Capt David A. Peiffer and his all-41st ALS crew. His Hercules was equipped with

(Above) **Captains Darren Maturi and Mike Brignola pose for the camera in front of C-130E 64-0529 (4017) in the 41st ALS, 43rd ALW from Pope AFB, at Rhein-Main just before take-off for the night airdrop at Bjelimici, Bosnia.** Author

The sun dips below the horizon as Capt Maturi taxies out at Rhein-Main. Mike Brignola, in the right-hand seat, checks the details. Note the AN/APN-169A SKE (Station Keeping Equipment) scope mounted atop the instrument panel. Author

AWADS (Adverse Weather Aerial Delivery System) and was thus able to navigate to its own release point. There were six Hercules in the 'package': two AWADS and their wingmen. Maturi was to have led to gain lead experience – what was termed 'spreading the wealth' – but an enforced delay aboard Capt Warren H. Hurst's C-130, who was to have been the No. 2, meant that he flew his slot. Hurst's co-pilot was Capt Catherine A. Jacob, one of three female pilots in the 37th ALS; Hurst would catch up as the mission progressed. To the left, Capt Gallagher nosed out to take the third slot, then a fourth with Captains Mike Hampton and Ed Brewer at the controls. Hampton's aircraft was an AWADS-equipped Hercules. Capt Jones, who was to have flown the fifth slot, had a malfunction and the spare aircraft, piloted by Maj Douglas D. Delozier, filled in.

Peiffer was soon climbing away into leaden skies, and UN43 followed. Maturi opened the throttles and the C-130 rumbled along the runway; there was a slight judder as it gained height and the wheels were retracted. The orange scope of the AN/APN-169A SKE (Station-Keeping Equipment) atop the instrument panel showed a reassuring line of five red blips with a circle (us) behind the lead blip. To the left of the SKE, the flight command indicator, or the 'fluter phone', waited to be used to pass commands to the other aircraft. The layer of black cloud grew wider. On intercom Maturi said, 'We are now entering the "bumpy zone"!' Peiffer's white-flashing tail-navigation lights disappeared into the cloud; he turned, and Maturi turned also. The conga-line on the SKE followed a fraction later. At 7,000ft (2,000m), the C-130 started to pick up icing and leading-edge de-icers had to be turned on; only the faithful line of red blips following on the SKE lit up the console.

Priorities for drops over Bosnia were provided by US European Command (EUCOM) from the UNHCR office in Geneva. EUCOM would pass the information to Joint Task Force at Naples, where a targeting board convened daily to assess information and determine where formations would drop. The information was then passed to planners and schedulers at Rhein-Main who put together the actual mission. Airdrops had concentrated mainly on Mostar recently due to the large numbers of refugees there.

West of Munich Maturi followed Peiffer in the turn; Maturi applied 20 degrees of bank. Intercom conversation was staccato, short, and to the point. Maturi and Brignola agree that it is harder to be element leader, which they are, than formation leader. At this point Jim Carezas, the satcomm operator, has informed Naumann that a fighter pilot has reported triple A in the area. However, it was made on VHF in the clear, so the two pilots agree that it cannot be too sensitive. On intercom someone says, 'On some nights I hear word of twenty sightings – let's press on.'

The moon was high above as the C-130 skimmed the clouds below. Misty gossamer trails scudded past, while in front huge clouds loomed like polar ice caps; Maturi banked away slightly to avoid turbulence. There was a city below: lights, lots of them. There were no stars visible, only the twinkling of Peiffer's nav' lights. Maturi had got a little high, so he banked lightly to the left; the blips followed obediently like carriages being pulled by a locomotive. There was a brief, tantalizing glimpse of the Alps in a rare shaft of moonlight, though the pilots were seemingly oblivious to the majestic sight. They were thinking ahead, fully aware of the dangers a full moon presented over the drop zone.

'Full moon out there.'

'Means we'll be visible over Bosnia.'

'Yeah, could do with some cloud.'

On the interphone came a chilling reminder of the recent shooting down, on 28 February, by F-16Cs, of four Serbian SOKO G-4 Super Galeb jets – the first confirmed violation of the UN aid resolution by fixed-wing aircraft since NATO began Operation *Deny Flight* in April 1993: 'Unidentified aircraft land immediately or I will have to take action. You are in violation of UN Resolution 816.' Nothing further is heard, and the pilots showed no more concern in their voices than they did before. Mark Naumann cut in, 'Twenty minutes off our combat checklist'.

The formation headed inexorably into Croatian and then Bosnian airspace. Somewhere out there F-16 escort fighters were patrolling, protecting their 'assets', as the C-130s are termed. Apart from the Hercules there was another, smaller 'package' of French and German Air Force Transalls heading for their drop zone at Tesanj.

The crew donned their flak vests. Maturi discarded his lucky cap, put on his light-blue helmet and clamped his oxygen mask on. Everyone followed suit. Thumbs up showed that everyone's oxygen system was working normally as Carezas turned the controls to depressurize the cabin and the hold. Everyone was now breathing pure oxygen. Navigation and cabin lights were extinguished, and the cockpit was bathed in a red hue; Naumann called out the time to the IP (Initial Point), and Higginbotham checked the fuel gauges above his head.

WHOOMPF!

Alarmed, Naumann exclaimed 'What was that?' He didn't wait for an answer – 'Did we make a hit? Did any pieces fly off?' Fortunately it was nothing more than an air pocket.

The DZ was Bjelimici, south-west of Sarajevo. Naumann explained the drop procedure: 'AWADS enables us to make airdrops at night or in bad weather when we cannot visually see the drop zone. We have a GPS NAVISTAR navigational computer so we can programme radar targets into the computer, call up the targets, and it projects cross-hairs onto the radar scope over the targets; we can then see if the cross-hairs are accurately placed on the target. If not, the navigator can manually move the cross-hairs over the target to update the navigational computer. Then we fly off the navigational computer to the release point to make the drop. The rear ramp is lowered. Coming into the drop we slow down a certain distance out, making a series of warning calls – thirty seconds slow down, five seconds slow down, then the slow-down call itself, slowing down to our drop zone air-speed, which is 140 knots.

Naumann made a one-minute advisory call. He added 'Confidence high – "Dee Zee" ahead,' and sends a 'Down Prep' on the SKE system, which our followers receive. He then made a ten-second call, and sent another 'Down Prep' which our wingmen following us received.

Through all of this he has been evaluating wind speed and altitude, and passing on flight directions to Maturi. The biggest variable that occurs after the load exits is the wind. For example, a 10-knot crosswind airdropping at, say, 10,000ft (3,000m), causes the load to drift about 800 yards (730m) over the ground. The Hercules is travelling at about 100 yards (90m) per second, at a drop airspeed of 140 knots. Naumann used his equipment to evaluate the winds, speed of aircraft and all of these sorts of parameters, forecast versus the actual, to come up with the CARP, or computed release point. Maturi eased the control column back to reduce his airspeed, and raised the nose about 8 degrees to allow the CDS to exit from the rear cargo door.

Once Naumann had the DZ in the cross-hairs he informed the pilots: 'Green light, Green light, Green light!' Brignola threw the switch that released the cargo-restraining strap, and the extraction process was set in motion: slowly at first the six pallets of food bundles, medical boxes, clothing, blankets and tetanus serum, slid down the rollers towards the black void. The small chemical green pen-lights which stay lit for more than eight hours to aid recovery of the CDS on the ground, swung pendulously on the webbing straps. It took only about four seconds but it seemed longer – and then suddenly they were gone. Each bundle was attached to a conventional 26ft (8m) ring-slot parachute, opened by static line; the parachutes bring the bundles in at about 60mph (100kmph). Special packing techniques ensure the survival of the contents: on one occasion, 4,000 glass vials of penicillin were dropped near a hospital, and not one broke!

Meanwhile, in the six C-130s leaving the area above, the loadmasters confirmed, 'Load clear!' Down below, Bosnia was illuminated by many hundreds of lights – and aboard UN43, Capt Brignola remarked on how strange it was that a country at war had so much electricity. The total flight-time was going to be around six hours by the time the C-130 touched down at

Frankfurt, and upcoming vacations were discussed to help while them away.

At last the two parallel runways at Frankfurt appeared, their green landing and red exit bars glowing against the skyline. Minutes later the C-130 was down, and one by one the superb Hercules were marshalled into position by ground signallers using illuminated batons. Engines were cut, and the cabin lights came on. Another six cargoes of supplies had been delivered to Bosnia, and for the crews, a day of rest would be taken before it all began again – if not here, then somewhere else in Europe, or the Far East, or Africa: wherever the US air forces would be needed next.

Air-drop: The View from the Ground

Capt Jim Stockmore had the opportunity to observe an allied air-drop; here is his eye-witness account of it: 'The effort was well organized, with strict control measures in place. Prior to the drop, a crew of about sixty local residents under the control of the local police chief, Hurem Sahic, were in place around the drop zone. Most of the crew had walked the rugged uphill route from Zepa, a 15-kilometre trek, which takes about three hours by foot. They now huddled around a small fire, attempting to stay warm in the wind and snow on the high, flat drop site.

Before the drop, small sorties of NATO aircraft went over the area, an indication that the C-130 Hercules aircraft were not far behind. The window for the drop had been passed the day before, through the UNMO CAPSAT communications net, the only link to the outside world. Within the announced time-window, the aircraft arrived over the drop zone. An eerie silence fell on the hilltop.

The crew knew instinctively that at any moment the pallets would drop somewhere in the area. The rate of descent – about 50mph – also meant that any one of them could be crushed to death; however, through experience they had learned where to position

themselves to minimize the threat. Even so, their silence was indicative of their anxiety.

The pallets began to hit with a loud thud. Three struck the south side of the drop zone ahead of the others; then minutes later, a ripple of impacts, similar to the sound made by dud artillery rounds, echoed across the field. There was a chorus of cheers from the crew, and after waiting about fifteen minutes to ensure there were no more drops, they rushed to find the pallets. Each was guarded throughout the cold night by a member of Hurem's crew.

'The Bosnians expected fifty-six pallets, based on the information passed though the UNMOs. Altogether, three US planes dropped a total of forty-one CDS bundles, and by 06:00 hours, thirty-five pallets had been found. Three had come down without fully deployed parachutes, but without damage to the contents. Hurem's crew made inventories of the contents of the pallets, and loaded them on Ukrainian trucks for the trip down the hill to Zepa. On arrival the cargo was again inventoried, then warehoused and distributed by the local government. Two persons were arrested for attempting to enter the drop zone and pilfer cargo.'

EC-130 62-1863 (3827) The Iron Horse **in the 42nd AACS, 355th Wing, at Aviano, Italy during Operation Deliberate Force in Bosnia, September 1995. Behind is EC-130 62-1836 (3799).** Gary Madgwick/The Aviation Workshop

CHAPTER SEVEN

Civvy C-130s

In 1959 Lockheed announced that Pan American Airways had ordered twelve GL-207 Super Hercules for delivery in early 1962, and that Slick Airways was to receive six later in the year. They were to differ from the C-130B in being 23ft 4in (7.11m) longer, with wingspan increased by 12ft 5in (3.78m), and were to have a maximum take-off gross weight of 204,170lb (92.610kg). The intention was to power the Super Hercules with 6,000 eshp Allison T61 engines, and in 1960 a GL-307 version with 6,445 eshp Rolls-Royce Tynes and gross weight of 230,000lb (104,326kg) was also proposed. Moreover in that same year a jet-powered version with four 22,000lb/9,979kg thrust Pratt and Whitney JT3D-11 turbofans, a 250,000lb (113,398kg) gross weight, and with a maximum cruising speed of 564mph at 20,000ft (907kmph at 6,095m) was put forward. However, Pan American and Slick cancelled their orders for GL-207s, and these other versions did not progress beyond the initial study phase. Since then, all commercial versions of the C-130 have been straightforward developments of the production aircraft. To date, civil Hercules have been produced in three versions: L-100, L-100-20, and L-100-30.

L-100 (Models 382 and 382B): A total of 114 L-100 commercial models have been built. They differ from the military Hercules in that the underwing fuel tanks have been omitted, and most military equipment removed, although the aircraft can be fitted with retractable combination wheel-skis. The L-100 demonstrator (382-3946 N1130E) made a very impressive first flight on 20/21 April 1964, when it remained airborne or 25 hours 1 minute; and all except 36 minutes of this time were flown using just two of the 4,050 eshp Allison 501-D22 engines (the commercial version of the C-130's T56). N1130E was used to obtain a type certificate on 16 February 1965. It was subsequently modified to Model 382E/L-100-20, being 'stretched' with a 5ft (1.52m) fuselage plug forward of the wing, and a 3.3ft (1.02m) plug aft to bring cabin-hold volume from 4,500cu ft (127.4cu m) to 5,335cu ft (151cu m). Eight more L-100s were later stretched to become L-100-20 models. Only one unmodified L-100 (4144) remains in service, with Pakistan air Force. This aircraft, and another unmodified L-

Only one unmodified L-100 (4144) remains in service, with the Pakistan Air Force. This aircraft, and another unmodified L-100 (4145), were acquired by the Pakistan government for Pakistan Airlines in October 1966, and were given the registrations AP-AUT and AP-AUU respectively. Both aircraft subsequently passed to the Pakistan Air Force, but AP-AUU was lost on 30 April 1968, when it crashed near Chaklala and was written off. W.F. Wilson, MCE via Frank Mason

100 (4145), were acquired by the Pakistan Government for Pakistan Airlines in October 1966, and were given the registrations AP-AUT and AP-AUU respectively. Both the aircraft subsequently passed to the Pakistan Air Force, but AP-AUU was lost on 30 April 1968 when it crashed near Chaklala and was written off.

The first commercial L-100 operator was Alaska Airlines which, on 8 March 1965, put into service the Hercules demonstrator, on lease from Lockheed. It later leased four more L-100s and purchased one, but by the end of the 1960s had disposed of all of them. Twenty-one production aircraft (Model 382B) were built as follows:

Airlift International Inc
N759AL (4225) and N760AL (4229).
Alaska Airlines
N9227R (4208); N9248R 842219;
N9267R 841469.
Continental Air Services
N9260R (4101); N9259R (4176);
N9268R (4147).
Delta Airlines
N9258R (4170); N9529R (4176);
N9268R (4147).
International Aerodyne
N9262R (4248).
Lockheed
N1130E (3946).
National Aircraft Leasing
N7999S (4234); N9266R (4250).

Pacific Western Airlines
CF-PWO (4197); N9263R (4134).
Pakistan International Airlines
AP-AUT and AP-AUU (4144/4145).
Zambian Air Cargo
9J-RBW, 9J-RBX (4129, 4137).

The first delivery of L-100, to Continental Air Services, took place on 30 September 1965. L-100s did not carry underwing fuel tanks and had most military equipment removed. They could be fitted with retractable combination wheel-skis.

The demonstrator and six Model 382Bs (4147, 4170, 4176, 4221/22 and 4125) were modified as L-100-20s, with their fuselage stretched an additional 8.3ft (2.54m) by fitting a 5ft (1.52m) plug forward of the wing, and a 3.3ft (1.02m) plug aft. 4129 and 4150 were modified likewise (but with 4050 eshp 501-D22s instead of 4510 eshp 501-D22As) to become Model 382F/L-100-20s.

L-100-20 (Models 382E and 382F)
The first L-100 versions were severely limited in cargo-carrying capacity, so to rectify this situation, Lockheed produced the L-100-20 version. Some twenty-seven L-100-

20s have been produced, nine of them modified from L-100s with their fuselage stretched an additional 8.3ft (2.54m) by fitting a 5ft (1.52m) plug forward of the wing, and a 3.3ft (1.02m) plug aft (3946, 4147, 4170, 4176, 4221/22 and 4125, and 4129 and 4250 likewise, but with 4050 eshp 501-D22s instead of 4510 eshp 501-D22As).

The L-100-20 was certificated on 4 October 1968, and entered service with Interior Airways one week later. Eight L-100-20s were later modified to L-100-30 configuration. 4412, an ex-Kuwaiti L-100-20, was modified as the experimental HTTB (High Technology Test Bed) for the C-130J etc., as part of a multiphase development programme to obtain STOL data for use in designing aircraft to meet USAF requirements for an advanced tactical transport. Phase 1 began on 19 June 1984, with the first flight of the modified L-100-20 which was then specially instrumented and fitted with a head-up display, a dorsal fin extension, and lateral strakes (horsals) ahead of the stabilizers. For Phase II trials, it was fitted in 1968 with double-slotted flaps, drooped wing leading edge, wing spoilers, extended chord ailerons and

Ex-Delta Airlines L-100 N105AK (4176) in Alaska International Air livery. This aircraft was delivered to Delta in October 1966 and modified to L-100-20 in December 1968 before being sold to Air Finance in September 1979 who leased it to AIA in October 1973. N105AK, now registered D2-FAF, was sold to CTA in September 1977 and operated during the late 1970s by Angola Cargo and TAAG-Angola Airlines; it was damaged in a landing at Sao Thomé on 15 May 1979, which resulted in it having to be written off. Lockheed

A Transamerica Airlines L-100 takes aboard a Rolls Royce RB-211 engine for flight from England to Lockheed-California Company's L-1011 commercial airliner assembly plant at Palmdale, California in December 1982. Three of the engines could be carried on one flight, a complete set for the TriStar *Lockheed*

Specification – Lockheed L-100-30

Powerplant:	Four Allison 501-D22A turboprops, each rated at 4,508eshp
Weights:	Operating 77,905lb (35,337kg); max. take-off 155,000lb (70,308kg); max. payload 50,885lb (23,081kg)
Dimensions:	Span 132ft 7in (40.41m); length 112ft 9in (34.37m); height 38ft 3in (11.66m); wing area 1,745sq ft (162.12sq m)
Performance:	Max. cruising speed at 120,000lb, 363mph (583km/h); rate of climb 1,700ft/min (518m/min); take-off 6,200ft (1,890m); landing at 135,000lb from 50ft 4,850ft (1,478m); range with max. payload and reserves 1,569 miles (2,526km); range with zero payload and reserves 5,733 miles (9,227km)

rudder, and a high-sink-rate undercarriage. Prior to Phase III, the HTTB received a steerable turret housing an FLIR (forward-looking infra-red) and a laser ranger and was later re-engined with 5,250 eshp T56A-101 propeller-turbines.

The L-100-20 civil customers are as follows:

Air America
N7951S (4301) (for Southern Air Transport). Air America also operated USAF C-130s in Laos in the war in south-east Asia.
First National Bank of Chicago
N9265R (4300) (for Interior Airways).
Flying W Airways
N60FW and N70FW (4358 and 4364).
Gabon
TR-KKB (4710).
Girard Trust
N7952S and N9237R (4302 and 4303) (for Flying W Airways).
Kuwait
317 and 318 (4350 and 4412).
National Aircraft Leasing/Maple Leaf Leasing
N7906S (4355).
Pacific Western Airlines
CF-PWX (4361).
Peru
382/384 (4706, 4708, 4715) 396/398 (4450, 4850, 4853).
Philippine Government
RP-C100 and RP-C101 (4512 and 4593).
Safmarine
ZS-GSK (4385).
Saturn Airways
N10ST (modified to L-100-30, April 1974 – leased to Southern Air Transport, July 1986 and registered to them in October 1987. Re-reg N911SJ, March 1988. Engine failed on take-off from Juba, Sudan, 12 August 1990. Returned for landing, over-ran runway, burned).
N11ST and N7957S (4383, 4384 and 4333).
Southern Air Transport
N7984S, N9232R (4362 and 4299).
TAAG-Angola Airlines
D2-EAS, D2-THA (4830 and 4832).

L-100-30
The main commercial version of the Hercules, with the delivery of twelve converted L-100s, stretched 15ft (4.6m), followed by fifty-three new-build examples. Power is provided by 4510 eshp 501-D22A engines. Aft doors are an optional fit.

Five L-100-30s (4950, 4952 – configured as a dental clinic – 4956/57, and 4960) were modified for use in Saudi Arabia as airborne

L-100-20 (4593), bought by the Philippine government in May 1975 and registered RP-C101, was leased to Philippine Aero-transport. Early in 1984 the civil registration was cancelled and the aircraft became 4593 in the Philippine Air Force. Lockheed

hospitals. In 1992 and 1993 respectively, 4950/HZ-MS05 and 4957/HZ-MS10 were demodified to L-100-30 with their hospital equipment removed.

Two other L-100-30s were sold to Armoflex for purported use in Benin, but finished up in the hands of the Libyan government. The L-100-30 entered service with Saturn airways in December 1970.

AFI International
N4248M (4992) N4269M (5000).
Advanced Leasing Corporation
N82178 (5048).
Air Algerie
7T-VGH (4880); 7T-VHK (4883) – w/o 1 August 1989); 7T-VHL (4886).
Air Gabon
TR-LBV (5024).
Alaska International Air
N108AK (4763); N501AK (4798).
Canadian Armed Forces
(5320) (modified to C-130H-30); (5307) (modified to C-130H-30).
China Air Cargo
B-3002 (5025); B-3004 (5027).
Dubai (now United Arab Emirates)
311 (4834).
Ecuador
893 (4893).

Ethiopian Airlines
ET-AJK (5022); ET-AJL (5029); ET-AKG (5306).
Frameair
PJ-TAC (5225); (5307 – not sold), to CAF (C-130H-30).
Gabon
TR-KKA (4582); TR-KKD (4895).
Indonesia
A-1314 (4800).
Indonesian Government
PK-PLR (4889); PK-PLS (4917); PK-PLT (4923).
Kuwait
322 (4949); 323 (4951); 324 (4953); 325 (4955).
Lockheed
N4110M (4839); (for Wirtschaftsflug); N4170M (4891); (for LADE).
Mitsui Corporation
PK-PLU (4824); PK-PLV (4826); PK-PLW (4828).
Pacific Western Airlines
C-GHPW (4799).
Pemex
XC-EXP (4851).
Safair Freighters
ZS-JIV (4673); ZS-JIW (4679); ZS-JIX (4684); ZS-JIY (4691); ZS-JIZ (4695); ZS-JJA (4698); ZS-JVL (4676); ZS-JVM

(4701); ZS-RSB (4472); ZS-RSC (4475); ZS-RSD (4477); ZS-RSE (4558); ZS-RSF (4562); ZS-RSG (4565); ZS-RSH (4590); ZS-RSI (4600); ZS-RSJ (4606).
Saturn Airways
N12ST (4388); N15ST (4391 – leased to Southern Air Transport, crashed into hangar, night take-off from Kelly AFB, 4 October 1986).
N20ST (4561); N21ST (4586).
Saudi Arabia
HZ-MS05 (4950); HZ-MS06 (4952); HZ-117 (4954); HZ-MS09 (4956); HZ-MS10 (4957); HZ-MS14 (4960).
SCIBE Zaire
9Q-CBJ (4796) (leased).
Southern Air Transport
N108AK (4763); N251SF (4590); N921SJ (4586); N519SJ (4562); N20ST/N920SJ (4561); N106AK (4477); N905SJ (4472).
Transporte Aereo Boliviano
CP-1564/TAM-92 (4833) (for Bolivian government).
Uganda Airlines
5X-UCF (4610).
Worldwide Trading
N4281M (5032).

In an effort to boost the Hercules' commercial market, Lockheed had proposed, and continues to market, a number of derivatives, including the L-100-50 (with a fuselage stretched by another 20ft/6.10m), the L-100-PX passenger transport with 100 seats, the L-100-30QC cargo/passenger convertible, and the L-100-30C combined cargo/passenger version. It also announced in January 1980 its decision to proceed with development and production of the L-400 Twin Hercules, a smaller and lighter version powered by two 4,910 eshp Allison 501-

D22Ds; however, this decision was later rescinded and development of the L-400 was shelved.

Operators, Past and Present

Algeria Three L-100-30s have been operated by Air Algérie, Algiers: 4880/7T-VHG has been operated since May 1981, and 4886/7T-VHL since July 1981; 4883/7T-

VHK was operated form June 1981 until August 1989, when it was written off after a ground loop during landing at Tamanrasset. Two other L-100/-20s have been leased.

Angola Twenty L-100, -20 and -30 have been operated by Angola Air Charter, Luanda, and TAAG Angolan Airlines, Luanda. L-100-20 (4176) (D2-FAF) was damaged whilst landing at Sao Thomé on 15 May 1979 while operating with TAAG,

(Above) **Air Algérie L-100-30 (N4152M/4883) 7T-VHK:** this aircraft was operated as a cargo plane by IAS from August 1988. It was damaged in a ground loop landing at Tamanrasset on 1 August 1989, and as a result was written off. via Frank Mason

(Below) **L-100-30 PK-PLV (4826) Hanonen of Pelita Air Service.** This aircraft was sold to Mitsui Corporation in August 1978 and leased to Pelita. In August 1989 it operated on lease in Angola; later it was leased to Heavylift, and subleased to TAAG before being operated by Heavylift, and finally for Heavylift by Pelita, in September 1994. It suffered a no. 4 engine overspeeding propeller, and crashed into water taking off from Kai Tak, Hong Kong on 24 September 1994. via Frank Mason

L-100-30 (4891) was registered N4170M in June 1981, and was used as a Lockheed demonstrator in May 1982; it was then sold in December 1982 to the Fuerza Aérea Argentina (FAA) where it was assigned to I Escuadron Brigata (LQ-FAA). It was re-registered LV-APW in January 1983 and is operated by Lineas Aéreas del Estade (LADE), Buenos Aires. via Frank Mason

and was written off. L-100 (4222) L-100-20 (D2-THA), bought by TAAG in October 1979, made a wheels-up landing at Dondo, Angola on 8 June 1986, caught fire, and was written off. L-100-20, also sold to TAAG (D2-EAS) at the same time, was shot down near Menongue, Angola, on 16 May 1981. (D2-THB), on lease to Transafrik, was hit by a missile at Menonque, Angola, on 5 January 1990, crash-landed and was written off. L-100-30 (4679) (D2-TAD) was damaged beyond repair by fire from overheated brakes landing at Malenge, Angola, on 7 April 1994. L-100-30 (4839)

D2-EHD, belonging to ENDIEMA, Angola, operated by Transafrik, and chartered by the UN, was lost after take-off from Huambo, Angola, on 2 January 1999 with all nine passengers and crew (possibly shot down by UNITA). This aircraft had previously been damaged by UNITA taking off from Luena in February 1993.

Argentina L-100-30 (4891) was operated by Lineas Aéreas del Estade (LADE), Buenos Aires.

Bolivia The Fuerza Aérea Boliviana's

Grupo Aereo de Transporte 71, based at BA General Walter Arze, La Paz, is operated on a peacetime basis as an internal domestic airline: Transporte Aereo Boliviano (TAB).

Canada L-100-30s operated by Canadian Airlines International, Vancouver, and Northwest Territorial Airways, Yellowknife, (leased).

China Two L-100-30s operated by China Air Cargo, Shanxi, currently for fish charter Tianjin-Japan.

Ecuador One L-100-30 operated by the government of Ecuador.

Ethiopia Two L-100-30 operated by Ethiopian Airlines, Addis Ababa.

France L-100-30 operated by EAS Air Cargo, Perpignan.

Gabon L-100-30 operated by Air Gabon, Libreville. L-100-30 operated by the Republic of Gabon government.

Indonesia L-100-30 operated by Merpati Nusantara Airlines, Jakarta, and Pelita Air Service, Jakarta.

Libya L-100-20s and -30s operated by Libyan Air Cargo. L-100-20 and -30 operated by Jamahiriya Air Transport, Tripoli.

Mexico Two ex-USAF C-130H military

L-100-30 (4851) XC-EXP of Pemex (Petroléos Mexicanos), who purchased the aircraft in April 1980 and operated it until April 1993 when it was acquired by FAM for operation by Escuadron 301. The aircraft was sold Protexa in September 1994. via Frank Mason

(56-0487 and 56-0537) and two ex-USAF RC-130As (57-0517 and 57-0518) were operated by Aeropostal, Mexico City. C-130A 56-0487 was sold in 1994 and both RC-130As were withdrawn from further use in 1996. L-100-30 operated by Petroleos, Mexicanos (Pemex), Mexico City.

Morocco The fourteen C-130 military transports operated by the Royal Maroc Air Force carry civilian-style registrations; these are worn with the aircraft construction number on the fin.

Netherlands L-100-30 leased by Schreiner Airways, Leiden.

Netherlands Antilles Frameair (TAC Holidays) has leased four L-100-30s at various times, and purchased one (5225); the latter was damaged in August 1993 during lease to TAAG Angola Air Charter, when a hand-grenade detonated accidentally in a cargo compartment while the aircraft was on the ground. It was sent to Luanda for repair; it is now in Mozambique. A second L-100-30 (5307) was contracted in February 1992 but not purchased; it went to the Canadian Armed Forces instead.

Philippines C-130A operated by Aboitiz Transport.

Sao Thomé L-100-20 and -30 operated by Transafrik. L-100-30 (4561) Sao Thomé registered S9-CA0, belonging to Transafrik, was lost after take-off from Huambo, Angola, 26 December 1998. All fourteen aboard, including eight members of the UN Observer Team were killed (possibly shot down by UNITA).

Saudi Arabia A fleet of five L-100-30s (4950, 4952, 4956/57, and 4960), and one C-130H-30 (4986) medically-configured Hercules, were operated by Saudi Special Services, Jeddah, in conjunction with No.1 Squadron (4952 is configured as a dental clinic). In 1992 and 1993 respectively, 4950 and 4957 were demodified to L-100-30, their hospital equipment removed.

South Africa SAFAIR Freighter (Pty) Ltd, Johannesburg, have operated nineteen L-100-20s/L-100-30s at various times; these are also available as a military reserve airlift asset. SAFAIR is a wholly owned subsidiary of Safren – Safmarine and Rennies Holdings Ltd the independent holding company which has grown to be one of Africa's giants in the fields of aviation, shipping, cargo services and security. The airline currently operates its charter services on Boeing 707 and Hercules aircraft, and operates freight and passenger charter flights across the length and breadth of the continent. Its facilities at Jan Smuts Airport, Johannesburg, is fully equipped to accommodate Airbus, Boeing 707 and Boeing 737 jets as well as L-100 aircraft. SAFAIR's Hercules are leased by private individuals and businessmen as well as some of the largest corporations on the continent. Approximately six remain in operation with SAFAIR, or on lease from the company.

Sudan Of the six C-130Hs operated, one aircraft has occasionally been seen in civilian guise wearing the markings of Sudan Airways and varying registrations.

Tunisia Two C-130Hs, which wear quasi-civilian markings.

Uganda L-100-30 (4610) was purchased in August 1975 by Uganda Airlines (5X-UCF) and was operated by Uganda Air Cargoes, Kampala, from August 1981 until September 1985 when it was impounded, and from September 1987 until April

L-100-30 (4695) ZS-JIZ Swiss Boogie **of SAFAIR, carrying out a 'Snowdrop' (food sachets) on the Piet Joubert Training Range, north of Pretoria, on 19 August 1993. This aircraft, like many civilian Hercules, has had a chequered career, operating from Nairobi for the Lutheran World Food, LWF in September 1995, and being leased to Transafrik for work in Angola, TAC Holdings (Frameair) and EFIS Cargo.** via Geoff Woodford

L-100-30 (4562) was bought by SAFAIR in November 1974. It is pictured in the colours of NW Territorial Airlines (C-FNWF) who operated it on lease from October 1978 to February 1982. Since October 1997 the aircraft has been operated by Transafrik. via Frank Mason

L-100-30 A2-ACA (4701) was sold to SAFAIR (ZS-JVM) in December 1976, who leased it to Air Botswana (A2-ACA) from 1979 until February 1987. During this time it was employed by the Red Cross in 1980, and it also flew relief supplies to the Lebanon during June and July 1982. In February 1987 it was registered to Zimex Aviation (HB-ILF); that same year it crashed after take-off from Cuito, Angola, on 14 October 1987. Starliner Aviation Press.

L-100-30 (4610) was purchased by Page Airways in August 1975 and sold the same month to Uganda Airlines under registration 5X-UCF. It was passed to Uganda Air Cargos in August 1981 where it became The Silver Lady, but it was impounded at Marshall of Cambridge in September 1985 because of German debts. In September 1987 it was returned to Uganda Air Cargo who used it until April 1993 before it was stored at Entebbe. The aircraft was impounded again, in Zaire in December 1995. It suffered a brake fire and wheel-bay damage in March 1996; repaired, in May 1997 it was sold to Medecair Foundation. MAP

(*Above*) **C-130A (3189) N133HP (formerly 57-482) of Hawkins & Powers, pictured at Greybull, Wyoming, in August 1989. The aircraft was retired from the Air Force, and in March 1989 was registered to Hawkins & Powers as N8026J, one of three Hercules water-bombers currently by H & P, which at one time or another has leased or purchased ten C-130s. The majority have either been scrapped or used for parts, while N135FF (ex C-130A 56-0540) crashed at Pallette Mountain, 19 miles (30km) south-east of Palmdale, California, after an explosion in no. 2 engine, probably a fuel leak, on 13 August 1994.** Author

1993. It is currently operated by Medecair Foundation.

United States of America
Advanced Leasing Corporation (L-100-30).
Aero Firefighting Services, Anaheim, CA (C-130A).
African Cargo Inc, Miami, FL (C-130A).
Butler Aircraft Co, Richmond, OR (C-130A).
Flight Cargo Leasing Inc, Dover, NY (L-100-30).
Hemet Valley Flying Service Inc, Hemet, CA (C-130A).
IEP IEPO, Chatsworth, CA (C-130A).
Military Aircraft Restoration Corporation, Anaheim, CA (C130A).
National Aeronautics and Space Administration (NASA), Moffett Field, CA, (NC-130B), and Wallops Island, VA (EC-130Q).
National Oceanic and Atmospheric Administration, Miami, FL (L-100-30, EC-130Q).
National Science Foundation (EC-130Q).
Pacific Gateway Investments, Orange, CA (C-130A).

L-100-30 (4796) was bought by SAFAIR in November 1978 and leased to SCIBE-Zaire (9Q-CBJ) the same month. It was then stored at Brussels from October 1988 to January 1989, when it was registered to Pegasus Aviation, Houston, Texas, as N123GA. It was then registered to Rapid Air Transport, Washington DC as N8183J in February 1989, and leased to Tepper Aviation, who have used it on operations for the US government. Lockheed

Pacific Harbor Capital Inc, Portland, OR (C-130A).
Pegasus Aviation Co (L-100-30).
Rapid Air Trans, Washington DC (LC-100-30).
Snow Aviation International Inc., Columbus, OH (C-130A)
Southern Air Transport, Miami, FL (L-100-20/-30).
T&G Aviation, Chandler, AZ (C-130A).
TBM Inc., Redmond, OR (C-130A).
World Wide Trading Inc., Delray Beach, FL (L-100-30).

Yemen Yemenia, Sanaa (C-130H).

Zambia Five L-100s have been used by the Zambian government and Zambia Air Cargoes, and possibly the air force, too. 4109 was destroyed in a ground collision with 4137 at Ndola on 11 April 1968. 4209, operated by ZAC from April 1964 until 1969, was sold by the insurance company to AIA; it was destroyed on the ground when the cargo exploded at Galbraigh Lake on 30 August 1974, 4101 was operated on lease by ZAC from August 1968 until

early 1969. It was modified to L-100-30 configuration in 1972 and, after being operated by several users, was destroyed on the ground at Caafunfo, Angola, during a UNITA guerrilla attack on 29 December 1984. C/No. 4129 *Alexander* was bought by ZAC in 1966 and sold to Maple Leaf Leasing in 1969. It was rebuilt as L-100-20 and enjoyed a colourful career with St Lucia Airways, operating as *Juicy Lucy* transports to UNITA, and *Grey Ghost* in Tepper Aviation; it crash-landed at Jamba in Angola on 27 November 1989.

L-100-20 and L-100-30s of Southern Air Transport photographed at Moi International Airport, Mombasa, Kenya, in February 1993 during Operation Provide Relief to supply Somali refugees. Author

N226LS Feed the Hungry, ex-TAC C-130A 55-0025 and ex-Peru FAP381, pictured in Turkey in 1991. In November 1990 this aircraft was registered N226LS to the Lester Sumrall Evangelistic Association. In June 1991 the aircraft became Mercy Ship Zoe, and in December 1991, N226LS Feed The Hungry, before being repurchased by the Peruvian Air Force in 1997 for service with Grupo 41. Mick Jennings

CHAPTER EIGHT

Albert RAF

Throughout its very long and distinguished history, RAF Transport Command – renamed Air Support Command on 1 August 1967, and reduced to a group of Strike Command a year later – boasted one of the finest indigenous transport fleets in the world. This all came to an abrupt end when the standard medium-range tactical transports, the piston-engined Handley

three months after the Beverley. By late 1967 only two transport squadrons of Hastings remained in service with the RAF, while Beverleys were finally withdrawn from RAF service at the end of the year.

No British replacement would be found, because two years earlier the UK government had seen fit to cancel the Hawker-Siddeley AW 681 V/STOL jet-powered

1965 the RAF operated no less than nineteen different types of transport aircraft – Britain of course had, and continues to operate, American-built aircraft; the ubiquitous C-47 (DC-3) Dakota is one of the few American transports to see service in the RAF. The decision to go for the Hercules was not difficult, particularly when it was agreed that British companies could be

C-130K/C.Mk.1 Hercules XV190 (4210) and XV303 (4271) of the Lyneham Wing. RAF Air Support Command in 1974 in the early high-gloss sand/brown upper surface and black under surface scheme. Sixty-six C-130K models were purchased by Great Britain for the RAF. The first flew on 19 October 1966, and as the Hercules C.MK.1, entered service with No. 242 OCU at Thorney Island in April 1967. XV190 was delivered to Marshall Engineering in May 1967, it was modified to C.Mk.3 in May 1985 and received SKE in July 1989; it was modified again, to C.Mk.3P, in June 1991. It was named Betty Boop in July 1994. XV303 was modified to C.Mk.3 in March 1981 and to C.Mk.3P in July 1996. Mick Jennings

Page Hastings and Blackburn Beverley, were replaced in the late sixties by the Hercules. Its introduction to RAF service marked a massive increase in performance over these types, cruising some 160mph (257kmph) faster than the Beverley, and it is even more amazing when one remembers that the Hercules had flown in production form only

tactical transport project. The late-lamented Short Belfast strategic freighters could not cope with the RAF freight needs by themselves – only ten were ever built – and these were phased out in 1976 when No. 53 Squadron was disbanded on 14 September 1976. During World War II and after – and it is worthy of note that between 1945 and

permitted to sub-manufacture avionics equipment and other components, and since the only home-produced contender had been cancelled.

The version chosen for issuing to RAF Transport Command was essentially the C-130H-130 airframe with 4,508 eshp T56-A-15 engines. Although re-engining

C.Mk.1 XV181 (65-13026/4198) engaged on mercy flights, pictured at Lyneham in 1985. This aircraft joined
No. 36 Squadron in June 1967, and then No. 242 OCU in March 1975. It was damaged in June that year,
repaired, and in December 1988 was fitted with an in-flight refuelling probe to become a C.Mk.1P. In
December 1997 XV181 was chosen to test the C-130J engine. Mick Jannings

the aircraft with Rolls-Royce Tynes was suggested in some quarters, its supporters failed to win the day, perhaps because of the problems at that time with the re-engined, Spey-powered RAF Phantoms. Although the Hercules retained the Allison engines, Britain's subcomponent contribution was politically as well as financially expedient, and so significant that it led to the RAF Hercules production versions being given their own designation. Thus the C-130K was born. In RAF service the new transport would be designated the Hercules C.Mk.1. In 1965 an order for sixty-six C-130Ks was placed by the British Government, making the RAF the second-largest Hercules user after the USAF (Iran later received sixty-four C-130s). Some components would be manufactured by Scottish Aviation, and British electronics were to be fitted by Marshall of Cambridge (Engineering) Ltd, the prime British sub-contractor, responsible for the support and co-ordination of all engineering development.

The first C-130K (65-13021/XV176) flew at Marietta, Georgia, on 19 October 1966. This remained in the US for six months of flight-testing, and the second aircraft (XV177) became the first Hercules

delivered to Marshall, on 16 December. This, together with the third aircraft (XV178), underwent Service trials at the A&AEE (Aircraft and Armament Experimental Establishment) at Boscombe Down, in February and March 1967 respectively. No. 36 Squadron, which had flown the Hastings at Colerne, moved to Lyneham, Wiltshire, and became the first squadron in the RAF to begin re-equipment with the C.Mk.1., in July and August 1967. The only other Hercules in RAF service at this time were six operated by No. 242 OCU at Thorney Island, Hampshire, which had received its first C.Mk.1 in April. C.Mk.1s were flown out to Singapore to equip a second ex-Hastings squadron, No. 48, at RAF Changi, in October 1967.

Final deliveries to the RAF of the C.Mk.I were made in 1968. During February, May and June, Nos 24, 47 and 30 Squadrons respectively converted to the Hercules, No. 24 joining No. 36 Squadron at Lyneham, and the other two being based at RAF Fairford. In 1970, No. 70 Squadron at Akrotiri, Cyprus, became the sixth Hercules squadron when it began receiving C.Mk.1s. that November to fly alongside its Argosys.

During the period 1971 to 1975 all Hercules squadrons came together in one wing

and operated from Lyneham. No. 70 Squadron returned to England in January 1975, and No. 48 Squadron left Changi in September, both to join the Lyneham Wing, although the later disbanded there, in January 1976. No. 36 Squadron disbanded in November 1975. The end result of all these changes left the Hercules equipping four front-line squadrons (Nos 24, 30, 47 and 70 Squadrons), and No. 242 OCU at Lyneham (in July 1992 the OCU was renumbered as No. 57, (Reserve) Squadron). Along the way four aircraft were written off between 1969 and 1973: XV180, operated by No. 242 OCU, stalled on a three-engined take-off from RAF Fairford on 24 March 1969. XV216, belonging to No. 242 OCU, crashed in the sea after take-off from Melovia, Italy, on 9 November 1971. XV194, used by No. 48 Squadron, veered off the runway when landing at Tromsö, Norway, on 12 September 1972, and was scrapped for parts. XV198, also belonging to No. 48 Squadron, crashed when an engine failed on a three-engined touch-and-go training flight at Colerne on 10 September 1973.

Introduction into service for any aircraft type is never straightforward, and the Hercules also had its problems. In 1969,

Marshall's discovered that the service use of contaminated fuel had corroded many of the C.Mk.1s' integral wing tanks; this resulted in eleven Hercules being withdrawn from front-line squadrons, and each had its 48ft (15m) long tanks either completely or partially replaced with new components manufactured by Lockheed. In 1972, XV208 was taken out of service with No. 48 Squadron and delivered to Marshall's for extensive modification as the Hercules W.Mk.2 for weather reconnaissance and research by the Royal Aircraft Establishment's Meteorological Research Flight at Farnborough. Once completed, *Snoopy*, as this aircraft is affectionately known, flew on 31 March 1973.

During 1972–85, Marshall's modified the Hercules' outer wing structure, wing joints and engine truss mounts to extend the life of the C.Mk.1 airframes. (In 1975 the company was appointed by Lockheed as an authorized Hercules Service Centre, which meant that Marshall's could now carry out engineering support of any Hercules operator in the world.) When a structural test programme conducted by Marshalls in January 1975 revealed a major failure in the test aircraft, the decision was taken to modify all the C.Mk.1s with a redesigned centre section; this had been first introduced by Lockheed for the USAF's C-130A, E and HC-130H aircraft in 1968. Marshall's completed this modification in 1979. In addition to all of this work, beginning in 1976, Marshall Engineering began major servicing of the RAF Hercules fleet, dealing with each aircraft on a three-year cycle. For three years, from 1976–79, all the C.Mk.1s were also put through an anti-corrosion programme to extend their service life.

In 1978 meanwhile, the MoD had decided to fund a 'stretch' programme to bring thirty C.Mk.1s up to C.Mk.3 standard to increase the available cabin volume by 37 per cent and so increase capacity from ninety-two to 129 infantrymen, or from sixty-four to ninety-two paratroops. This decision followed Lockheed's success in extending the commercial L-100-20 and -30 by using a 5ft (1.52m) 'plug' forward of the wing and a 3.3ft (1.02m) 'plug' aft. XV223 was therefore flown back to Marietta late in 1979 to become the prototype of the Hercules C.Mk.3. XV223 first flew in modified form on 3 December 1979. It returned to Britain in January 1980 to undergo Service trials with 'B' Flight at the A&AEE. Plugs were manufactured by Lockheed and shipped to Marshall's where the remaining twenty-nine C.Mk.1s were stretched to be brought up to C.Mk.3 standard. All were completed by the end of November 1985.

Bending a C-130 wing on the test rig at Marshall Engineering. During 1972–85, Marshall's modified the Hercules' outer wing structure, wing joints and engine truss mounts to extend the life of the C.Mk.1 airframes. When a structural test programme conducted by Marshall's revealed, in January 1975, a major failure in the test aircraft, the decision was taken to modify all the C.Mk.1s with a redesigned centre-section first introduced by Lockheed for the USAF's C-130A, E and HC-130H aircraft in 1968. Marshall's completed this work in 1979. Marshall Aerospace

Humanitarian Airlifts, 1970–1981

The Hercules' range of over 4,500 miles (7,240km) carrying a payload of nearly 20,000lb (9,080kg), or 2,500 miles (4,022km) with 45,000lb (20,430kg) gave the RAF a transport equally suited to tactical and strategic roles. It could carry and airdrop (if necessary by the 'ultra low-level airdrop' (ULLA) method only yards above the ground) a wide range of military equipment, or sixty-two paratroops or ninety-two

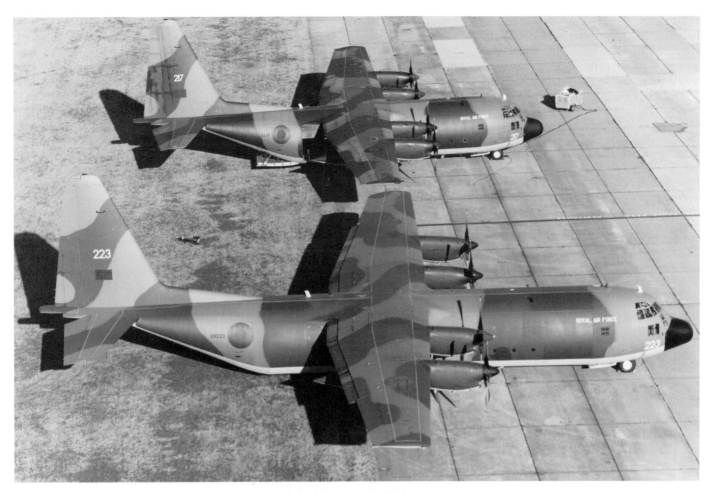

(Above) **XV223 (4253) was modified by Lockheed as the prototype of the Hercules C.Mk.3. with fuselage 'stretched' by 15ft (4.57m) to increase capacity from ninety-two to 129 infantrymen, or from sixty-four to ninety-two paratroops. This aircraft first flew in modified form on 3 December 1979. Twenty-nine C.Mk.1s (including XV217) were subsequently stretched by Marshall Engineering, to be brought up to C.Mk.3 standard.** Lockheed

XV189 and XV217 undergoing the -30 stretch for conversion to C.Mk.3s at Marshall Engineering in April 1982. In the background is XV200, then in the process of being modified to the C.Mk.1P prototype. XV217 was completed in October, and XV189 in December that year. Both were later modified to C.3P standard. Marshall Aerospace

passengers. The Spartan facilities in the hold in a Hercules mean that it is not the most comfortable place in which to find oneself, but when you are fleeing from danger in the world's troublespots or delivering aid to oppressed regions in far-off lands, a task for which the RAF has been renowned for almost the past thirty years, then comfort is usually the last consideration.

In 1970 RAF Hercules assisted in earthquake relief operations in Turkey and Peru, and cyclone relief operations in East Pakistan. During the 1971 war between India and Pakistan, in eighteen sorties between 10 and 12 December, Hercules transports evacuated 909 British and friendly foreign nationals from West Pakistan, and 434 from a bomb-cratered runway in East

Pakistan. In 1972 Lyneham's Hercules helped with typhoon relief in the Philippines, earthquake relief in Nicaragua, as well as reinforcement of Belize to counter threat of invasion by that country. In March 1973, No. 46 Group was involved in Operation *Khana Cascade*, the biggest airlift since Berlin in 1948, in which Hercules dropped almost 2,000 tons (2,032 tonnes) of grain, maize and rice to Himalayan villagers in Nepal. (In 1980 the RAF Hercules returned, in *Khana Cascade* 80.) In 1973 also, Hercules assisted in famine relief in

Phnom Penh, Cambodia. An evacuation of the British Embassy in Saigon, South Vietnam, was made under fire. Emergency reinforcement of Belize and earthquake relief in the Van region of Turkey was carried out, but all RAF units in Cyprus were withdrawn to the UK, except a few Whirlwind helicopters but including transports.

All operations were mounted despite economic factors which saw huge reductions in British overseas commitments. The transport force perhaps suffered more than most, certainly during the late 1960s and early

Red Cross in Kampuchea, and delivered civil relief to Nicaragua during the civil war there. For three months during 1979–80, six RAF Hercules were used in Operation *Agila* to resupply British forces in Rhodesia (later to become Zimbabwe) stationed there to help monitor the ceasefire and the setting up of free elections after a long and bloody civil war. Main operations were flown from the capital, Salisbury, and about five other towns, as well as remote air drop zones (DZs). The latter posed the biggest threat to air operations. There had been no time to fit the RAF Hercules with defence against infra-red guided surface-to-air missiles (SAMs), but the main danger came from Patriotic Front small arms and anti-aircraft artillery (AAA). The 'Fat Alberts' were flown at lo-lo altitudes of 250ft at a speed of 210 knots to minimize the SAM threat. Operations were flown without accident, although there were a few near-misses, the main problem being a few bird strikes.

On 3 August 1981 a stretched C.MK.3 of No. 70 Squadron left Lyneham to rescue British holidaymakers stranded in the Gambia following an attempted coup. Operating from Dakar, Senegal, the RAF crew, under the command of squadron leader Rod Caffady, evacuated approximately 200 refugees from Banjul airport during the following week.

Nepalese children at Surkhet sift grain just brought to them by C.Mk.1 XV200 (4223) of No. 46 Group (RAF) Transport Command during the March 1973 Operation Khana Cascade. **This aircraft became the C.Mk.1P prototype in April 1982.** RAF

Operation *Bushell*

On 31 October 1984 the RAF flew a detachment of two Hercules, four aircrews and fifty ground staff at short notice to Addis Ababa to assist in the distribution of famine-relief supplies in Ethiopia. Within hours of arriving in Addis Ababa the RAF detachment was in action flying up-country, delivering grain into some of the roughest and most inhospitable airstrips in the world. The RAF transports were joined in due course by military aircraft from five other nations. Operation *Bushell*, as it was called, was initially intended as a three-month effort (by year-end, the Hercules had ferried more than 3,500 tons of supplies), but it continued into 1985, making it the longest sustained relief effort ever. It involved aircraft from Nos 47 and 80 Squadrons, specially trained in low-level air-drop techniques, with crews rotating regularly. The tropical heat and the altitude of the Ethiopian plateau posed problems similar to those which the RAF had experienced in Rhodesia in 1980.

Sudan, Mali, and West Africa, and deployed UN peacekeepers to the Middle East after the Yom Kippur war.

In 1974, Hercules dropped relief supplies to St Helena, and gave assistance to cyclone relief in north Australia, and famine relief in North Africa. 1974 was also the first year that the Hercules first began deploying troops to Northern Ireland. In July, during the war in Cyprus, the RAF airlifted 13,430 service and civilian families by Hercules, VC-10s, Britannias, Belfasts and Comets. One Hercules alone airlifted 139 people from Dhekelia to Akrotiri. On 10 March 1975, Hercules of No. 48 Squadron evacuated civilians from

1970s. It had started in November 1967 when British forces had left Aden. In November 1971 the Far East Air Force was disbanded, and in December, the withdrawal of all units in the Arabian Gulf was complete. In March 1976 a Short Belfast became the last RAF transport to leave this island outpost in the Indian Ocean. Although by September the last of the Belfasts followed the same fate as the Comet C.Mk.4s, the Andovers and the Brittanias, aircraft that represented high-operating costs, the Hercules fleet remained relatively intact.

In 1979, RAF Hercules evacuated Western nationals from Iran, assisted in earthquake relief in Yugoslavia, supported the

Corporate: The Hercules' Finest Hour

Britain suddenly had a war on its hands in the South Atlantic on 2 April 1982 when Argentinian forces invaded the Falkland Islands. The UN attempted to persuade the ruling junta in Buenos Aires that it should withdraw its forces of occupation from the islands, but to no avail. Even though the British government had already decided to mount an operation to retake the islands, Britain's action was legitimized by the UN following this failure to resolve the situation diplomatically.

The RAF was not the only combatant to operate the Hercules in the war. At the start of the conflict, the Fuerza Aérea Argentina (Argentine Air Force) had nine Hercules – two C-130Es, five C-130Hs, and two KC-130H tankers – in its operational strength. On 3 April eight Hercules left Lyneham and staged through Gibraltar to Wideawake airfield on the British-owned island of Ascension (4,260 miles/6,855km from Britain, and 3,915 miles/6,300km from Stanley). One aircraft carried a six-man team from the UK Mobile Air Movements Squadron (UK MAMS) in order to establish an airhead for the Hercules fleet from the UK. Apart from the need to organize, equip and deploy a large naval task force to repossess the islands, one other major consideration centred on how the very long-range supply mission could be best carried out. On 21 April, the first airdrop by Hercules from Ascension Island to ships of the Task Force took place. In the first three weeks of *Corporate*, as the

operation to retake the Falklands was called, some 163 flights were made by Hercules aircraft and they delivered almost 1,500 tons of stores and equipment for the Task Force. In addition, two chartered Boeing 707s and even some ex-RAF Belfasts, supplemented the RAF Hercules effort.

These supporting operations posed no immediate problems to the RAF. Hercules crews were already familiar with this route, staging through Gibraltar (southbound) and Dakar (northbound), where they ground-refuelled for the legs to and from Ascension Island. However, the range performance of Nos 47 and 70 Squadron's Hercules would have to be substantially increased if they were to support the Task Force as far as Port Stanley in the Falklands itself. Provision for in-flight refuelling would have to be made. In the interim, beginning on 16 April, the Engineering Wing at Lyneham adapted and began fitting surplus 825 Imperial gallon (3,750 litre) auxiliary tanks intended for use in Andovers and Argosys, subsequently held in store, in the forward fuselage of the C.Mk.1s. This added some 13,200lb (5,990kg) of fuel to the Hercules' standard 63,000lb (28,580kg), increasing the range by approximately 1,000 miles and extending the maximum endurance by about four hours. The converted aircraft became known as LR2s and adaption was completed in just five days. A further increase in range was effected by installing four tanks in the forward fuselage instead of two, and these aircraft became known as LR4s. The first LR version was deployed to Ascension on 4 May.

Marshall Moves It

Meanwhile, a further increase in range was being achieved, when on 15 April Marshall of Cambridge was urgently directed, as a matter of high priority, to design, install, test and fit, 15ft (4.5m) in-flight refuelling probes (modification 5308) to twenty-five C.Mk.1s, which, when completed, would be designated C.Mk.1Ps. On 30 April, Marshall also received word from the MoD that it should prepare a TI (trial installation) for a Hercules tanker using the standard Flight Refuelling Ltd hose-drum unit (HDU, or 'hudu') Mk.17B, which British Aerospace were using to help convert six Vulcan K.Mk.2 tankers at Manchester. In all, six modified C.Mk.1s, designated C.Mk.1Ks, would be required to serve as tankers. In-flight refuelling conversion on this scale had never been attempted before, except for a small number of EC-130Es in the USAF which had received underwing probes. In Britain the Vulcans were the only aircraft already 'probed', but their in-flight refuelling systems had not been used for some fifteen years, and crews were not current in the refuelling technique.

The task facing Marshall's was huge, and it would mean working right around the clock. Since no new probes could be made in the time available, Marshall Engineering produced a probe installation fashioned from a standard Flight Refuelling Ltd probe with a Mk.8 nozzle fitted to a surplus Vulcan. Using as the prototype C.Mk.1P, XV200 (which was at Cambridge for routine engineering), it was

The prototype C.Mk.1P, XV200, completed by Marshall Engineering in just ten days, made its first flight fitted with the probe installation on 28 April 1982; it was delivered the next day to the A&AEE. The aircraft passed its first test with flying colours on 2 May when it successfully transferred fuel to a Victor K.2; on 5 May it was redelivered to No. 47 Squadron at Lyneham. Marshall Aerospace

C.Mk.1s nearing completion at Marshall Engineering after having their in-flight refuelling equipment fitted to C.Mk.1P standard. The furthest aircraft is XV218. Marshall Aerospace

installed in the upper forward fuselage of the Hercules, offset to starboard. The in-flight refuelling pipe (of 3in/7.6cm diameter) was routed along the upper surface of the fuselage to enter the wing trailing edge-to-fuselage fairing on the starboard side, where it connected with the vertical ground refuelling pipe. The latter was modified to have a 'Y'-branch, adjacent to which a non-return valve was included to isolate the in-flight refuelling system when the aircraft was refuelled on the ground. Another non-return valve was fitted just aft of the probe to contain fuel in the event of nozzle failure at the weak link, which could result from excessive side loads during air-to-air refuelling. Two floodlights were fitted to the side of the co-pilot's instrument panel and positioned to illuminate the probe from the right-hand windows, and the refuelling control panel was located above the navigator's station on the flight deck.

Marshall completed this first C.Mk.1P in just ten days. XV200 made its first flight fitted with the probe installation on 28 April and was delivered the next day to the A&AEE. The aircraft passed its first test with flying colours on 2 May when it successfully transferred fuel to a Victor K.2, and on 5 May XV200 was redelivered to No. 47 Squadron at Lyneham. Problems manifested during trial 'prods' with Victor K.2s were gradually eliminated, and a new air-to-air refuelling 'toboggan' technique was adopted. The Victor's minimum speed at 23,000ft (7,000m) the Hercules' optimum range-height with load – was 264mph (425kmph), compared with the transport's maximum speed at high all-up weight of 242mph (389kmph). This disparity in speeds meant that the Victor had to approach the Hercules from above and astern, the latter beginning a 500ft (152m) per minute descent as soon as visual

XV201 and XV296 (4262) at Marshall's airport, Cambridge, in July 1982. XV296 became the C.Mk.1K tanker prototype, being modified at Marshall Engineering from 11 May to 13 July that year; XV201 was also so modified. Marshall Aerospace

contact was made. The Victor then slowly had to overtake, allowing the Hercules to move into the six o'clock low position to engage the drogue, and continue the descent at about 500ft per minute for fifteen minutes at a speed of 270mph (434kmph).

XV200 reached Wideawake on 12 May, and the first Hercules' air-refuelled, long-range, airdrop sortie to the total exclusion zone (TEZ), imposed by British Forces around the Falklands, went ahead on 16 May. The operation, which involved a distance of 7,247 miles (11,660km), was made by Victor K.2 tankers, and Flt Lt Harold Burgoyne's crew in the Hercules, which air-dropped 1,000lb (454kg) of special stores and eight members of the SAS parachuted out. For this extraordinary achievement, Harry Burgoyne was awarded the Air Force Cross.

Each of the remaining twenty-four C.Mk.1s, fitted with two internal auxiliary tanks, was converted to the same standard as XV200; for a time, these aircraft were referred to as PLR2s. The last of these was delivered on 25 October 1982. Meanwhile, Marshall Engineering was also required to carry out modification 5309, which involved fitting CMA 771 Omega navigation equipment (similar to that installed in the USAF C-130H) to RAF Hercules for use on the long overwater flights in the Atlantic. This involved mounting the display and control panel in the navigation station, and the small antenna in the upper rear fuselage, on the port side behind the fin. XV179, which had been delivered to Cambridge for the probe modification, became the first RAF Hercules to be fitted with the navigation device.

Also, installation of the HDU Mk.17B in the fuselage of six C.Mk.1K tankers (MoD 5310) proceeded apace. XV296 was fitted out first, the HDU installation being sited on the rear loading ramp with the auxiliary carriage and drogue deployment box on the cargo door so that the Hercules could remain pressurized while not refuelling. (Much later, Marshall Engineering retrofitted a system which enabled in-flight

refuelling to take place while retaining pressurization.) Fuel supply to the HDU came from the C.Mk.1K's main tanks (and not from the cabin auxiliary tanks), by tapping the standard fuel dump pumps, refuelling pressure being supplied by a bleed-air turbine-driven fuel pump. Two ram-air intakes and a pair of exhaust ducts were mounted in the sides of the pressure hull to provide cooling for the HDU components. Standard

On 18 June 1982, Flt Lt Terry Locke and his crew in No. 70 Squadron set a new world duration record for the Hercules in C.Mk.1P XV179 on an airdrop mission to East Falkland lasting 28hrs 4mins. Marshall Aerospace

external external tanker lights were fitted, together with their switches adjacent to the in-flight refuelling panel above the navigation station.

XV296 successfully deployed its drogue in two flights from Cambridge on 8 and 10 June. On the 11th, the aircraft was despatched to the A&AEE to make its first dry coupling with a Harrier. Not everything went according to plan, however: the HDU projecting from the rear ramp caused some buffeting, and the HDU oil cooler

overheated. XV296 was therefore returned to Marshall Engineering, where strakes added to the loading ramp solved the buffeting defects, and a third ram-air intake solved the air cooler problem. On 21 June, XV296 carried out an entirely successful in-flight refuelling, transferring 5,900lb (2,676kg) of fuel to a Buccaneer at 1,000lb/min (454kg/min). XV296 returned to the A&AEE on 22 June and was equally successful in 'wet' coupling with Hercules, Nimrod, Sea Harrier and Phantom Aircraft. The tanker was delivered to Lyneham on 5 July, but problems with the heat exchangers persisted and it was eventually decided to introduce alternative heat exchangers. With this final modification, four C.Mk.1Ks – XV296, XV210, XV204, and XV192 *Horatius* – were delivered to Lyneham by 26 July. The first operational use of a C.Mk.1K was made early in August, seven weeks after the Argentinian surrender at Port Stanley, during a round trip from Ascension. (By the end of the year, two were based on Ascension Island and two at Stanley. The two remaining tanker conversions were completed in early 1983.) Meanwhile, on 3 June 1982 the RAF notched up its 10,000 hour of Hercules operations since *Corporate* began. In fourteen weeks of operation, the UK MAMS teams at Ascension handled over 18,000 tons of freight and 42,000 passengers, all without loss. On 18th June, Flt Lt Terry Locke and his crew in No. 70 Squadron, set a new world duration record for the Hercules in C.Mk.1P XV179, on an airdrop mission to East Falkland lasting 28 hours 4 minutes.

The Fuerza Aérea Argentinia operated Hercules on thirty-one resupply sorties, mostly under cover of darkness at very low level, in appalling weather, to the Port Stanley garrison from 1 May until 13 June, less than twenty-four hours before the surrender. They carried 400 tons of cargo in, and brought out 264 casualties, plus a captured RAF Harrier pilot who was evacuated to the mainland. Two airdrop sorties were also flown to remote locations on the

The final battles made Stanley's runway untenable for RAF Hercules aircraft until 24 June, when the first one landed with a UK MAMS team aboard, its mission to help restore the island's war-torn economy. Next day a Hercules flown by Harry Burgoyne landed at Stanley, triumphantly returning Rex Hunt, the former governor, to the Falkland Islands. C.Mk.1P XV218 was modified in May 1982. Marshall Aerospace

An RAF Hercules comes in to land at RAF Port Stanley after the Argentinian surrender. Abandoned Fuerza Aérea Argentinia Pucaras litter the side of the runway. Marshall Aerospace

XV192 (4212) Horatius, one for four C.Mk.1K tankers delivered to Lyneham by 26 July 1982, about to refuel C.Mk.1P XV187 (4205). The first operational use of a C.Mk.1K was made early in August, seven weeks after the Argentinian surrender at Port Stanley, during a round trip from Ascension. XV192 was modified to C.1P in March 1992. Marshall Aerospace

Islands. Grupo 1 operated one of its C-130Hs (TC-68) as a bomber on 29 May, when the fuel-laden 15,000-ton *British-Wye* was the target for a salvo of eight bombs. One of the bombs hit the ship but fortunately failed to explode, bouncing off into the sea. (A week later, on 8 June, a US-leased oil tanker, coincidentally named

Hercules, on its way round Cape Horn in ballast, was also hit, and again the bomb failed to explode – but this time the weapon finished up lodged below decks and the ship eventually had to be scuttled.)

Just after dawn on 1 June, an Argentinian C-130E (TC-63) flew supplies into Port Stanley; it was piloted by Capt Ruben

Martel, who exploited the dull and overcast conditions to good effect and hugged the sea. On the return flight that morning, 20 miles (32km) north of San Carlos Water, Martel decided, apparently on his own initiative to climb above the radar horizon and conduct a brief search for British shipping. He was observed on the

(Above) **Local Air Defence FGR. 2 Phantom of No. 23 Squadron from Stanley after the Falklands War takes on fuel from a C.Mk.1K. The plumes from each wing is excess fuel being dumped, as the tanks have overfilled.** via Pete Nash

A C.Mk.1P takes on fuel from a C.Mk.1K near the Falkland Islands late in 1982. From April 1986, four (later two) C.Mk.1Ks of No. 1312 Flight have been stationed at RAF Mount Pleasant to support the Phantom air-defence detachment there. Mick Jennings

C.Mk.1K XV204 (4228) at Stanley late in 1982. This aircraft received Racal 'Orange Blossom' ESM pods beneath its wingtips in December 1986 and it joined 1312 Flight in March 1988. In March 1996 XV204 was flown to Marshall Aerospace for storage and cannibalization, and by March 1998 it had no wings or radome. Mick Jennings

C.Mk.1K XV203 (4227) of 1312 Flight at Stanley in 1984. This aircraft was stored at Marshalls of Cambridge (MoC) in March 1996. Pete Nash

search radar of the frigate *Minerva*, and two Royal Navy Sea Harriers, on patrol in the area, were immediately vectored to intercept. TC-63, which was flying about 200ft (60m) and 'going flat out', could not possibly outrun the Sea Harriers, and it was intercepted 50 miles (80km) north of Pebble Island. The second of Lt Cdr 'Sharkey' Ward's two Sidewinders found its mark, and he finished it off with bursts of 30mm cannon. TC-63 struck the sea and cartwheeled before breaking up. Martel and six other crew were killed.

The final battles made Stanley's runway untenable for RAF Hercules aircraft until 24 June, when the first RAF Hercules landed with a UK MAMS team aboard whose mission was to help restore the islands' war-torn economy. Next day a Hercules flown by Harry Burgoyne landed at Stanley to triumphantly return Rex Hunt, the former governor, to the Falkland Islands. Between 15–28 August, the runway at Port Stanley was closed for landings while it was repaired and extended, so the Hercules had to make the 7,830-mile (12,600km) round trips without landing. These usually required around four in-flight refuellings. To enable a single Hercules to reach Port Stanley, the primary C-130 flew from Wideawake accompanied by a C.Mk.1K tanker, followed by a pair of Victor K.2s. The primary Hercules would be refuelled by the Victors before they returned to Ascension to be refuelled themselves, the Hercules tanker would then refuel the primary Hercules which would fly on to Port Stanley, while the C.Mk.1K also returned to Wideawake. The Victor K.2s would then take off and rendezvous with the primary Hercules on its return flight.

The Hercules carried mail and supplies on these air drops, and picked up mail using an air-snatch technique devised at Brize Norton some six weeks before. This involved trailing a grappling hook from the Hercules' lowered ramp and engaging a nylon rope, suspended between two 22ft (6.7m) poles on the ground, to which the mailbag was attached.

The contribution made by the Hercules fleet in the Falklands War was, as we have seen, immense. The part played by the Harrier – in undeniably its finest hour – by the Royal Navy and the land forces, is rightly recorded in the annals of history. Often the unsung and largely unheralded role performed by the RAF Hercules fleet in sustaining the Task Force is understated

---

Falklands Fall-Out

Lessons learned in the Falklands were manifold, and many have since been put to excellent use around the world. From April 1986, four (later two) C.Mk.1K Hercules of No. 1312 Flight have been stationed at RAF Mount Pleasant. Beginning in 1986, Marshall Engineering began fitting in-flight refuelling probes to the thirty C.Mk.3s to convert them to C.Mk.3P configuration. Starting in 1987, C.Mk.1Ps and C.Mk.1Ks began receiving AN/ALQ 157 IR jamming equipment and chaff/flare dispensers. At least five C.Mk.1Ps were fitted with Racal 'Orange Blossom' ESM pods beneath their wing-tips to give some degree of surveillance capability.

---

and overlooked. (Perhaps this is because events immediately following such successes have usually resulted in cutbacks in the RAF transport fleet.) That the Hercules was able to operate over such vast distances and in such inhospitable climes in the first place, is due entirely to the engineering staff at Marshall Aerospace and at Lyneham, while the professionalism of the air- and ground-crews in the Lyneham Wing is unsurpassed. In all, 2,004 RAF personnel received the South Atlantic Campaign medal, and seventy-four honours for the South Atlantic Operation were bestowed on members of the RAF, including fifty 'in-theatre' meritorious and gallantry awards.

Albert of Arabia

Nine years after the Falklands War the RAF was faced with an even bigger logistics challenge when Iraq invaded neighbouring Kuwait on 2 August 1990, quickly overran this small Arab kingdom, and massed its armies on the border with Saudi Arabia. King Fahd of Saudi Arabia invited friendly nations to assist in the defence of his country, and the UN response led to the largest deployment of military hardware since World War II. RAF Lyneham's contributions to Operation *Granby*, as the RAF involvement in *Desert Shield/Desert Storm* was called, began on the morning of 8 August 1990 when three Hercules crews left for Cyprus on a VC-10 bound for Akrotiri. These crews were to found a pool on the Mediterranean island that was to remain there without break until May 1991.

The RAF Air Transport Detachment (ATD) at King Khalid International Airport, Riyadh, was formed on 30 October

with three Hercules and six crews, plus engineering movements and support personnel from Lyneham. Two Hercules and three crews from No. 40 Squadron RNZAF joined the ATD on 23 December; this was expanded to four crews in mid-January 1991, making a total of about sixty RNZAF personnel during the war period. The ATD was expanded on 14 January 1991, three days before the start of *Desert Storm*, to seven Hercules and fourteen crews, and the number of personnel increased to about 200. That month over 7,500 hours were flown in support of the operation alone.

In the main, support equipment for operational squadrons was airlifted direct from normal operating bases in the UK, with station Mobility Flight personnel playing a major role in the planning and preparation for airlift. In the UK, RAF Lyneham and Brize Norton movers prepared and loaded the majority of the air freight, and it was here that the strain of the huge out-load task was felt the most. Initially, the basis of operations was a 'hub-and-spoke' system. RAF TriStars and VC-10s fed the 'hub' at King Khalid with freight and passengers, and the Hercules flew these out to locations like Seeb and Thumrait in Oman, Minhad in the UAE, Bahrain, and Saudi airfields such as Dhaban, Tabuk, Jubail and Qaisumah, and to other airfields and strips within the theatre of operations. From August 1990 to the end of February 1991, over 46,000 Army, RAF and Royal Navy personnel were moved out to the Gulf by air alone, along with over 46,000 tonnes of equipment.

At the outset of the war the Hercules used short strips for moving troops of the 1st British Armoured Division. These flights employed 'combat loading', a procedure in which the aircraft fuselage is left empty of all seats and the troops simply sit on the floor. During this time the Hercules crews became skilled at desert low flying, which increased as the land war got underway. Their rôle then was to have been CASEVAC (Casualty Evacuation) from the field hospitals back to Riyadh for onward flights to the UK, but thankfully, little was required, and fortunately the elaborate plans were not needed. ATD began operating into Kuwait International Airport on 28 February 1991. Subsequently, crews were faced with the horror of having to fly into the thick black choking smoke caused by the Iraqi mass destruction of Kuwait's oil wells. From the beginning of

C.Mk.1P XV306 The Baron, **the first piece of RAF Gulf nose art, devised and painted by J.A. Osborough of the Lyneham Wing. Osborough also painted XV192** Sid the Sexist, the Silver-Tongued Cavalier **(from** Viz **Magazine), while Cpl Ali Attwater painted** Sharon and Tracey, the Fat Slags **(also from** Viz**) on C.Mk.3P XV215, and Osborough again,** Garfield's Where's the Beach? **on C.Mk.1P XV297. It was suggested by some that this be changed to** Life's A Beach, **but since it was used in the CASEVAC role, Osborough thought this might be inappropriate. C.Mk.1P XV206** Foxy Lady **(the only nude painted on the Hercs, but which received a bikini back in Britain!), which moved the Special Forces around, was by an artist unknown. Finally, Osborough painted C.Mk.1P XV292** Dennis the Menace, **in outline only, saying** Let me at Him!. Steve Jefferson

March, the Hercules operated regularly from Riyadh to Dubai and Kuwait City, the Saudi seaport at Al Jubayl, and the two Tornado bases, at Tabuk in northwest Saudi Arabia, and Muharraq, Bahrain, as well as to desert airstrips.

By the time the fighting was over, the Airlift Co-ordination Centre (ALCC) at HQ, Strike Command at RAF High Wycombe had despatched over 2,250 RAF and 550 civil air transport flights. In the main, these carried deploying forces and their equipments, or the vast quantities of supplies which were required to sustain them. In total, the ATD had flown 2,990 hours on 2,231 sorties, delivering 19.9 million lb (9 million kg) of freight and over 22,800 passengers. Before the homeward rush began, the ATD notched up other firsts, as they flew the first fixed-wing aircraft into Kuwait itself, delivering the men to secure the British Embassy, and then a mere two days later, returning the Ambassador himself to his rightful place.

Despite the ending of the Gulf War, Lyneham's work was far from complete. Most of the equipment used in the conflict was to come home to the UK by sea, but still an enormous amount was too expensive or valuable to be left too long. By May the main operation was complete, but the Hercules mission continued with a schedule every other day to Turkey in support of the Marines, then extending into Iraq itself, as the US forces opened the small airfield of Sirsenk in the Anatolian Mountains. The RAF Hercules detachment, now reduced to two crews and one aircraft, moved to Bahrain; there they continued until the end of June 1991 and 50,000 flying hours later, when it was all over. In July the plight of the Kurds of Northern Iraq, following their failure to overthrow Saddam Hussein, led to more effort, and the RAF launched in to Operation *Warden* (the UK contribution to the US-led *Provide Comfort* relief operation for the UN *Safe Haven*).

XV292 (4257) has received several changes to its appearance since it was delivered to Marshall Engineering in February 1968. It joined No. 47 Squadron in March that year and served in No. 48 Squadron from 1970, and the Lyneham Wing from 1971. In October 1982 it was modified to C.Mk.1P and that same year was flown from Punta Arenas, Chile, in FAC markings '996'. In June 1991, in the Gulf War, it became Dennis the Menace, **and in December 1991 appeared with a large '25' on its tail to celebrate twenty-five years of the Hercules in the RAF. It carried these markings, which included the badges of all the Hercules squadrons and units on the sides of the fuselage, for two more years. It is pictured here, flying over Kemble.** RAF via Gary Madgwick/The Aviation Workshop

'Behold, I Will Rain Bread From Heaven For You' (Exodus 16)

Where there is famine or when warring factions use food – or lack of it – as a weapon, as in the case of Bosnia, inevitably the UN High Commission for Refugees (UNHCR) attempts to provide the innocent bystanders with the basic essentials for survival. Lacking any resources, they quite naturally ask individual nations to contribute aid. In the case of the UK, that request comes to the Foreign & Commonwealth Office who, if they agree, will inevitably 'contract' the MoD to do the task, who in turn order Strike Command, who pass it to No. 38 Group and their Hercules fleet.

C.MK.1K XV213 (4240) at RAF Mount Pleasant, Falkland Islands, in 1994. Note the Racal 'Orange Blossom' ESM pod beneath the wing-tip. This aircraft was flown to Marshall Aerospace in March 1996 for storage. Mick Jennings

C.Mk.1P XV206 pictured in Nevada during the 1989 Red Flag exercise in the experimental 'pink' scheme applied that August. It has had a colourful career, colliding with an RN helicopter in the Falklands in June 1985, operating in 'desert pink' in the Gulf War, and returning to 'normal' camouflage in January 1991. Note the Racal 'Orange Blossom' ESM pods beneath the wing-tips, installed in May 1984. Pete Nash

The activities and personnel involved in 38 Group's response to humanitarian tasks involved three very different categories: Operation *Martock*, the evacuation of British Nationals from Luanda in November 1992; Operation *Vigour*, the UK contribution to the US Operation *Provide Relief* involving the delivery of aid to Somalia from December 1992 to March 1993; and Operation *Cheshire*, the on-

going provision of humanitarian aid to the people of Sarajevo.

In August 1992, the multi-national air operation known as *Provide Relief* was launched to airlift supplies to feeding centres and clinics for Somali refuges. By 25 February 1993, some 28,050.86 tonnes of food had been delivered by the American, German and Royal Air Forces based at Moi International Airport, Mombasa, in

1,924 sorties to Somalia and 508 to Kenya. During Operation *Vigour*, in three months two Hercules and four crews of 38 Group delivered some 3,500 tons of supplies to all areas of Somalia, flying just short of 1,000 hours in the process.

Operation *Cheshire* began in the summer of 1992 when the UN asked nations to provide aircraft to deliver aid to Sarajevo. The UK government responded

C.Mk.1P XV185 (4203) and C.1P XV293 (4258), the two RAF Hercules used in Operation Vigour, at Moi International Airport, Mombasa, Kenya, 28 February 1993, the day before they routed home to Lyneham. In three months these two Hercules and four crews of 38 Group delivered 3,500 tons of supplies to all areas of Somalia, flying just short of 1,000 hours in the process. Author

C.Mk.1P VX291 (4256) at Sarajevo in 1995 during the Bosnian airlift. Gary Madgwick/The Aviation Workshop

with an offer of one Hercules, and a No. 47 Squadron aircraft began flying into Sarajevo three times a day from 3 July 1992. Group Capt D.K.L. McDonnell OBE RAF, Head of Air Transport and Air-To-Air Refuelling Branch, HQ No. 38 Group at High Wycombe, has written the following account of the operation:

Regrettably, the aircraft are regularly tracked by radar-layed AAA, and occasionally pick up transmissions from potentially hostile systems. Clearly they are at their most vulnerable during approach and departure at Sarajevo; therefore the ground situation is continuously monitored. As at the end of October 1993, the RAF had delivered some 12,500 tons of aid to Sarajevo in some 880 visits and flown close to 2,000 hours in the process. This represents some 18 per cent of all aid delivered by air – not bad when we represent only 12 per cent of the aircraft dedicated to the airlift … We have been fortunate so far, in that there has been little damage to our aircraft – only two bullet holes. Others have been less so; for instance, the Italians lost a Fiat G222 aircraft to missile fire in 1993, and it was only through the quick reaction of the crew that the Germans did not lose a C-160 in February 1994

[there were no UK casualties during the course of Operation *Cheshire*, but there were more than 260 security incidents involving other relief aircraft]. The hazards are evident. Our hope is that we shall continue to get the balance right and not exceed it. We get it wrong at our peril.

A Hercules crew from No. 47 Squadron, with two Hercules from the French and US air forces, carried out the last relief flight (IFN 94) into Sarajevo on 9 January 1996. The RAF contribution to the airlift, the longest in history, was immense: a total of 1,977 sorties carried 28,256 tonnes of relief supplies into the city over the 1,279 days of operation, and overall, the UN effort totalled 160,370 tonnes of aid and included flights from the air forces of Canada, the US, Germany and France.

Meanwhile in 1995, Hercules crews from Lyneham were involved in relief missions to the tiny Caribbean island of Montserrat which was threatened by volcanic eruptions. About 3,000 of the island's 12,000 inhabitants left Montserrat for Antigua and surrounding islands. The first appeal for assistance was answered by a Hercules which left Lyneham in early

August. This aircraft, crewed by No. 47 Squadron, spent a week in the area of relief duties. Its first flight carried food parcels and soft toys for children, and thereafter three flights each day took in food, fold-up beds, pillows and tents; the aircraft finally returned to Lyneham on 10 August. Following a second personal request from the island's governor, forty Royal Marines were flown from Lyneham on 24 August to help the beleaguered islanders. The aircraft flew to Goose Bay where it changed crew before flying on to Antigua.

A Dynamic Mix

In addition to the humanitarian and logistics operations, there are other operational considerations each and every year which involve the Lyneham Wing and its Hercules fleet. Each year Exercise *Dynamic Mix* involving land, sea and air forces from several NATO nations takes place in the Mediterranean. In order to support the substantial British participation in the exercise, a large amount of engineering equipment has to be transported to Turkey. As

Lyneham Transport Wing's Special Forces Flight C.Mk.1P XV206 Foxy Lady **at Brize Norton, 1994. AN/ALQ 157 infra-red jamming equipment and chaff/flare dispensers were installed in August 1991. The rear section of the sponson houses a 'disco light' infra-red jammer.** Gary Madgwick/The Aviation Workshop

well as the equipment needed for the day-to-day operations of the Tornados, a spares back-up is also required to provide replacement parts for aircraft and bulky ground engineering equipment. A large proportion of this equipment is sent by sea, but smaller items of equipment and the support passengers, including engineers and suppliers as well as aircrew, all travel from Lyneham to Akinci AB, Turkey, in up to six Hercules.

The overworked Hercules fleet had, by the early 1990s, reached a point whereby if the humanitarian and logistics support roles were to continue to function in times of extreme crisis, then replacement of the RAF's senior citizens was due. (The RAF has been operating the C-130K since 1967.) The UK is the largest operator of C-130s outside the US, with a fleet – at the time of writing – of sixty C.Mk.1, C.Mk.1P, and C.Mk.3P versions, and it has the highest utilization rate of any operator because of its rigorous training schedules, worldwide commitments and involvments in many peacekeeping and humanitarian tasks. In 1992 an LS82 project team was set up to oversee the Hercules replacement project. The subsequent decision to opt for the C-130J model was an obvious one, and twenty-five of the existing fleet are scheduled to be replaced by C-130Js/ -30s. Of

Ground personnel load a Hercules at Lyneham. Andy Sheppard

these, the first fifteen will be the stretched C-130J-30 version, an option being held on the last ten to switch all or some of them to the shorter version, should requirements change for which this version would be better suited. They will de designated Mks. 4 and 5 respectively (Mk.2 is *Snoopy*, the meteorological research vehicle). With these aircraft the RAF becomes the first operator of these new versions.

C.Mk.3P XV222 (4252), XV293 (4258), converted to C.Mk.1P in July 1987, and other RAF Hercules, on the line at Lyneham early in 1998. Andy Sheppard

CHAPTER NINE

C-130J, The Next Millennium Hercules

The design objective of the C-130J is to provide a replacement that makes good economic sense for any twenty-year-old Hercules. Buying a new C-130J is more cost-effective in the long run than extending the service life of old airplanes.

Al Hansen, Vice President for Airlift Programs at LASC, speaking in April 1994

At first glance the C-130J, the latest version of the Hercules family, does not look significantly different from the existing C-130H standard, and certainly it is built on the same basic platform. However, Lockheed-Martin Aeronautical Systems Company is selling the aircraft on the basis that the new version is significantly cheaper to operate and support than the C-130H, with substantial improvements in life-cycle costs. Certainly by the early 1990s, the faithful and ubiquitous workhorse was under-ranged and undersized for true strategic operations. Increasingly, tactical transport aircraft are being used to great effect in the strategic role. This was emphasized during the deployment and recovery phases of the Gulf War in 1990–91, and the reinforcement of Kuwait in 1994. These events particularly showed that the widening gap in the RAF transport inventory, one that had existed since the demise of the Short Belfast in 1975, had become a chasm. The Hercules Air Transport Force is crucial to the RAF's worldwide rôle for humanitarian and peacekeeping operations and in war.

The Hercules force will be less reliant in the future on fixed-base support, and far more concerned with mobile and deployed operations. Against this background, in December 1994 the Ministry of Defence (MoD) announced its intention to procure a first tranche of twenty-five C-130J and C-130J-30 aircraft (Hercules C.MK.4/5), the latter having a 180in (457cm) 'stretch' in the fuselage which can accommodate seven pallets (up from five in the C-130E/H/J; this would begin replacement, on a one-for-one basis, of the RAF's ageing and overworked Hercules fleet. A continuing need for a cost-effective strategic transport capable of operating from improvised airstrips therefore

As good as ever! Three generations of transport aircraft are represented in this photo at Air Fête 1998, RAF Mildenhall: C-130E, McDonnell Douglas C-17A Globemaster III, and C-141 Starlifter. C-130E 63-13187 (4012) 'ETI-187' was delivered under the US Military Assistance Program (MAP) to the Turk Hava Kuvvetleri in October 1964 and is still in first-line service with the Turkish Air Force. Author

seemed to rule out anything but a turbo-prop transport – and what better than the C-130J? Has it not always been said that the best replacement for a Douglas DC-3 is another DC-3? The same equally has often been said of the Hercules.

In the early 1990s the airlift market seemed to have been left – not quite, but almost – wide open for Lockheed and its next generation to fill, just as it always did with a succession of models tailored for almost every labour and every task. Though competition in the airlift market hotted up with the introduction of the custom-built, turbofan-powered McDonnell Douglas C-17A, which first flew on 15 September 1991, the Globemaster III still equips no more than one wing in the US transport inventory. It seems to have all the right credentials, being the first military transport to feature a full digital fly-by-wire control system and two-crew flight deck, with two full-time, all-function GEC-Marconi advanced HUDs and four Delco Electronic's multi-function electronic display systems. 'The C-17', championed the sales brochures, 'appeared to represent a new dimension in airlift, combining the benefits of both strategic and tactical airlift in one airframe. Flying

Specification – C-130J Hercules	
Powerplant:	Four Allison AE2100D3 turboprops, each rated at 4,591eshp
Weights:	Operating 79,090lb (35,875kg); max. take-off 155,000lb (70,308kg); max. payload 41,043lb (18,617kg)
Dimensions:	Span 132ft 7in (40.41m); length 97ft 9in (29.79m); height 38ft 3in (11.66m); wing area 1,745sq ft (162.12sq m)
Performance:	Cruising speed 365mph (586km/h); rate of climb 2,234ft/min (681m/min); ceiling at 100,000lb, 40,000ft (12,103m); range with max. payload 2,700 miles (4,563km); range with max. fuel 4,700 miles (7,562km)

intercontinental distances and landing at small, austere airfields with runways as short as 3,000ft (900m), it can transport outsized equipment, paratroops, military supplies or humanitarian aid to crisis areas around the globe – all traditional Hercules attributes.' By 1994, ten C-17As had established eighteen new world records for payloads to altitude, and three in the time-to-climb category. The makers declared that the C-17A would be able to operate routinely into small, austere airfields *previously restricted to C-130 Hercules*, and would be the first aircraft able to airland or to airdrop or extract outsize cargo in the tactical environments. Why then, in spite of all these attributes and achievements, have just forty C-17As been built?

There is the even less likely An-124, as well as derivatives of American civil jet airliner variants, while in Europe the much championed FLA concept, which has been on the drawing board since 1982, is an unknown quantity. Development costs alone were estimated at (£3–4.6 billion, and at £85m a copy, it would cost three to four times the price of C-130J. First-flight estimates varied between the year 2000 and 2002. However, even if it were to go into production there are doubts that it would be able to meet the strategic deployer's requirements.

In 1991 Lockheed-Martin began designing the C-130J. British industry participation started in the early 1990s, with a partnership between just two companies and Lockheed-Martin. By January 1998 almost fifty British firms were supporting the C-130J project on a risk-sharing basis, and more than £470 million of orders had been placed in the UK. British companies have played an integral rôle in the development and production of the C-130J, sharing in all orders, irrespective of customer. The aircraft's new, more powerful and efficient propulsion system is largely produced by British companies including Dowty Aerospace, GKN Westland, Lucas Aerospace and Rolls-Royce.

March 1994 marked two major milestones for the C-130J programme: initial cutting of metal began, with the fabrication of parts for the first five aircraft, a mock-up unit and two sets of spares – these were support panels for power-supply units that would provide low-voltage power to the cockpit control panels. In April – a point in time corresponding with more than 2,100 earlier models of the Hercules having been sold to over sixty-six countries

– Alfred G. Hansen, executive vice president for Airlift Programs at LASC and a former head of the USAF's Logistics Command, alluded to an equally bright future for the C-130J and its makers, sub-contractors and workers. According to Hansen, the contracts already awarded to UK companies translated into more than 3,000 current direct and indirect technology jobs. Financially, the contracts would mean more than £1.2 billion of revenues to UK companies over the next ten years. Said Hansen, 'When we began looking for partners on the C-130J programme, we expected a high interest from UK companies because of their recognized leadership in aerospace technologies. These companies survived tough competition and proved that they were technically competent and willing to invest in the programme.'

At this time, marketing forecasts showed anticipated sales of from 400 to 700 C-130J aircraft in the following ten years. Indeed between 1962 and 1975, Lockheed delivered more than 700 Hercules to air forces throughout the world. Hansen again: 'The design objective of the C-130J is to provide a preplacement that makes good economic sense for any twenty-year-old Hercules. Buying a new C-130J is more cost-effective in the long run than extending the service life of old airplanes.' Current Hercules' operators regard the C-130 as an important asset because of the emphasis being placed on mobility, rapid reaction, reach and flexibility. 'To accomplish this, operators need improvements in maintainability, reliability, performance and reduced manning costs. Significant technology advancements and modular manufacturing techniques allow us to offer the C-130J at an affordable price with lower operating costs, greater safety and reliability and with minimum risk.' Hansen said.

Lockheed, its sub-contractors and its competitors knew that even in the field of strategic transportation, the days when uncomplicated, workmanlike designs such as the original Hercules had long since disappeared. 'Significant technology advancements' and 'modular manufacturing techniques', while in themselves offering solutions to problems, can also cause problems to solutions – tradition often dictates nomenclature, but, as has been shown with the C-17A, although the name was the same, the aircraft lineage, because of dramatic technology changes, was quite different. So although Lockheed-Martin understandably wanted to

trade on the long-established and highly successful Hercules name, it is more accurate to say that the C-130J is not really an updated version of the pedigree, but essentially a whole new aircraft.

If the decision by Lockheed in the fifties to reject conventional piston engines in favour of the newer and less proven technology of turboprops had been a brave one, then the decision to create a state-of-the-art Hercules for the next century has been an unparalleled step. However, winning large new orders for a cost-effective airlifter now represents such a quantum-leap forward in many areas – notably in the field of avionics, software programming and propeller design – that it produces some challenging technological hurdles which if left unsolved, could have severe repercussions on the very future of an aircraft facing the next millennium. The C-130J development programme, funded independently, has revealed many technological barriers that have had to be surmounted, and it has cost Lockheed-Martin at least $400 million in the process. Ray Crockett, Lockheed-Martin communications director, was quoted in June 1998 as saying: 'We accept that we did not allow enough time for testing and certification, but the development of this aircraft, essentially a whole new aircraft, is still being accomplished in half the time that it would take for a new aircraft of this type to be produced.' At the start of the C-130J programme, Lockheed set very clear objectives: to develop a low-risk, off-the-shelf modern version of the Hercules, which could incorporate state-of-the-art technology. Certainly the new Hercules had to offer the military customer substantially reduced costs in areas such as manpower levels and life-cycle management so that he could achieve his primary objective: to carry out the mission at minimum cost. Therefore, all C-130J configuration features had either to contribute to the low-cost drivers, or to provide a life-cycle cost-reduction in their own right (life-cycle costs basically encompass reliability, maintainability and support activities). In addition, some significant improvements have come along: these are that it can take off in a shorter distance, cruise higher, and carry the same payload almost 50 per cent further. To do this, and to do it more cost-effectively than the C-130H, there have had to be tangible differences.

The most dramatic changes in costs and performance come from the fact that the C-

(Above) **C.Mk.1 (65-13026) XV181, one of five aircraft used in the flight-teat programme for the C-130J, fitted with one of the new Dowty-designed composite R391 scimitar-shaped six-bladed propeller unit in a C-130 nacelle modified by Westland. It was first flown for evaluation at Marshall Aerospace, Cambridge, on 19 March 1994 by Marshall Aerospace test pilots John Blake and 'Daz' James.** Marshall Aerospace

Close-up of the Dowty-designed composite R391 propeller unit tested on XV181. Marshall Aerospace

130J has two crew instead of four, also the avionics are modern state of the art, and there is the new Allison AE-2100D3 two-spool powerplant, complete with oil-bath engine starter and new modular gearbox. The T56 has been an outstanding performer – pilots trust it, and like its responsiveness – but the AE 2100 has added a new dimension to the C-130J: full authority, digital electronic control is incorporated; there is 29 per cent more take-off thrust; and 15 per cent better fuel economy. The engine is also modular and lighter in weight. Coupled to it is the Dowty-designed composite R391 scimitar-shaped six-bladed propeller unit, replacing the all-metal four-bladed propeller on the C130H. This new propeller is lighter, has fewer parts, and delivers 13 per cent more thrust. (The new propeller subsequently proved extraordinarily successful in live-firing tests, which analysed its ability to sustain damage from direct attack or shrapnel.)

A leased RAF C-130K/C.Mk.I (65-13026/XV181), one of five aircraft used in the flight-test programme, was fitted with one of the new powerplants in a C-130 nacelle modified by Westland. It was first flown for evaluation at Marshall Aerospace, Cambridge, on 19 March 1994 by Marshall Aerospace test pilots John Blake and 'Daz' James. It was airborne for 3¾ hours and flew at up to 270 knots and 35,000ft (10,700m). Dr Bill Mikolowski, director of the C-130J project, said: 'Invaluable data is being collected, with nearly 400 sensors measuring more than 550 points throughout the aircraft [engine, nacelle and propeller].' During a two-month, fifty-hour flight-test programme, testing was carried out for flutter clearance, powerplant response, propeller blade and shaft stress, airframe structural response, and near- and far-field noise characteristics. Marshall Aerospace was responsible for the overall conduct of the flight-test programme,

including the installation of the refuelling probe and new components onto the aircraft, the day-to-day flying operations, and much of the data acquisition and reduction. Lockheed analysed propulsion system performance, cabin and far-field acoustic characteristics, and airframe structural response to the new propeller excitation frequencies. Allison Engine Company accumulated data on the engine, and provided technical support during the flight-test. Dowty Aerospace Propellers monitored propeller performance on board the aircraft, as well as providing field support and data reduction. The test team included Westland Aerospace Ltd, who as well as providing technical support, evaluated the nacelle systems design, such as engine compartment ventilation. Aerostructures Hamble provided the ejector tailpipe; IMI Marston, the engine oil cooler; Lucas Aerospace, the electrical generator; and Kaiser-Sargent, the throttle quadrant for the test engine.

The carbon-fibre flaps and flap shrouds are manufactured by Shorts.

It was soon established that the forgiving and predictable stalling characteristics normally associated with the Hercules had suffered because the six-bladed propellers were causing the airflow over the upper-wing surfaces to separate. Many would-be solutions, including leading-edge stall strips, wing fences and vortex generators, were all tried in an attempt to alleviate a greater-than-20-degree wing drop at stall. Despite these aerodynamic fixes, the wing drop could not always be eliminated in all configurations. (The FAA requires less than 20-degree wing drop at stall.) Lockheed then chose to install a stickpusher to force down the aircraft's nose at any sign of a stall: if the airflow over the wing was disturbed, no doubt the airflow around the rear fuselage was disturbed also. These setbacks prevented Lockheed from testing live paratroops drops, with serious consequences for the C-130J's paratrooping role.

Other innovations on the new aircraft include Mk.IV carbon brakes coupled with an automatic braking feature, and a new anti-skid system to shorten landing distances. A new modular wheel and integral self-jacking struts greatly reduce the time required to change a wheel, and make it possible to replace tyres at remote sites without ground-support equipment. A new nose-gear strut improves the stability to taxi on rough airstrips. An updated electronic system with two new converters provides stable power to all avionics and electronic loads. The C-130J is now equipped with dual VHF, and HF radios. The new AiResearch auxiliary power unit provides more output, especially for heating and cooling the aircraft on the ground, and the service life of the APU has been doubled from the previous model in the C-130H.

A new fuel system has a single cross-ship manifold, with half as many fuel-control valves. Foam installed in the dry bays provides added safety and survivability. Because the new engine/propeller combination and reduced drag increase range by 20 per cent, there is no real need for external fuel tanks, although the C-130J can carry an additional 18,700lb (8,482kg) of fuel in external tanks if required. Lockheed has relocated the in-flight refuelling probe from the centre of the fuselage to the left side over the pilot's head; this is designed to make it easier for the co-pilot when in-flight refuelling is being performed, than in earlier versions. Lockheed-Martin also

plans a boom tanking version for refuelling US Air Force-type aircraft, and this will be offered as future modification. The company is also looking at a variable speed basket to install on its probe-and-drogue refuelling system, which would permit in-flight refuelling of an F/A-18 and a Bell-Boeing V-22 using the same basket, rather than the two separate baskets required now.

Cruising at an average of 310 knots, at up to 30,000ft (9,000m), the 'old' C-130 burns approximately 5,000lb (2,270kg) of fuel every hour. The C-130J and C-130J-30 have a maximum internal fuel load of 45,900lb

The flight engineer and navigator stations have been eliminated in the C-130J cockpit, which is equipped with four flat-panel liquid-crystal (LCD) head-down (HDD) colour displays which present all the information needed to fly the aircraft and make available data and navigation plans, traffic and ground collision avoidance, Advisory Caution and Warning System (ACAWA) messages and SKE-2000 (Station Keeping Equipment) information. Two Flight Dynamics holographic head-up (HUD) displays permit both pilots to maintain a constant out-of-the-window view while monitoring all the data necessary to control the aircraft. Lockheed-Martin

(20,820kg): the maximum is reduced by slightly over 2,000lb (907kg) when foam is introduced into the tanks – though international C-130Js are not normally equipped with the foam. Lockheed estimates the range of the C-130J to be about 3,000 nautical miles without external tanks. The C-130J-30's added length adds 3,729lb (1,729kg) to the aircraft's empty weight, and reduces payload by the same amount. However, the stretch C-130J can carry two additional pallets as compared to the C-130J, and ninety-two paratroops as opposed to sixty-four for the standard C-130J.

The cockpit is still approached via a near-vertical ladder, (although there is no fold-down floor panel to cover the ladder well) and the two crew-rest bunks remain at the rear of the cockpit. Although the flight engineer and navigator stations have been eliminated, there is provision for a third crew member (check-out pilot, etc) to sit behind the centre console between the two pilots to monitor the flight, or to operate the aircraft's systems, as required. The superb 'greenhouse' windowing, providing unparalleled all-round vision, has also been retained (although two in the nose have been blanked off). The galley has been turned through 90 degrees to face into the cockpit instead of over the ladder as previously. The control yokes, the nose-wheel steering wheel and the parking-brake handle, are all throwbacks to the familiar C-130s of yore – but all this said, the C-130J cockpit is still revolutionary because in terms of electronics on the aircraft, it is a wholly different world. The systems include a digital autopilot, a fully integrated global positioning system, colour weather and ground-mapping radar and a digital map display, plus an advisory caution and warning system that allows for fault detection.

Mission effectiveness has been infinitely improved thanks to a mission computer allied to electronically controlled engines and propellers, databus architecture and digital avionics. The new configuration includes the USAF-developed Self-Contained Navigation System (SCNS). System architecture is centred around dual Electronic Flight Instrumentation System (EFIS) MIL-STD-1553B databuses with analog and digital interfaces. (Replacing the conventional wiring systems with this databus architecture reduced wire assemblies by 53 per cent and wire terminations by 81 per cent. The new design reduced line-replaceable units by 53 per cent.) A new Digital Avionics Flight Control System (DAFCS) is installed for the autopilot and flight director system. An Integrated Diagnostic System (IDS) offers fault detection and isolation, and is integrated with the ACAWS greatly to improve maintenance troubleshooting. The 'virtual systems' on the aircraft cover automatic thrust control and engine monitoring. The Lucas Aerospace full-authority, digital engine-control (FADEC) for the Allison AE2100D3 engines provides automatic starting cycles, with automatic shutdown for overspeeding, and warnings should other malfunctions occur. It has also meant that the need to line up all four engine powers by setting each power lever is no longer necessary.

Engine status is present on one of the four flat-panel, liquid-crystal (LCD), head-down (HDD) colour displays on vertical bars, while system data is presented as digital readouts on the display. The Westinghouse AN/APN-241 weather/navigation radar display – which equipment includes the only *proven* forward-looking windshear mode available today – presents the primary navigation plan, showing the aircraft proceeding along a flight-plan course on a map overlay. Eight different navigational tasks are carried out automatically. An Enhanced Traffic Avoidance System (E-TCAS) and a

C-130J-30 (Model 382V-01J) N130JN (5443)/ZH868 for the RAF. Lockheed-Martin

Ground Avoidance System (GCAS) are also fitted. A second display presents Advisory Caution and Warning System (ACAWA) messages and SKE-2000 (Station Keeping Equipment) information. The fourth display presents all information necessary to fly the aircraft. Two flight dynamics holographic head-up (HUD) displays permit both pilots to maintain a constant out-of-the-window view while monitoring all the data necessary to control the aircraft. All the panels and consoles in the cockpit have been redesigned, and the aircraft is compatible with night-vision imaging systems. As a fail-safe, there are two mission computers, although one computer is capable of doing all tasks.

Much of the protracted flight-test programme has concentrated on proving the complex software systems. Lockheed tested the systems heavily in the laboratory, and then released the software loads in a staged process involving a flight simulator and the test aircraft. There are almost 600,000 lines of software code in the aircraft, and Lockheed-Martin were determined to carry out more comprehensive testing on this aircraft than on any military or civil aircraft before.

Problems with the liquid-crystal cockpit displays and the totally unexpected problem with stalls during flight-testing, caused long delays to the C-130J development programme and a consequent lag in production-aircraft delivery. N130JA, the C-130J (Hercules C.4/ZH865) prototype, was rolled out of Lockheed's huge hangar at Marietta on 18 October 1995 in front of distinguished guests from the US and Britain, with AM Sir John Allison, deputy C-in-C of Strike Command, the guest of honour. One of the most interested observers was Group Capt Brian Symes, station commander at Lyneham, where the first squadron to receive the aircraft will be No. 24, to be followed by No. 70 Squadron. A diminutive figure in the crowd turned out to be eighty-two-year-old Willis Hawkins, the chief engineer of the original C-130; in 1951 his late boss, Kelly Johnson, had reluctantly signed the right bit of paper, saying the aircraft was 'too ugly' to succeed! What Johnson would have had to say about this new generation of tactical transport aircraft is open to question. Sir John Allison greeted Hercules ZH865 as a milestone aircraft, the latest example of a line which would go down in aviation history as one of the truly great designs.

ZH865 flew for the first time on 5 April 1996. In-flight refuelling tests were carried out in January 1998. A new airflow difficulty emerged when it was found that the aircraft's tail-fin iced up in freezing conditions. Lockheed came up with a solution, however: a pneumatic rubber boot wrapped around the foot of the tail-fin; this was during 'cold-weather' trails Argentina in mid-1998. (Lockheed-Martin had rejected the Falklands for 'cold-weather' trials, apparently because the islands have only one runway, in favour of Rio Gallegos, 400 miles (640km) from the Falklands base at Mount Pleasant, and the home of Argentina's Exocet force in the 1982 Falklands War.)

The MoD were originally promised that the first production versions for launch customer, the RAF, would begin arriving in the UK in November 1996. However, two years on, none had arrived, and in the summer of 1998 it was predicted that actual deliveries would not start until late in the year, and that it would be at least February 1999 before any were in RAF service. Orders received by January 1998 had reached eighty-three firm contracts and sixty-two options for C-130Js, with Italy ordering eighteen aircraft, the RAF twenty-five, the Royal Australian Air Force twelve (looking to replace twelve C-130Es and twelve C-130Hs), and the USAF, AFRes and ANG, twenty-eight, and the USMC, seven. As a result of the delays, huge penalty charges were imposed – some reports indicated that Lockheed-Martin were forced to pay the Ministry of Defence more than £25 million in penalty charges for late delivery, and that these could rise to almost £60 million if the delays continued.

C-130J/C-130J-30/Construction Nos/Service Allocations

Model		C/n	Serial No.	Delivery To
382V-49F	C-130J-30	5408	N130JA/ZH865	RAF*
382U-49F	C-130J	5413	94-3026/N130JC	ACC
382V-49F	C-130J-30	5414	N130JE/ZH866	RAF
382U-49F	C-130J	5415	94-3027/N130JG	ACC
382V-49F	C-130J-30	5416	N130JJ/ZH867	RAF
382V-03J	C-130J-30	5440/42	A97-440/442	RAAF
382V-01J	C-130J-30	5443/46	ZH868/871	RAF
382V-03J	C-130J-30	5447/50	A97-447/450	RAAF
382V-04J	WC-130J	5451/53	96-5300/02	US AFRes
382U-02J	C-130J	5454/55	96-	ACC
382V-05J	C-130J-30	5456/63	ZH872/ZH879	RAF
382V-03J	C-130J-30	5464/68	A97-464/468	RAAF
382V-05J	C-130J-30	5459	ZH875	RAF
382V-07J	WC-130J	5469/72	97-5303/06	AFRes
382V-08J	C-130J	5473/77	97-	ANG
382V-06J	C-130J	5478/85	ZH880/887	RAF
382V-12J	WC-130J	5486/87	98-	AFRes
382U-11J	KC-130J	5488/89	97-	USMC
382U-10J	C-130J-30	5490/95		RNoAF
382U-11J	KC-130J	5496	97-	USMC
382U-13J	C-130J	5497		ItAF
382U-17J	EC-130J	5489/99	98-	ANG
382U-06J	C-130J	5500	ZH888	RAF
382U-13J	C-130J	5501/02		ItAF
382V-06J	C-130J-30	5503	ZH889	RAF
382U-16J	C-130J	5504/06	98-	ANG
382U-11J	KC-130J	5507/08	98-	USMC
382	WC-130J	5509	99-	AFRes
382	C-130J-30	5510/11	99-	ARC
382	C-130J	5512/14	99-	ItAF
382	C-130J-30	5515/16	99-	ARC
382	EC-130J	5517	99-	ARC
382U-11J	KC-130J	5518/19	99-	USMC
382	C-130J	5520/37	No order	
382	C-130J	5538/39		ItAF
382	C-130J	5540/44	No order	
382	C-130J	5545/46		ItAF

*(C.4/C-130J prototype)

Glossary

A&AEE	Aeroplane and Armament Experimental Establishment, RAF	EAF	Egyptian Air Force	RNorAF	Royal Norwegian Air Force
		ECS/W	Electronic Countermeasures Squadron/Wing	RNZAF	Royal New Zealand Air Force
ABCC	Airborne Battlefield Command and Control Centre			RSAF	Royal Saudi Air Force
		ESD	Electronic Systems Division, AFSC	RTAF	Royal Thai Air Force
ABDR	Aircraft Battle Damage Repair			SAAF	South African Air Force
ABW	Air Base Wing	ETR	Eastern Test Range, Systems Command	SAMSON	Special Avionics Mission Strap On Now
ACC	Air Combat Command				
ACCS	Aerospace Cartographic and Geodetic Squadron/Service	FAA	Fuerza Aérea Argentina	SiAF	Republic of Singapore Air Force
		FAB	Forca Aérea Brasiliera	SKE	Station Keeping Equipment
AD	Abu Dhabi Air Force	FAC	Fuerza Aérea Colombiana	SLAR	Side Looking Array Radar
AFB	Air Force Base	FAE	Fuerza Aérea Ecuatoriana	SOAF	Sultanate of Oman Air Force
AFFTC	Air Force Flight Test Centre	FAM	Fuerza Aérea Mexicana	SOG/S/W	Special Operations Group/Squadron/Wing
AFMC	Air Force Mobile Command	FAP	Fuerza Aérea del Peru		
AFRes	Air Force Reserve	FAU	Fuerza Aérea Uruguaya	SOTS	Special Operations Training Team
AFSC	Air Force Systems Command	FAV	Fuerza Aérea Venezolana	SpAF	Spanish Air Force
AFSOC	Air Force Special Operations Command	FCS	Facility Checking Squadron	SRS/W	Strategic Reconnaissance Squadron/Wing
		FTS	Flight Transport Squadron		
AFSWC	Air Force Special Weapons Centre, AFSC	FV	Flygvapnet (Swedish Air Force)	STAR	Surface To Air Recovery
		HAF	Hellenic (Greek) Air Force	SVAF	South Vietnam Air Force
AG	Airlift Group	IDFAF	Israel Defence Force/Air Force	SwAF	Swedish Air Force
ALC	Air Logistics Centre	IIAF	Imperial Iranian Air Force	TAC	Tactical Air Command
ALS/ALW	Airlift Squadron/Wing	LAAF	Libyan Republic Air Force	TACAMO	Take Charge And Move Out
AM	Aeronautica Militare (Italian Air Force)	LAC	Lockheed Aircraft Corporation	TAF	Turkish Air Force
		LAPES	Low Altitude Parachute Extraction System	TAS/G/W	Tactical Airlift Squadron/Group/Wing
AMARC	Aerospace Maintenance and Regeneration Centre				
		M&CS	Mapping and Charting Squadron	TATS	Tactical Airlift Training Squadron
AMC	Air Mobility Command	MAC	Military Airlift Command		
ANG	Air National Guard	MAFFS	Modular Airborne Firefighting System	TAW	Tactical Airlift Wing
APCS	Air Photographic and Charting Service, MATS			TCS	Troop Carrier Squadron
		MAP	Military Assistance Programme, USA	TCW	Troop Carrier Wing
ARRS	Aerospace Rescue and Recovery Squadron/Service			TDS	Tactical Drone Squadron
		MSADC	Military Storage and Disposition Centre	TNI-AU	Indonesian Air Force
ARRW	Aerospace Rescue and Recovery Wing			TS/W	Test Squadron/Wing
		MATS	Military Air Transport Service	TTC	Technical Training Center
AS	Airlift Squadron	MCS	Mapping and Charting Service	TUDM	Malaysian Air Force
ATS/W	Air Transport Squadron/Wing	NAF	Nigerian Air Force	USACC	United States Air Combat Command
AURI	Angkaten Udari Republik Indonesia (Indonesian Air Force)	NAS	Naval Air Station, USN		
		NATWP	Naval Air Transport Wing Pacific	USAETC	United States Air Education and Training Command
AW	Airlift Wing				
AWACW	Airborne Warning and Control Wing	NAWC AD	Naval Air Warfare Centre, Aircraft Division	USAF	United States Air Force
				USAFE	United States Air Force in Europe
AWADS	All Weather Airborne Delivery System	NWT	Northwest Territorial Airways		
		OCU	Operational Conversion Unit, RAF	USAF-SOPC	United States Air Force Special Operations Command
BAF	Belgian Air Force				
BLC	Boundary Layer Control	OG	Operational Group	USCG	United States Coast Guard
BolAF	Bolivian Air Force	PACAF	Pacific Air Forces	USMC	United States Marine Corps
CAF	Canadian Armed Forces	PAF	Pakistan Air Force	USN	United States Navy
CAS	Continental Air Services	PMW	Photo Mapping Wing	USPACAF	United States Pacific Air Forces
CCTW/G	Combat Crew Training Wing/Group	PortAF	Portuguese Air Force	VFMA	US Marine squadron
		PSYOP	Psychological Operation	VLAGES	Very Low Altitude Gravity Extraction System
CFB	Canadian Forces Base	RAAF	Royal Australian Air Force		
CSS/W	Combat Support Squadron/Wing	RCAF	Royal Canadian Air Force	VMGR	US Marine in-flight refuelling squadron
CTA	Consorcio Technico de Aeronautica, Luanda, Angola	RDAF	Royal Danish Air Force		
		RJAF	Royal Jordanian Air Force	WRS	Weather Reconnaissance Squadron
CW	Composite Wing	RMAF	Royal Maroc Air Force		

Index